Beautiful Child

Also by
Torey Hayden

One Child
Ghost Girl
Just Another Kid
The Tiger's Child
Twilight Children

This book is based on the author's experiences. In order to protect privacy, names and some identifying characteristics, dialogue and details have been changed or reconstructed. Some characters are not based on any one person but are composite characters.

Torey Hayden

Beautiful Child

HARPER element

HarperElement
An Imprint of HarperCollins*Publishers*
77–85 Fulham Palace Road,
Hammersmith, London W6 8JB

The website address is: www.thorsonselement.com

and *HarperElement* are trademarks of
HarperCollins*Publishers* Ltd

First published in the US by William Morrow 2002

1

This paperback edition 2008

A catalogue record of this book is
available from the British Library

ISBN 978 0 00 783874 5

Printed and bound in Great Britain by
Clays Ltd, St Ives plc

This book is proudly printed on paper which contains wood from well-managed forests, certified in accordance with the rules of the Forest Stewardship Council.
For more information about FSC,
please visit www.fsc-uk.org

FSC
Mixed Sources
Product group from well-managed forests and other controlled sources
www.fsc.org Cert no. SW-COC-1806
© 1996 Forest Stewardship Council

Beautiful Child

Chapter One

The first time I saw her, she was atop a stone wall that ran along the west side of the playground. Lolling back with one leg outstretched, one drawn up, her dark hair tumbling opulently down behind her, she had her eyes closed, her face turned to the sun. The pose gave her the aura of some long-forgotten Hollywood glamour queen and that's what caught my attention, because she could, in fact, have only been six or seven.

I went on past her and up the walk to the school. Seeing me coming, the principal, Bob Christianson, came out from the school office. "Hey, darned good!" he cried heartily and clapped me on the shoulder. "Great to see you. Just great. I've been so looking forward to this. We're going to have good fun this year, hey? Great times!"

In the face of such enthusiasm I could only laugh. Bob and

I had a long history together. When I was just a struggling beginner, Bob had given me one of my first jobs. In those days he was director of a program researching learning disabilities, and his noisy, casual, hippy-inspired approach to dealing with the deprived, difficult children in his care had alarmed many in our rather conservative community at the time. Admittedly, it had alarmed me a little in the beginning too, because I was newly out of teacher training and not too accustomed to thinking for myself. Bob had provided me with just the right amount of encouragement and direction while bullishly refusing to believe anything I claimed to have learned from my university course work. As a consequence, I spent a heady, rather wild couple of years learning to defend myself and finding my own style in the classroom along the way.

At the time it was an almost ideal working environment for me, and Bob almost single-handedly molded me into the kind of teacher I would become, but in the end he was too successful. I learned not only to question the precepts and practicalities of the theories I was taught in the university, but I also began to question Bob's. There was too much insubstantial pop psychology in his approach to satisfy me; so when I felt I'd grown as much as I could in that setting, I moved on.

A lot of time had passed for both of us in the interim. I'd worked in other schools, other states, other countries, even. I'd branched out into clinical psychology and research, as well as special education. I'd even taken a couple of years away from education altogether. Bob, meantime, had stayed local and moved in and out of the private and public sectors, in and out of regular and special education. We'd stayed in touch in a rather casual way, although neither of us had kept close track of what the other was doing. As a consequence, it had been a delightful surprise to discover Bob was now the principal of the new school I was being sent to.

Our state school system was in the midst of one of its seemingly endless reorganizations. The previous year, I'd worked in an adjacent district as a learning support teacher. I was going from school to school to work with small groups of children and to provide backup support for teachers who had special education students integrated into their classrooms. Although this program had been in place only two years, the system decided it wasn't working effectively enough with the bottom-end children. Consequently, a third of the learning support teachers were given permanent classrooms to allow children with more serious and disruptive behaviors to have longer periods of special education placement.

I jumped at the chance to give up the peripatetic lifestyle and have a classroom again, because I enjoyed that milieu enormously and felt it best suited my teaching style. Ending up in Bob's school was a bonus.

"Wait till you see this room," Bob was saying as we climbed the stairs. And stairs. And stairs. "It's such a super room, Torey. From the time I knew you were coming,

I wanted to give you someplace you could really work in. Special ed. so often gets the leftovers. But that's the beauty of this big, old building." We climbed yet *another* flight of stairs. "Plenty of room."

Bob's school was a hybrid building, part old brick lump from 1910, part prefab extension tacked on in the 1960s to cope with the baby boomers. I was given a room on the top floor of the old building and Bob was good for his word, because it was a wonderful room, spacious with big windows and bright freshly painted yellow walls and a little cloakroom-type niche for storing outerwear and students' things. Indeed, it was probably the nicest room I'd ever been assigned. The downside was that three flights of stairs and a corridor separated me from the nearest toilet. The gym, cafeteria, and front office were almost in another galaxy.

"You can arrange things the way you want," Bob was saying as he walked among the small tables and chairs. "And Julie's coming in this afternoon. Have you met Julie yet? She'll be your teaching aide. What's the current politically correct term? Paralegal? No, no… para-educator? I don't remember. Anyway, she's only going to be in here half days. Sadly. I couldn't finagle you more. But you'll like Julie. We've had her three years now. She comes in the mornings as a support person for a little boy of ours who has cerebral palsy, but he goes for physiotherapy in the afternoons. So once she has him onto his transport, she's all yours."

As Bob talked I was walking around the room, peering here and there. I paused to check the view from the windows.

That girl was still sitting on the wall. I regarded her. She looked lonely to me. She was the only child anywhere near the playground on this last day of summer vacation.

Bob said, "I'll have your class list up for you this afternoon. The way we've arranged it, you'll have five kids full-time. Then there'll be about fifteen others who'll come and go, depending on how much help they need. Sound good? What do you think?"

I smiled and nodded. "Sounds great to me."

I was trying to shove a filing cabinet back out of the way when Julie arrived.

"Let me give you a hand with that," she said cheerfully and grabbed hold of the other side. We wrestled it into the corner. "Bob told me you were hard at work up here. Are you getting on all right?"

"Yes, thank you," I said.

She was a pretty girl – not a girl, really – she had to be older than she looked, but she was slightly built with delicate bones, pale, dewy skin, and clear green eyes. She had thick bangs and long, straight, reddish blonde hair, which was pulled back from her face in a sweet, schoolgirl style. Consequently, she appeared about fourteen.

"I'm looking forward to this," she said, dusting off her hands. "I've been supporting Casey Muldrow since he was in first grade. He's a super little kid, but I'm looking forward to something different."

"If it's 'different' you're looking for, you've probably

lucked out," I said and smiled. "I usually do a good line in 'different.'" Picking up a frieze, I let it drop to its full length. "I was thinking of putting this up over there between the windows. Do you want to give me a hand?"

That's when I saw the child again. She was still on top of the same wall, but now there was a woman standing beneath her, talking up to her.

"That little girl has been on that wall for about four hours," I said. "She was there when I arrived this morning."

Julie looked out the window. "Oh yeah. That's Venus Fox. And that's her wall. She's always there."

"Why?"

Julie shrugged. "That's just Venus's wall."

"How does she get up there. It must be six feet high."

"The kid's like Spiderman. She can get over anything."

"Is that her mom with her?" I asked.

"No, it's her sister. Wanda. Wanda's developmentally delayed."

"She looks old to be the girl's sister," I said.

Julie shrugged again. "Late teens. She might be twenty. She used to be in special ed. at the high school, but she got too old. Now she seems to spend most of her time trailing around after Venus."

"And Venus spends most of her time sitting on a wall. This family sounds promising."

Julie raised her eyebrow in a knowing way. "There's nine of them. Nine kids. Most of them have different fathers. I think every single one has been in special ed. at one point or another."

"Venus too?"

"Venus, definitely. Venus is *way* out to lunch." Julie gave a little grin. "As you'll get to find out for yourself soon enough. She's going to be in here."

"'Way out to lunch' how?" I asked.

"For one thing, she doesn't talk."

I rolled my eyes. "Surprise, surprise there." When Julie looked blank, I added, "Elective mutism is my research specialty. In fact, I got my start on it when Bob and I were working together in a different program."

"Yeah, well, this kid's mute all right."

"She won't be in here."

"No, you don't understand," Julie replied. "Venus doesn't talk. I mean, *doesn't talk.* Doesn't say zip. Anywhere. To anyone."

"She will in here."

Julie's smile was good-humored but faintly mocking. "Pride goeth before a fall."

Chapter Two

As I ran my finger down the class list, I came to one I knew well. Billy Gomez. Aged nine, he was a small boy of Latino origin with an unruly thatch of black hair, a fondness for brightly colored shirts, and the grubbiest fingernails I'd ever seen on a kid. But while Billy was small, he was not puny. He had the sleek, sturdy musculature of a weasel and a fierce aggressiveness to match. Ruled by an explosive temper and a very bad mouth, he'd gotten kicked out of two previous schools. I'd worked extensively both with him and his teacher the year before, but I hadn't been particularly successful. Billy still ranted, raved, and fought.

The other three boys I did not know. The fifth child, as Julie predicted, was Venus.

When I arrived the next morning, Venus was again up on her wall.

"Hello, Venus," I said as I passed.

No response. She didn't even turn her head in my direction.

I stopped and looked up. "Venus?"

There was not even the faintest muscle twitch to indicate she was aware of being spoken to.

"I'm your new teacher. Would you like to walk into the building with me?"

Her failure to respond was so complete that the first thing I thought was she must have a hearing loss. I made a mental note to check on what tests she had had. Waiting a few minutes longer, I finally gave up and went on into the school alone.

The first student to come into class was Billy. "Oh *no*! Not *you*!" he cried and smacked the center of his forehead with his palm. Hard. He almost fell backward with the blow. "Oh no. No, no, no. I don't want to be in here. I don't want *you*."

"Hi, Billy. I'm glad to see you too," I said. "And guess what? You're the first person here. So you get your pick of any table."

"Then I pick the table in the cafeteria," he said quickly and bolted for the door.

"Hey ho!" I snagged him by the collar. "Not literally *any* table. One in here."

Billy slammed his things down on the nearest one. "I don't want any of *these* tables," he said gloomily. "I just want to get the fuck out of here."

I put a finger to my lips. "Not in here, okay? You're the oldest in here, so I need you to set a good example of how to talk. Do you think you can watch your tongue for me?"

Billy put his fingers into his mouth and grabbed hold of his tongue. "I'll try," he garbled around his fingers, "but I don't think I can pull it out far enough for me to watch."

"Billy, not literally."

Billy laughed hysterically. So much so, in fact, he fell off his chair.

Just then Bob appeared, shepherding in two little boys with the most startlingly red hair I'd ever seen. It was *red*. Bright, copper penny red, worn in a floppy style over small, pointed faces that were generously splattered with raindrop-size freckles.

"This is Shane," Bob said, putting a hand a little more firmly on the boy to his right. "And this is Zane."

Shane and Zane? God, why did parents do this to their kids?

They were identical twins, dressed in what I can only describe as ventriloquist's dummy style: polyester pants, striped shirts, and, quite incredibly, bow ties.

Billy was as amazed by their appearance as I was. "Are they Dalmatians?" he asked incredulously.

Before I could respond a heavyset African–American woman wearing a bright, flowery dress appeared and pushed forward a slender, almost lanky-looking boy. "This here's Jesse," she said, keeping both hands on the boy's thin shoulders. "This here's Jesse's classroom?"

Bob stepped aside, and the woman propelled the boy into the room. "You be good for Grandma. You be special for this here lady and Grandma'll hear all the good things you done today." She kissed him soundly on the side of the head. The boy flinched. Then she departed out the door.

"Here," I said. "Do you want to take a chair here?"

The boy tossed his belongings down with an angry-sounding thud.

"Oh no, you don't. Not here. You're not sitting here," Billy cried. "No ugly black kid's going to sit here, because I'm sitting here. Teacher, you put him someplace else."

"You want to fight about it?" Jesse replied, making a fist.

The boys lunged at each other right over the tabletop and went crashing to the floor. I leaped in, grabbing Billy by the collar and pushing Jesse aside.

Bob grinned with rather evil relish. "I see you have everything in hand, so I'll leave you to it," he said and vanished out the door.

"I'm not sitting with him. He's crazy," Billy said and grabbed his stuff from the table. "I'd rather sit with the Dalmatians. Come here, you guys. This here's our table. That ugly kid can sit alone."

I grabbed Billy's shoulder again. "For now I think everyone's going to sit alone. One person per table. You sit here. Zane? Are you Zane? You sit here. Jesse, there. Shane, over here. Okay, these are your tables. And your chairs. So remember where they are, because I want your bottoms glued to those chairs unless you have permission to be somewhere else."

"Glued on?" cried Billy and leaped up. "Where's the glue?" He was over to the bookshelves already, rummaging through a basket. "Got to glue my bottom to that chair."

"Billy, sit down."

"But you said 'glued on.' I'm just doing what you said."

"Sit *down*."

With a cheerful smile, he sat. "We got whole tables to ourselves?" he said. "These are our tables?"

"Yes, those are your tables."

"Wow," he said and smoothed his hand over the wood surface. "Cool. My own table. Wonder where I'm going to put it when I get home."

"*Billy*!"

"Is there only going to be four of us in this here class?" Jesse asked.

Suddenly I remembered Venus. The bell had rung, and she wasn't in the classroom.

I crossed to the window. Venus was still on the wall, but below her was Wanda, arms reaching up. Gently she lifted Venus down. I saw them approach the school building.

Wanda came all the way up to the classroom door with her sister. She was a big, ungainly girl, at least thirty pounds overweight, with bad acne and straggly hair. Her clothes were wrinkled, ill-fitting, and noticeably smelly.

"Hello," I said.

"Her come inside now," Wanda said in a cheerful manner. "Come on, beautiful child. Time to go to school."

Venus looked up at me with a full, open gaze, making unabashed eye contact. I smiled at her. She didn't smile back; she just stared.

"Here." I offered my hand. "Shall I show you to your table?"

"Her no talk," Wanda said.

"Thank you for your thoughts," I replied, "but now it's time for Venus to be in school." I kept my hand outstretched to Venus. "Time to get started."

"Her no come to school."

"I don't think you go to school, do you, Wanda? But Venus does. Come on, sweetheart. Time to find your seat."

"Go on, beautiful child," Wanda whispered and put her hands on Venus's back. She pushed the child gently into the room.

"Good-bye, Wanda," I said. "Thanks for bringing her. Do you want to say good-bye to Wanda, Venus? Shall we say, 'See you after school, Wanda'?"

"Bye-bye, beautiful child," Wanda said. Then she turned and ambled off.

"Beautiful child" was not the epithet I would have given Venus, now that I had a chance to look at her up close. She was neither clean nor well cared for. There was the dusky cast of worn-in dirt to her dark skin, and her long hair hung in matted tendrils, as if someone had tried to make dreadlocks out of them and failed. Her clothes were too big and had food stains down the front. And like her sister, she smelled.

"Okay, sweetheart, you can sit in this chair."

"How come you're sitting her at the Dalmatian's table?" Billy asked. "How come you don't make her sit with that ugly black kid. You should put all the black kids together."

"Actually, Billy, we don't sort people by color in here, so I would prefer it if you stopped going on about it," I replied. "I'd also prefer it if you'd stop saying 'Dalmatian.' He's not a dog. He's a boy and his name is Zane."

"My name's Shane," the boy said in an annoyed tone. "And you shut up, stupid kid."

"I'll tell *you* who's stupid!" Billy shouted angrily. "You want me to punch your lights out?"

Before I knew what was happening, Billy lunged at Shane.

But no quailing from Shane. He lunged back. "Yeah! I wanna beat your head in!" he shouted. "I'm gonna pound you to a bloody little zit on the sidewalk and then step on you!"

"Yeah!" Zane chimed in. "Me too!"

And I was thinking, Gosh, this is going to be a fun year.

I was pathetically glad to see Julie when she showed up at one o'clock. The morning had been nothing but one long fistfight. Shane and Zane, who were six, had arrived in the classroom with a diagnosis of FAS – fetal alcohol syndrome

– which is a condition that occurs in the unborn child when alcohol is overused in pregnancy. As a result, they both had the distinctive elflike physical features that characterize fetal alcohol syndrome, a borderline IQ, and serious behavioral problems, in particular, hyperactivity and attention deficit. Even this glum picture, however, was a rather inadequate description of these pint-size guerrillas. With their manic behavior, identical Howdy Doody faces, and weird, out-of-date clothes, they were like characters from some horror film come to life to terrorize the classroom.

Jesse, who was eight, had Tourette's syndrome, which caused him to have several tics including spells of rapid eye blinking, head twitching, and sniffing, as if he had a runny nose, although he didn't. In addition, he obsessively straightened things. He was particularly concerned about having his pencils and erasers laid out just so on his table, which was *not* a promising road to happiness in this class. The moment the others realized it mattered to him, they were intent on knocking his carefully aligned items around just to wind him up. Also not a good idea, I discovered quickly. His obsessiveness gave Jesse the initial impression of being a rather finicky, fastidious child. However, beneath this veneer was a kid with the mind-set of Darth Vader. Things *had* to be done his way. Death to anyone who refused.

Compared to these three, Billy seemed rather tame. He was just plain aggressive, a cocky live wire who was willing to take on anyone and everyone, whether it made sense or not; a kid whose mouth was permanently in gear before his brain. Permanently in gear, period.

I'd been forced to more or less ignore Venus over the course of the morning because I was too busy breaking up fights among the boys. She didn't appear to mind this inattention. Indeed, she didn't actually appear to be alive most of the time. Plopped down in her chair at the table, she just sat, staring ahead of her. I'd offered some papers and crayons at one point. I'd offered a storybook. I'd offered a jigsaw puzzle. Admittedly, all this was done on the run, while chasing after one of the boys, and I'd had no time to sit down with her, but even so… Venus picked up whatever it was I'd given her and manipulated it back and forth in a sluggish, detached manner for a few moments without using it appropriately. Then, as soon as I turned away, she let it drop and resumed sitting motionlessly.

Once Julie arrived, I gave her the task of refereeing the boys and then took Venus aside. I wanted to get the measure of Venus's silence immediately. I wasn't sure yet if it was an elective behavior that she could control or whether it was some more serious physical problem that prevented her from speaking, but I knew from experience that if it was psychological, I needed to intervene before we developed a relationship based on silence.

"Come with me," I said, moving to the far end of the room away from Julie and the boys.

Venus watched me in an open, direct way. She had good

eye contact, which I took as a positive sign. This made it less likely that autism was at the base of her silence.

"Here, come here. I want you to do something with me."

Venus continued to watch me but didn't move.

I returned to her table. "Come with me, please. We're going to work together." Putting a hand under her elbow, I brought her to her feet. Hand on her shoulder, I directed her to the far end of the room. "You sit there." I indicated a chair.

Venus stood.

I put a hand on her head and pressed down. She sat. Pulling out the chair across the table from her, I sat down and lifted over a tub of crayons and a piece of paper.

"I'm going to tell you something very special," I said. "A secret. Do you like secrets?"

She stared at me blankly.

I put on my most "special secret" voice and leaned toward her. "I wasn't always a teacher. Know what I did? I worked with children who had a hard time speaking at school. Just like you!" Admittedly, this wasn't such an exciting secret, but I tried to make it sound like something very special. "My job was to help them be able to talk again anytime they wanted." I grinned. "What do you think about that? Would you like to start talking again?"

Venus kept her eyes on my face, her gaze never wavering, but it was a remarkably hooded gaze. I had no clue whatsoever as to what she might be thinking. Or even if she was thinking.

"It's very important to speak in our room. Talking is the way we let others know how we are feeling. Talking is how we let other people know what we are thinking, because they can't see inside our heads to find out. They won't know otherwise. We have to tell them. That's how people understand each other. It's how we resolve problems and get help when we need it and that makes us feel happier. So it's important to learn how to use words."

Venus never took her eyes from mine. She almost didn't blink.

"I know it's hard to start talking when you've been used to being silent. It feels different. It feels scary. That's okay. It's okay to feel scared in here. It's okay to feel uncertain."

If she was uncertain, Venus didn't let on. She stared uninhibitedly into my face.

I lifted up a piece of paper. "I'd like you to make a picture for me. Draw me a house."

No movement.

We sat, staring at each other.

"Here, shall I get you started? I'll draw the ground." I took up a green crayon and drew a line across the bottom of the paper, then I turned the paper back in her direction and pushed the tub of crayons over. "There. Now, can you draw a house?"

Venus didn't look down. Gently I reached across and reoriented her head so that she would have to look at the paper. I pointed to it.

Nothing.

Surely she did know what a house was. She was seven. She had sat through kindergarten twice. But maybe she was developmentally delayed, like her sister. Maybe expecting her to draw a house was expecting too much.

"Here. Take a crayon in your hand." I had to rise up, come around the table, grab hold of her arm, bring her hand up, insert the crayon, and lay it on the table. She kept hold of the crayon, but her hand flopped back down on the table like a lifeless fish.

Picking up a different crayon, I made a mark on the paper. "Can you make a line like that?" I asked. "There. Right beside where I drew my line."

I regarded her. Maybe she wasn't right-handed. I'd not seen her pick up anything, so I'd just assumed. But maybe she was left-handed. I reached over and put the crayon in the other hand. She didn't grip it very well, so I got up, came around the table, took her left hand, repositioned it better and lay it back on the table. I returned to my seat. Trying to sound terribly jolly, I said, "*I'm* left handed," in the excited tone of voice one would normally reserve for comments like "I'm a millionaire."

No. She wasn't going to cooperate. She just sat, staring at me again, her dark eyes hooded and unreadable.

"Well, this isn't working, is it?" I said cheerfully and whipped the piece of paper away. "Let's try something else."

I went and got a children's book. Putting my chair alongside hers, I sat down and opened the book. "Let's have a look at this."

She stared at me.

It was a picture dictionary and the page I opened to was full of colorful illustrations of small animals driving cars and doing different sorts of jobs. "Let's look at these pictures. See? They're all in a bus. And what are they? What kind of animals are they? Mice, aren't they? And there's a police car, and look, one of the policemen is a lion. What kind of animal is the other policeman?"

She stared up at me.

"Here, look down here." I physically tipped her head so that she'd look at the page. "What's this other animal? What kind of animal is he?"

No response.

"What is he?"

No response.

"What is he?"

No response. Absolutely nothing. She just sat, motionless.

"Right here." I tapped the picture. "What kind of animal is that?"

I persisted for several minutes longer, rapidly rephrasing the question but keeping at it, not letting enough silence leak in to make it seem like silence, taking up the rhythm of both sides of the conversation myself, all with just one question: what animal is that?

Bang! I brought my hand down flat on the table to make a loud, sudden noise. It was a crude technique but often a very effective one. I hoped it would startle her over the initial hurdle, as it did with many children, but in Venus's case, I was also interested just to see if it got any reaction out of her. I hoped to see her jump or, at the very least, blink.

Venus simply raised her head and looked at me.

"Can you hear that?" I asked. "When I bang my hand like that on the table," I said and banged it suddenly on the tabletop again, "can you hear it?"

"I sure can!" Billy shouted from the other side of the classroom. "You trying to scare the shit out of us over here?"

Venus just sat, unblinking.

Leaning forward, I pulled the book back in front of me and started to page through it. "Yes, well, let's try something else. Let's see if we can find a story. Shall I read a story to you?"

Eyes on my face, she just stared. No nod. No shake of the head. Nothing. There was very little to denote the kid was anything more than a waxwork accidentally abandoned in the classroom.

"Yes, well, I have an even better idea. What about recess?"

She didn't react to that either.

Chapter Three

"All right," I said, pouring myself a cup of coffee in the teachers' lounge, "joke's over. What's wrong with Venus Fox?" I looked pointedly at Bob.

Bob took a sip from his mug. "That's what you're here to tell me, I believe."

"So far I'm still working on whether she's alive or not."

"Oh, she's alive all right," Bob replied.

A moment's silence intruded. Julie was making herself a cup of tea over by the sink, and she turned to look at us when the conversation paused.

"My first impression is that she's deaf," I said.

Bob took another swallow of his coffee.

"Has anyone had her tested?" I asked. "Because it would be a shame to put a kid in my kind of class, if she's actually hearing impaired. I don't sign well at all."

"She was sent to an ENT specialist at the hospital last year," Bob replied. "Apparently they had such a hard time testing her that they ended up giving her an ABR."

"What's that?" I asked.

"Auditory brainstem response," Julie answered.

"It's a test that tells whether the brain is registering any sound. The test measures the brain's response to sound stimulation, so you can determine if someone is hearing, even if they aren't verbal."

"And?" I asked.

"And she seems to be hearing fine."

"Oh," I said and a faint sense of dismay settled over me. After working with her, I'd become so convinced that Venus's problems stemmed from hearing loss that I'd felt I pretty much had a handle on her. We'd make arrangements for hearing tests and off she would go for the appropriate equipment and, eventually, the appropriate classroom. I looked around, first at Julie, then back at Bob. Really, I hadn't expected that answer.

One of the other teachers, a third-grade teacher named Sarah, looked over. "I think what we're going to discover with Venus is that she just doesn't have much. Up there, if you know what I mean." Sarah touched her temple. "Venus looks blank because, basically, she is blank. It's a family thing. Every one of the Fox kids. They're all..." Her voice trailed off and she didn't finish the sentence, but then she didn't have to. I knew what she was saying.

Bob sighed. "I'm hoping that's not going to be the case, but no, it's not a bright family."

Noise of a tremendous commotion on the playground began to filter in through the window. For just the briefest moment all the teachers in the lounge paused, alert, before going to the window to see what was happening.

I didn't bother with the window because I knew immediately it was one of mine. An identifying factor of disturbed children, I'd discovered, was the uninhibited scream. Ordinary kids could yell, shout, or squeal loudly with delight, but by six or seven, they'd been pretty much socialized out of screaming in that peculiarly high-pitched, desperate way. Not so my kids. So, I didn't bother peering out the window. Setting down my coffee, I zipped out the door and down the hallway to get to the playground.

There on the far side beneath the spreading sycamore trees were the two playground supervisors, prying kids apart. Recognizing Billy's brightly colored shirt amid the fray, I sprinted across the asphalt.

As well as Billy, there was Shane (or Zane) and – the two teachers were battling to separate the kids, so I couldn't immediately tell who the third one was – Venus!

Venus, all right. Venus, as a virtual buzz saw of arms and legs, whizzing fiercely at Billy. More shocking yet, it was Venus who was making most of the noise. And what a weird noise it was – an eerie ululating sound, so loud and high pitched that it made my ears hurt. She kept at it, screaming and thrashing, until she broke free of the teacher's grip and threw herself viciously at Billy, who already had a bloody nose. The other teacher was holding on to both Billy and Shane; but when Billy saw Venus coming at him again, he pulled himself free and started running. Venus went in hot pursuit.

I took off after the two of them, as did Julie, who had just come out of the building, as did Bob and another teacher. We were like the characters in the children's story "The Gingerbread Boy," all chasing one after another after Venus, who was after Billy. When Billy reached the wall at the end of the playground, Venus cornered him and started to pummel him with unrestrained fury. She wasn't ignorant of us bearing down on her, however, because the moment I came within touching distance, Venus scurried up and over the wall.

Spiderman, indeed, I thought. With a not-too-graceful leap, I hoisted myself up and over the wall too, leaving Bob and Julie and the other teacher to scrape what remained of Billy off the pavement and put him back together.

Venus had the advantage of knowing where she was going while I did not. She bolted out through the underbrush, cut across someone's backyard, and ran down the alley. I pelted after her, doing the best I could to keep up with her. She was surprisingly lithe when it came to getting over or under things, but I had the longer legs. About half a block from the school I finally outran her, catching her by snatching hold of the material of her dress.

"Stop! Right there!"

She tried to jerk away, but I had a good hold of the fabric. With my other hand, I grabbed her arm.

For a moment we just stood, both panting heavily. Venus had scraped knees but otherwise looked none the worse for her altercation with Billy. She eyed me carefully and there was a lot more life in her glare than anything I'd seen earlier.

"This isn't how we do things when you are in my class," I said and secured my grip on her arm. "Back to school we go."

She dug her feet into the grass.

"No, we're going back to school. It's schooltime. You belong there."

Venus was not going to cooperate. There seemed no alternative but to pick her up and carry her back. Realizing what I was trying to do, she exploded into a furious array of arms and legs, hitting and kicking. As a consequence, we made very slow progress getting back to the playground. The total distance was about two blocks and she made it impossible for me to carry her for more than a few yards at a time before I had to set her down and get a better grip. Finally Bob came to my rescue. Seeing me struggling up the street, he joined me and took hold of Venus's other side. Together, we frog-marched her back into the building.

Venus hated this. The moment Bob touched her, she began to scream in her odd, high-pitched way again. She struggled, screamed, struggled more.

Finally we managed to get her into the school building and all the way up the stairs to my classroom. Bob, between pants, said, "Maybe it wasn't such a good idea, putting you way up here."

Once we reached the room, Bob let go, but I kept hold of Venus's arms. Julie was in the classroom with the other children and they all watched us warily. Bob, seeing the situation was more or less in hand, bid good-bye, closed the door, and left me to sort things out.

There wasn't a lock on the door, so I told Julie to stand in front of it. Hauling Venus across the room, I tugged out the chair assigned to be a "quiet chair" with my foot. I plopped her in it. "You sit there."

She screamed and struggled. I held her in the chair.

"You need to stay here. Until you can get control again and not fight, you need to sit here." Very cautiously I removed my hands, expecting her to dart up and run for the door, but she responded just the opposite to what I'd anticipated. The moment I let go, Venus immediately fell silent. She slumped forward in the chair, as if she were very tired.

"In this room we do not hurt others. We don't hurt ourselves. That's a class rule."

"That's two rules," Billy piped up from his table.

"That's *one* rule, Billy," I said fiercely. "The rule is: we do not hurt. *Anything*."

"Not even flies?" Billy asked. "We're not allowed to hurt flies in here?"

Julie, recognizing a flash-point situation when she saw one, quickly intervened, ushering Billy over to join the other boys, who were working with clay.

I turned back to Venus, who remained sitting in the time-out chair. She was watching me carefully, her heavy, hooded eyes so unreadable as to be virtually vacant.

"I'll set the timer for five minutes," I said. "When it rings, you may get up and rejoin us."

Putting the ticking timer on the shelf in front of the chair, I backed off carefully, half expecting her to make a bolt for the door when my back was turned.

Not so. Venus didn't move.

The timer rang. Venus still did not move.

"You may get up now," I said from the table where I was working with Jesse.

No response.

I excused myself from Jesse and went over to her. "This is the quiet chair. It's for when you get out of control and need a quiet moment to get yourself back together again. But once you've calmed down, you don't have to sit in the quiet chair anymore. Come on. Let's get you started on the clay. We're making pinch pots. Have you done that before?"

Venus gazed at me. From her look of total incomprehension, I might as well have been speaking Hindi to her.

I put a hand under her elbow and encouraged her to rise from the chair, which she did. I guided her over to where we were all working with the clay. "Here. Sit here."

She just stood.

Gently, I pressed her shoulder with one hand to get her to sit in the chair. I pulled out the adjacent chair and sat down. Picking up a ball of clay, I showed it to her.

"Look, what's this? Clay. And see? See how Jesse's doing it? You just push your thumbs into the ball of clay..."

Her eyes didn't even move to the clay. They stayed on my face, as if she hadn't even heard me.

Did she hear? It seemed hard to believe. I'd come across a lot of kids with speech and language problems in my time but none so unresponsive as this. Was this ABR test really accurate? Could there be some kind of failure between the brain and the ears that they hadn't noticed?

I rose up. "Come here, Venus," I said. Which, of course, she didn't. I had to go through the whole rigamarole again of getting her up out of one chair and over to another part of the classroom. Guiding her to the housekeeping corner, I sat down on the floor and looked through the toys. My sign language was rusty and what little I did remember seemed primarily to be signs for abstract concepts like "family" or "sister," but here was a concrete word I knew. "Doll," I signed and held up a baby doll. "Doll."

Venus watched me, her brow faintly furrowed, as if she thought I was doing something really odd.

I signed again. "Doll." I made the sign very, very slowly.

Reaching over, I lifted her hand. Putting it on the doll, I made her fingers run over the plastic features of the toy. Then I endeavored to make the sign with her fingers. I held the doll up. I signed again myself. "Doll."

The last twenty minutes of the school day passed thus. Venus never responded once.

At last the end-of-day bell rang. Julie escorted those who went by bus down to their rides while I saw out the ones who walked home. Then I retreated to the file cabinets in the main office to have a better look at the children's files. I pulled out Venus's and sat down.

Julie came in, carrying mugs of coffee for us both. She took out a chair on the other side of the table and sat down.

"Well, that was an experience," she said.

"I'd like to think this is first-day jitters and everything will settle down." I looked over. "Has that happened with Venus before, do you know? Have you seen her attack kids before?"

A pause, a hesitancy almost, and then Julie nodded. "Yes. Truth is, I think that's more why she's in this class than because of her speech. Last year they ended up having to keep her in during recesses because she does nothing but pick fights."

"Oh great. Five kids, all with a mission to kill."

"Kind of like being in the OK Corral in your room, isn't it?" Julie said rather cheerfully.

I looked up.

"Didn't you notice all the cowboy names? Billy – Billy the Kid. Jesse – Jesse James. And Shane. And Zane. And everything's shoot 'em up." She laughed.

"I don't remember any cowboys named Venus."

"Well, not cow*boys*," Julie said. She considered a moment.

"Her name doesn't fit," I said.

Julie gave a slight shrug. "Neither does the kid."

Venus's file made depressing reading. She was the youngest of nine children fathered by three different men. The man who fathered the four eldest children, including Wanda, had been committed to the penitentiary for grievous bodily harm, had been released, had robbed a bank, had been jailed again, released again, and finally died three years later while in detention on drug-dealing charges. The second man, who fathered the next two children, had beaten Venus's mother so severely when she was pregnant that the baby was stillborn. He was convicted of abuse toward three of the children, released, then later charged on animal cruelty for throwing a puppy onto a freeway from a bridge. The third man fathered the remaining three children, including Venus. He had a string of burglary convictions and other crimes related to drug and alcohol problems, but had also been charged with pedophile activity. He was currently out of prison and living elsewhere, as he'd been banned from having any contact with the children.

Venus's mother had a long history of prostitution and had been in and out of detox centers for drug and alcohol abuse. She now lived with seven of her nine children, three of whom had been officially labeled as mentally defective, and all of whom had been in one form of special education or another. The eldest, a son a year older than Wanda, was now in prison. A fifteen-year-old son was in a juvenile detention center. The next eldest daughter, who was seventeen, had suffered a seizure while in police custody the previous year and was now brain damaged. Two other children, boys aged nine and twelve, were mentioned as having serious communication problems and were receiving speech therapy.

There was actually very little in the file that was specific to Venus herself. I think the general opinion was that by including her family history, Venus's problems were self-evident. There were no notes on pregnancy or birth complications, nothing to denote whether or not her early development was normal. She had first come to the attention of the authorities when she reached age five and was registered for kindergarten. It was noted at this time that she was almost totally silent and, in general, very unresponsive. Except on the playground. Except when challenged or threatened. Then Venus seemed to call on an inner strength of almost comic book proportions. She screamed. She shouted. Some people even thought she swore. The idea would have seemed almost laughable – silent, unprepossessing seven-year-old girl metamorphoses into vicious little killing machine – if I hadn't witnessed it for myself.

I flipped the file shut.

Chapter Four

When I arrived the next morning, Billy was already there, sitting in the classroom.

"What's this?" I asked in surprise. "It's only eight-ten."

"I gotta come early. My god-damned bus don't come no later."

I put a finger to my lips.

"My god-darned bus don't come no later."

"How about just 'darned.' Darned bus doesn't come any later?"

He curled his lip up in an irritable snarl.

"So why aren't you out on the playground?" I asked. "The bell doesn't ring until eight-thirty-five."

"Fucking girl's out there."

I put a finger to my lips again. "We've got to remember.

You're oldest in here. I'm depending on you to set a good example for the others."

"I don't care. Fucking girl's out there and *I'm* not gonna take my chances. Ain't no teacher out there guarding us poor kids. Fucking girl's gonna knock the shit out of me again."

"Did she say that to you?"

Billy didn't answer.

"Did she tell you she was going to beat you up?" I asked again.

Head down, he just shrugged. "She's just got a crazy look in her eyes. Girl's a fucking psychopath or something. That's what she is. Like in one of them movies. Like maybe she's Freddy's little sister from Elm Street or something."

"Well, just for this morning you can stay in. But not every morning, Billy. The school rules say that everyone must be outside until the bell rings."

"You're not outside."

"All the *children* stay outside. You know what I meant. We'll sort something out so that you don't feel threatened."

Billy flopped dramatically across his table and sighed in a world-weary way. "I hate this school. I hate being here so much. Why did I have to come here anyway? Why couldn't I stay at my other school? My brother's there. My brother'd never let me get beat up by some psycho girl. This is the worst thing in the whole world that could have happened to me. I'm so unlucky. I'm the unluckiest kid in the world."

"If you work hard in here, Billy, and get your mouth and your temper under control, then maybe you can go back to your old school."

"Really? Is that all I got to do?" He said this with friendly surprise, as if no one had ever mentioned his behavior to him before. "Well, I can do that. I'm gonna be good as gold."

"That'd be super. I'd be very proud of you. For now, however, I'd be satisfied if you just got off that table. Please take your seat."

Cheerfully Billy leaped up and grabbed his chair, swinging it gleefully over his head. "Take my seat? Okay, sure, anything you say, Teach. Here it is. Where you want me to take it?"

The next to arrive in our doorway was Jesse, accompanied by a woman I recognized as one of the school bus drivers. She had him by the collar. She pushed him ahead of her into the room.

"This kid isn't going to last long," she said testily.

"What happened?"

"Well, on my bus you've got to take your seat, stay seated, and keep your hands to yourself. Those are about the only three things he didn't do."

"He was sticking his head out the window and swearing at people," Billy added.

"You weren't there, Billy, so please don't interrupt."

"He *was* doing that," the bus driver said. "And he wouldn't stay in his seat. That kid can't keep something you tell him in his head for more than three seconds. I *told* him. I told him to sit down and shut up and quit bothering everybody. He tripped one of the first graders when she got on and then when she tried to get up, he pushed her down again. I said, 'Keep that up, mister, and you're going to walk,' and what he said back, I'm not going to repeat. So I told him when I get him here, his life wasn't going to be worth living."

I nodded. "Okay, sit down over there, Jesse."

In burst Shane and Zane.

"Oh fuck, here come the damned Dalmatians again," Billy cried.

Shane didn't even pause to put down his things. He shot across the room and bashed into Billy, thunking him soundly over the head with his lunch box. The crack was audible and Billy let out a howl.

"You *girl*," Jesse sneered, as if that was the worst possible insult.

Zane joined the fray, kicking hard at Billy. Jesse leaped from his seat to join in. Recognizing discretion to be the better part of valor, the bus driver stopped her complaining and left immediately.

All four boys were in a tangle of flailing arms and legs by the time I reached them and the noise level in the room was absolutely deafening. I was shouting as loudly as anyone else.

Throwing myself in among them, I grabbed one of the twins by his leg and pulled him out. I ripped off his shoes, because shoeless he couldn't hurt so much when he kicked, and I slammed him into a chair. "*Stay there.*"

Billy was next. He was screaming, half in pain, half in rage. I flung him into another chair. "Take your shoes off."

He howled.

"Take them *off*!" I demanded.

Then I grabbed the other twin by the waistband of his pants and lifted him right off the floor. Wrenching his shoes off, I tossed them, one after the other, out of reach. I pushed him into a chair.

Last was Jesse, who was just so angry that there seemed no way to control him other than pin him to the floor until he calmed down. Once he'd stopped thrashing, I took his shoes off too.

"Okay, the four of you," I said and stood up. Three of the boys were in chairs in a ragged semicircle. Jesse was still sitting on the floor. "From now on, wearing shoes in this room is a privilege, not a right."

"What do you mean?" Billy asked.

"I mean, I'm not going to be kicked black and blue. Shoes aren't for kicking. Until everyone knows how to behave when they are wearing shoes, no shoes."

"You've got shoes on," Billy said.

"Yes, that's right. Because I'm not going to kick anyone with mine. But until you earn that privilege by showing me you aren't going to kick anyone, shoes will go off at the door when you come into the room and shoes will not go back on until you leave."

"You can't do that," Jesse said. His facial tic had started – blink, blink, blink, squint, jerk of the head – and it made it hard for him to speak clearly at the same time.

"Watch me," I said. Picking up a large plastic box, I crossed the room and collected up all the shoes I'd thrown over there.

"I'll tell my mom!" Zane shouted. "I'll tell her you're taking our shoes away and she'll make you give them back!"

"I intend to give them back when you go home. But in here, they're off and they're going to stay off. They'll be right here in this box." I put the box up on top of a tall cupboard.

"She'll make you give 'em back," Zane cried. "They're *my* shoes. My mom bought them for me!"

"They're still your shoes. And your mom will know I'm doing the right thing."

Zane rose from his seat.

"No, Zane, you sit," I said. "You too, Jesse. Get up off the floor and get in that chair."

Zane paused a long moment, clearly weighing the odds that I'd do something unpleasant if he didn't obey. My look must have been enough, because he plopped back down in the chair. Jesse rose and took the chair I'd indicated, but his body posture, his movements, even the air around him was heavy with barely controlled anger.

Pulling out a chair from the adjacent table, I sat down. We all sat, the boys fuming quietly or not so quietly, in a straggly semicircle.

A minute passed. Another minute, then another.

"How long we got to sit here?" Shane asked.

"Until everyone is calmed down."

"I'm already calmed down," he said. "We going to have to sit here all day?"

"I was never upset," Billy added. "It's him over there. Jerky Face. He caused all the trouble. If you're going to punish someone, you punish that ugly black kid."

"I never hit you!" Jesse retorted. "It's him that started it," he said and pointed at Shane.

"You're all fuckers," Billy muttered angrily. "I wish I wasn't in this fucking class. I wish I hadn't even *heard* of it."

"Yeah, me too," Jesse said.

"Me too," said Shane.

"And me," Zane added.

"Well, at least everyone agrees on one thing," I said.

"No sir," said Billy, "'cause you don't agree and you're part of everyone."

"Truth be known, Billy, I'm not very keen on this class at the moment either. I kind of wish *I'd* never heard of it," I said.

Billy's eyebrows rose, and an expression of genuine astonishment crossed his face. "But you *gotta* be in this class. It's *your* class."

"Yes. And it's yours too."

"But you're the teacher."

"But it isn't much fun this way, is it?" I said. "I don't like the way things are at the moment any better than you do. So what are we going to do about it?"

This seemed to puzzle the boys. Shane and Zane exchanged quizzical glances, but Billy, ever the class spokesman, offered his take on the matter. "Maybe you've gone nuts."

"What about that girl?" Jesse asked.

And that was the first moment I remembered Venus. She wasn't in the classroom. The bell had rung while we were having our group fight – which had been almost fifteen minutes earlier.

Rising so that I was still facing the boys, I edged carefully toward the window and glanced out. Sure enough, there was Venus on her wall.

"Don't you think we got enough problems already?" Billy said to Jesse.

I knew I couldn't go get Venus. I didn't dare turn my back on the boys, much less go out of the room. I had to just hope someone in the front office would notice her and get her off her wall, because it was more important that I get things settled down in here in the classroom first. I came back to the circle and sat down.

"So," I said, "what are we going to do about things in here to make it better?"

"What about that girl?" Jesse asked.

"That girl's out there and you're in here. I'm talking to you. And you and you and you. I don't want every day to be one long fight. I don't want it to be like now, where I'm making everyone sit in chairs until they calm down. Billy's right. This is definitely no fun. Nobody would want to be in a class like this, not even the teacher. So how are we going to change it?"

"Get rid of that ugly black kid," Billy said.

"Get rid of you, girlie."

"Get rid of everybody," Shane added. "Blow up the whole world."

"Yeah, kapow!" Zane shouted gleefully and threw his hands up in the air.

"Keep your bottom glued to that seat, Zane," I said.

"Glue! Glue! Got to get the glue!" Billy cried and jumped up.

"*Billy*!"

About ten minutes into my not-very-successful efforts to have a class discussion, the door swung open and Wanda loomed in with Venus trailing behind.

"Got to take her shoes off!" Billy shrieked. "Got to take your shoes off, psycho! Can't have shoes in here. Teacher says."

Wanda looked bewildered. Venus looked blank.

I went to the doorway. "Come on in, sweetheart. And thank you, Wanda, for bringing her up."

"Her don't want to come to school," Wanda replied.

"No, me neither!" Billy hollered. "It's a jail in here. Just like being sent to jail."

"Oh, shut up, would you, butthead?" Jesse muttered.

My feelings exactly.

Billy was undeterred. "Take off her shoes, Teacher. You got to take off her shoes. That girl's a psychopath."

"Billy, wherever did you learn a word like 'psychopath'?" I asked as I closed the door after Wanda.

He shrugged. "Just know it, that's all. Just a brain, that's me. But if I ever seen a real psychopath, that girl's one. So make her take off her shoes."

The morning proved absolutely ghastly. There seemed to be no way to keep the boys from fighting. The minute I relaxed my guard, they were at it again. I'd wanted to have everyone help come up with some ideas on how to handle all this aggressive behavior, but the entire time before recess was spent "sitting on chairs." I normally had a special "quiet chair" for disciplinary purposes, but in this room I very shortly had four. By 10 a.m. I had been forced to move the furniture so that there was one table in each corner of the room and two in the middle. The only way to maintain any kind of peace was by keeping everyone as physically separate as possible.

Venus repeated her previous day's performance. She sat, completely oblivious of the boys.

When the recess bell rang, the four boys leaped up and dashed for the door before realizing that none of them had shoes on.

"Hold it!" Billy cried. "What we gonna do?"

I lifted down the box with the shoes in it and started taking them out. I handed Shane his sneakers.

"Can't tie," he said.

I looked at Billy. "Please tie Shane's shoes for him."

"*Huh*?"

"He's not touching my shoes!" Shane cried.

"And Jesse, you tie Zane's for him."

"No way!"

"Well, I guess nobody's getting recess then," I said and put the box back up on the cupboard.

Loud shrieks of protest.

"You can't go out, if you haven't got your shoes on."

"Not *fair*," Billy cried. "I didn't *do* nothing."

"Neither did I."

"Or me!"

"Well, you four figure it out among you then. No one's going until Zane and Shane have their shoes tied."

"You tie them. You're the teacher," Jesse said.

"No, I'm going to help Venus put her shoes on. When you've come up with a solution, let me know." I grabbed Venus's shoes from the box.

"Go outside with*out* shoes," Shane suggested.

"Nope, sorry, that's not an option."

"Oh fuck," Billy said in a most world-weary way. "Give me the god-damned shoes then."

I put a finger to my lips.

"I don't care. Fuck, fuck, *fuck*!"

I didn't say anything but I pointed to the clock to indicate the passing minutes of recess.

"Okay. Give me the god-darned shoes then," Billy said. "Come here, poop face. Let me tie your stupid shoes."

I lifted Shane's shoes out and gave them to Billy. Then I took out Zane's. "Jesse?"

With a heavy sigh, Jesse accepted the shoes.

Defeated, the boys finally left for six minutes of recess.

But all was not over. As we hurried down the stairs for what remained of recess, Shane accidentally bumped against Venus. *Big* mistake.

She metamorphosed right then and there. Grabbing him by the shirt, she flung him down the remaining stairs, then, fists flying, she launched herself after him with the vicious grace of a leopard. Fortunately, it was only a few steps, so he was not hurt, and a passing sixth-grade teacher was able to help me subdue Venus and get her into the school office, where she spent the rest of the break sitting stonily in a chair.

When class resumed after recess, I made everyone take off their shoes again, collected them in what became known as the "shoe box," and put them back on top of the cupboard. I knew better than to try a group activity at this stage, so I endeavored to introduce the children to their work folders. Because I had always taught children who were at different levels academically, I was accustomed to putting each child's work for the day in a file folder. At the start of class I handed out the folders and the child did the work in it. While they were working, I circulated among them and gave help as needed. The system worked well once everyone figured out what was expected, but often during the first few weeks of a new school year there were teething troubles, usually because some children were not used to working independently.

I explained the system and let the children look through

their folders, but I didn't want to push the itty-bitty bit of order we'd managed to create in the ten minutes following recess. Consequently, I suggested that for today they might want to decorate the front of the folder with their name and things they liked so that I'd know whose folder was whose.

The boys all tucked into this activity with relish, and because I had them so far apart, they managed to start it peacefully enough, if a little noisily. Venus, however, just sat. I came over to her table and knelt down beside the chair. "Did you understand what you were supposed to do?"

Blank look. She wasn't even looking at me this time. Just staring into space, the same way she did when sitting outside on the wall.

"Venus?"

No response.

What was up with this kid? If she could hear, then why did she not respond? Not even to her name? Was she brain damaged? Did she hear but not process what was said to her? Or did she hear, process, and then not be able to turn it into action? Or, as I was beginning to suspect, was she so developmentally delayed that she wasn't really capable of much response?

"You and I are going to work on something else," I said. I pulled out the chair next to hers. I picked up a red crayon. I put the crayon in her hand. Venus didn't even pretend to take it. The crayon dropped through her fingers to the tabletop.

"Come on, now, Venus." I picked up the crayon again. "Here, put this in your hand." I uncurled her fingers and placed the crayon into it. Holding my hand over hers, I drew a straight line down the paper in front of her.

"Can you do that?" I asked.

Venus let the crayon drop through her fingers to the tabletop.

Taking the crayon myself, I made another line. "Now, you try."

Venus just sat.

I leaned very close to Venus's face. "Wake up in there." I said it quite loudly.

"Woo! What you doing back there?" Billy cried, whirling around in his seat.

"I'm talking to Venus."

"Well, I don't think you got to shout. She's right in front of you."

"I'm trying to get Venus to take notice."

"I can do that!" Billy said cheerfully, and before I could respond, he'd bolted out of his chair and trotted over.

"Ah-ah-ah!" he screamed in Venus's face and bounced up and down like a chimpanzee.

"Billy, get back in your seat this minute!"

"Look at me, psycho girl! Look at me! Ah-ah-ah-ah!" He was shouting at the top of his lungs and pulling stupid faces.

Venus responded to that all right. She went shooting right over the table after Billy, who hooted with fear and tore off. Stimulated by the excitement, the other boys leaped up. Shane and Zane ran, shrieking loudly, their movements wild and uncoordinated. Jesse, seeing a chance to get even, tripped Billy up as he ran by. In a split second, Jesse was on top of him pummeling him. A few seconds later, Venus was on top of both of them, ripping at Jesse's shirt, biting his hair.

Wearily, I pried everyone apart and forced them into chairs.

Chapter Five

The rest of that week passed in relentless chaos, and I spent most of it in damage control rather than teaching.

Every time the children came into the classroom, they had to remove their shoes. Of course this made getting ready for recess, lunch, and going home a pain, as only Billy and Jesse could tie their own shoes. However, it gave me the first small way to force bonding upon them because I made Billy and Jesse responsible for tying the twins' shoes and nobody could leave until it was done. Fortunately Venus usually wore slip-on shoes. I wouldn't have trusted her to let anyone help her.

For the first time in my career I was maintaining not one "quiet chair" but five – one for each student – because they all had a knack for getting into one big fistfight together.

Not a single day went by that week without my needing to use all five simultaneously at some stage. Indeed, most of the first three days were spent "sitting on chairs," as Billy termed it.

Bemused by having four feisty boys with cowboy names, I decided I'd capitalize on that in my efforts to bond us together as a group. I decided we'd become a cowboy "gang." We'd think up a name and a code of behavior and some fun things to do together to denote our "belongingness" and that would be the beginning of group harmony.

Unfortunately, no one told the kids that was the point of it.

I realized my mistake immediately. While cowboy gangs meant belonging and being loyal to an agreed code of ethics and sticking up for one another, they also meant guns and shooting and lots of macho behavior. In a word, outlaws. Not something I needed to encourage! It was Jesse who first noticed this. We'd be an outlaw gang, he said brightly when I was talking about us being a "gang." I said, no, that wasn't the idea. We weren't going to be outlaws. Billy, ever being Billy, then chirped up, "Oh? Does that mean we're going to be in-laws?"

I quickly quashed the opportunity to live out violent fantasies. The boys were thus left to come up with something different for our "gang." In the end, they chose to become "The Chipmunk Gang," which seemed ironically meek to me, but they were happy to make up rules about how to be a good Chipmunk. Billy really got into this. He wanted a pledge and a secret handshake to denote membership. Jesse then suggested that it ought to be a secret society and we could have other special signals too, to let one another know we were Chipmunks. By the end of the week, the Freemasons had nothing over on us.

Throughout all of this, Venus remained a world apart. She did nothing. Almost catatonic in her lack of response, she had to be physically moved from place to place, activity to activity. However, an accidental bump would result in her coming alive with such unexpected fury that it was almost as if someone had pushed an "on" button. Once in "on" mode, Venus screamed like a wounded banshee and indiscriminately took after anyone within range. There seemed to be no coherence to her rage. It was unfocused, all-embracing, and dangerous.

I tried to include her. Whenever we brought our chairs into a circle to talk about something, I always made sure Venus was there, although this involved moving her chair for her and then moving Venus. In the afternoons, when Julie was there to look after the boys, I endeavored to spend some time alone with her. To do what? I was never sure. Just get a reaction, I think. One day I tried coloring. She would do none of it herself. Another day I tried dancing. I put music on and pulled her through the motions. "Pull" was the operative word. On yet another day I piled building blocks up in front of her and stacked them one by one on top of one another to make what I felt was a very appealing tower. It just asked to be knocked over. Could she knock it over? I challenged. Nope. No response. I lifted her hand for her and knocked over the tower. It fell. Venus didn't even blink. I built the tower partway up and put a block in her hand. Could she add it to the stack? Nope. Her hand just lay there, the block loose in her fingers. I finished building the tower. Then again. And again. Each time I lifted Venus's hand and knocked the blocks down again. She didn't even so much as give an impatient sigh of boredom.

Perplexed and frustrated by Venus's behavior, I took my troubles with me into the teachers' lounge. I didn't really expect anyone to give me answers when I moaned about what was going on in my classroom. Indeed, I wasn't even upset, just frustrated. Being a rather noisy person by nature, this was my way of coping with the pressure. It was also a way of thinking for me. I'd go down to the lounge, complain about what was happening, and in the process of hearing myself articulate the problem, I'd often come up with alternatives.

Julie, however, appeared unsettled. "You're feeling really angry about Venus, aren't you?" she said to me one afternoon after school when we were alone.

Surprised, I lifted my eyebrows. "No. I'm not angry. Why?"

"Well, you just seem angry. In the things you say. You're always complaining."

"It's not complaining. Just letting off steam, that's all." I smiled reassuringly at her. "That's different from anger. I don't feel anger at all."

Julie looked unconvinced.

I was having to face the fact that I'd rather misguessed Julie. Her small size, her sweet face, her long hair with its thick bangs and girlish, beribboned styles gave the sense of someone young and, well ... naive and impressionable. I'd rather arrogantly assumed I'd have a protégée, someone I could introduce to my special milieu and help her grow into a competent educator, much the way Bob had done with me. Only a week on, however, and the cracks in this fantasy were already beginning to show.

For instance, on Wednesday, Shane picked up the fishbowl from the window ledge to bring it to the table. This was something he had attempted to do on two or three other occasions, and each time I'd intercepted him and explained very specifically that it was forbidden to carry the fishbowl around because it was heavy and awkward, which might lead to a nasty accident. Moreover, the fish didn't like it very much. This time, however, he managed to pick it up without my noticing, and disaster struck. The water sloshed, surprising him, and he dropped it. Water, broken glass, and goldfish went everywhere. Shane immediately started to bawl.

Julie was closest to him. She smiled, knelt down, and put her arms around him. "Poor you, did that frighten you?" she said in the most soothing of voices. "Don't cry. It was just an accident." She took a tissue and dabbed his cheeks. "That's okay. You didn't mean to drop it, did you? Accidents just happen."

Listening to her, I felt ashamed. My immediate reaction

had been serious annoyance and I would have said to him, probably not too pleasantly, that here was the natural consequence of picking up the fishbowl and, thus, why we didn't do it. I wouldn't have comforted him at all. I would have made him help me mop up the water and catch the poor fish. Julie's response was so much more humane.

Thus it was with Julie. I found her almost pathologically compassionate. Nothing the boys did seemed to upset her. If someone was perfectly horrid, she'd say, "That isn't thoughtful," in a quiet, even voice. Or "I'm sure you didn't mean to do that. It was an accident, wasn't it?" when the little devil was looking her straight in the face. So too with Venus. No, Venus didn't respond any more to Julie than to me, but that was okay. "I'm sure she just needs time to adjust," Julie would say. "It's a loud, active environment. I think if we allow her to move at her own pace, she'll become more comfortable and trust us enough to feel like joining in. Let's not force anything. Let's just wait and see."

Instinctively, I did not agree with Julie's approach to Venus, but there still seemed to be logic in it. I could see that. The problem was that it just wasn't my way of tackling things. I was not a wait-and-see kind of person. I was a do-it-now, a something's-got-to-work kind of person whose success rested largely on a terrierlike refusal to stop harrying problems until I got what I wanted. Just leaving Venus to sit like a lump on a log was anathema to my whole personality. But I didn't say this. In the face of Julie's serene patience, I felt ashamed of my restless need to intervene.

After so much failure with Venus, I decided I would go right back to basics; so, I arrived Monday morning with a bag of M&Ms.

"Remember these?" I said to Bob as I came through the front office to collect my mail. I rattled the bag of candy.

Bob smiled sardonically.

Back in our very early days together, Bob had caused something of a scandal in the school district by using M&Ms to reward his students. This was the early 1970s when behaviorism was considered a radical approach and classrooms were still quite formal. In our quiet, semirural backwater no one had yet thought of equating something like candy with learning. Bob changed all that. Like many of us of that generation, he was out to build a better world. In his case, he wanted to show that his ragtag group of unruly, deprived youngsters could rise above their various labels and depressing environments, learn and progress. He started very concretely with the children, giving them M&Ms when they cooperated and worked. Sure enough, he soon had impressive results. He also soon had the whole school board down on him too, irate that he should be bribing children to learn. From then on, the term "using M&Ms" became a code among staff at our school for any kind of subversive behavior.

Initially I'd been very impressed with Bob's M&M system because it did work so effectively. It appealed to the kids on such a basic level that virtually all of them responded positively to some degree, and as most of them had already been labeled "unteachable" or "hopeless," I felt the end justified the means. Moreover, I liked the obvious practicality of it all. Consequently, even though I didn't know much about the theory behind behaviorism, I participated happily during the time I worked with Bob.

Later, however, as I became more experienced and better educated, I could see flaws in such a system and now seldom used behavioral techniques in their stricter forms. However, I still knew them to be effective tools when used judiciously, and I was never someone to throw away something useful.

When Julie came in that afternoon, I had her supervise the boys while I sat down with Venus. This involved the whole cumbersome process of moving Venus to the table, putting her into a chair, and pushing it in. She did none of it herself.

I took the chair across the table from her. Lifting up the bag of M&Ms, I waggled it in front of her. "Know what these are?"

"I know what they are, Teacher!" Billy shouted from clear over on the other side of the classroom. This made all the other boys look up.

"Yes, and if you get your work done, you can have some afterward, just like Venus," I said. "*If* you get your work in your folder done. But for now I need private time with Venus, so I'd appreciate it if you didn't interrupt."

Julie endeavored to reorient the boys. I reached across

the table and moved Venus's face so that she was looking at me. I shook the bag in front of her again. "Do you know what this is?" I had hoped for a spark of recognition in her eyes, but there was nothing. She stared through me. "Candy. Do you like candy?"

Nothing.

I opened the bag and spilled several colorful M&Ms across the tabletop.

No response. She continued to stare at my face.

Picking up one of the candies, I reached over and pushed it between her lips. I did it cautiously because I didn't want to set her off and I feared that if she felt threatened by my movement, it might. The M&M just sat there, hanging half in, half out of her mouth.

"Hooo!" Billy cried gleefully. "Look at psycho! She doesn't even know what to do with it. It's candy, stupid! You're supposed to eat it. Here, Teacher, give me some. I'll show her." And before I could respond, Billy was galloping across the room toward me.

"Me too! Me too!" Shane and Zane cried, almost in one voice. They too bolted from their chairs.

Only Jesse remained behind. "I'm not supposed to eat candy," he said prissily. "It makes me hyperactive."

Billy lunged forward, grabbing up the M&Ms on the table between Venus and me. "I love these," he said cheerily and popped a handful in his mouth. "Here, girlie, see? You eat 'em. Crunch, crunch, crunch, like this." He made a big, open-mouthed show of masticating.

Billy hadn't touched Venus. He hadn't even bent close, but something in his behavior must have seemed threatening because Venus suddenly erupted. She let out a loud, ululating shriek and leaped up from the chair. Grabbing hold of Billy by the throat, she crashed to the floor on top of him. Bits of half-eaten M&Ms flew everywhere. Billy fought loose, got up, and tore off in terror. Venus leaped to her feet and took after him, all the while screaming her singular, high-pitched scream.

Julie and I took after both of them. Chairs fell. Tables screeched as they were pushed aside. The twins, manic with excitement, joined in the chase, screaming and yelling too. Convulsing with tics, Jesse leaped up on top of the bookshelf.

"She's gonna kill me! She's gonna kill me!" Billy shrieked.

"Billy, stop running. Come here. Don't keep running; you're making it worse."

"No way I'm gonna stop!"

"Zane, sit down! Shane!"

The noise level in the room would have drowned out a jet engine. At just that moment I was extremely *glad* we were not down near the office where we could be heard.

At last Julie caught hold of Billy. Venus flung herself against them, and I grabbed her, pulled her back in a bear hug.

Venus reacted violently to this. She fought against my grip, rocking back and forth rapidly, knocking her head repeatedly against my chest. She kicked viciously back at my legs. In an effort to force her into a sitting position so that she couldn't hurt me, I sank down to my knees. Even though I was much taller and heavier, I had a hard time bringing her into a sitting position.

"Julie, help me," I said.

Leaving the frightened boys over by the windows, Julie crossed to where Venus and I were struggling on the floor.

"I need to stop her legs. Take hold of them."

Tentatively, Julie reached forward.

"You're going to need to be more forceful than that," I grunted through the effort of keeping hold of Venus. "Just grab them and push down until they're against the floor."

Again, Julie reached down hesitantly.

"*Help* me. I'm going to lose my grip in a minute. Just grab her legs. Sit on them, if you must. I need to stop her kicking."

Julie managed to catch hold of Venus's legs. She leaned forward, pinning them to the floor.

This made things worse. Venus screamed louder and struggled harder.

"Calm down," I whispered in her ear.

She shrieked.

"Calm down, Venus. When you stop screaming, I'll let go. Until then, I need to hold you."

Louder still she went, so loud, in fact, that I could feel my eardrums vibrating.

"No. You need to stop screaming. When you stop, I'll let go."

Still she hollered painfully loudly.

"Calm down. Quietly, quietly."

"I can't do this," Julie moaned.

I couldn't tell what she meant, but assumed she had chosen a wrong position and didn't have a good grip on Venus's legs. "Just hang on. It'll be okay in a moment."

"I'm hurting her."

"No, you're not. You're fine. Just keep her legs against the floor."

"I'm really uncomfortable with this, Torey."

"Just hang on. Please. Just a little longer."

Throughout this exchange, Venus screamed nonstop.

"Come on, sweetheart," I said, bending close to Venus's ear. "Come on, now. Calm down. Quietly, quietly. Then I'll let go."

But as it turned out, the decision wasn't mine to make. "Torey, I just can't do this," Julie said. "I know I'm hurting her and it just feels wrong." And she let go, rising up and backing away.

That was all Venus needed. The small shift in balance was enough for her to break free of my grip. In an instant she was to her feet, to the door, through it, gone.

For a long, stunned moment I just stared after her. Then I glanced around quickly at the boys and Julie. "Look after them," I said. Then I took off out the door myself.

Chapter Six

Feeling panicky at losing Venus when she was so upset, I trotted through the school hallways, listening carefully for sounds of her. After the loud shrieking so close to my ears, I was finding it hard to hear properly. As I tried, all I could distinguish were the normal noises of a school in session: muffled voices, chairs moving, occasional coughs, teachers speaking. I ran down the stairs, down, down, down until I reached the ground floor. There was no sign of anything unusual. I opened the door out onto the playground.

There was Venus up on top of her wall. She was not in her normal relaxed glamor-queen pose but perched warily, poised to spring. Below her stood Wanda.

I approached very cautiously, fearful that Venus might bolt off if she saw me coming too close. The most notable thing to my mind – indeed, the most intriguing thing – was her wariness. Venus had not clocked out this time. She was watching me intently, not unusual in itself, but this was no vacant stare. The other interesting thing was that she did not appear upset. She had made a remarkable recovery from the incident in the classroom.

"Hello, Wanda," I said.

Wanda had a plastic baby doll in her arms. She smiled brightly. "Beautiful child."

I didn't know if she was referring to the doll or to Venus, who was definitely not being very beautiful at the moment. There was something atavistic about Venus's pose. She remained crouched, hands and feet on the wall, as if she'd spring off at me any time. With her wild hair and intent, rather fierce gaze, she reminded me of a drawing I'd seen once of a Neanderthal child, hunched over a kill.

"Venus's upset," I said to Wanda. "Do you suppose she will come down from the wall if you ask her?"

Wanda turned her head and looked up at her sister. "Her no come to school."

"She came today. She's upset now because we had a disagreement, but that happens sometimes, doesn't it? Sometimes we disagree. But no one is angry. And I'd like Venus to come back to the classroom."

Wanda turned her attention back to her doll. She hugged it, nestling it against her breast.

"Venus?" I asked. "Will you come down, please?"

Venus remained just as she was, tense, alert, and silent.

"I'm sorry if I upset you."

She watched me.

"Let's go back to the classroom."

"Her no go to school," Wanda interjected.

I looked at the older girl only to realize that she was talking about the doll. At least I think she was. Lifting the doll up, she squeezed it tightly, then she turned it over clumsily. The doll slipped out of its blanket and dropped headfirst onto the ground.

"Oh dear," Wanda said.

Without thinking, I bent down to pick up the doll. When I stood up again, Venus had disappeared off the other side of the wall.

"Oh *dear*," I said to Wanda. "She's gone."

"Beautiful child go home," Wanda replied and smiled blandly.

It seemed pointless to pursue Venus. The school day was only about fifteen minutes from being over; Venus was keyed up, and no doubt any attempt on my part to bring her back would only make things worse. So, I left Wanda to follow her home and went back inside.

Julie's efforts to calm down the boys, who'd clearly been distressed by the brouhaha, had been largely unsuccessful, so I returned to the classroom to find them running around chaotically. Feeling frustrated at having lost Venus in the manner I did and annoyed with Julie for her part in it, I was too irritable to deal calmly with them myself. So, in the end I decided we might as well do something to release all this pent-up emotion everyone was feeling.

"Let's have music," I said and went to lift down the box with cymbals, triangles, and tambourines in it, as I, for one, felt like bashing something.

The rest of the day passed effortlessly, although it had that walking-on-eggshells feel to it. The boys were remarkably well behaved for them, not even becoming overly boisterous when I gave them the chance to clash along to the music. Instead, they sat listening intently for the right places to play their instruments and so performed the song – an inane ditty about an amorous Mexican tomcat named Señor Gatos – with the seriousness of a Bach mass.

After the bell rang and the boys were seen off, I returned to the classroom, where Julie had remained to clean up. She was reshelving books when I came in.

"Look, I'm really, really sorry," she said before I could speak.

"Yes, we had a bit of a problem, didn't we?"

"I just found it really hard to hold Venus like that, Torey. She was so upset."

"I know it looked alarming," I said. "I know it looked like I was being too forceful with her, but I wasn't. She was seriously out of control. As the adults around her, our job is to bring order out of chaos. And that was chaos."

Julie regarded me.

I didn't want to get defensive over this, but I could see it wouldn't be hard. The problem with what I was doing with Venus was that it was gut-level stuff. I'd felt secure in my actions while I was doing them. Despite how it appeared, my sense was that this was a power issue. Venus appeared out of control, and on a cognitive level, she probably was. I doubt she had been knowingly thinking, "I want to impose my will on this woman and take control of this situation." However, on a deeper level, I sensed Venus was using her unresponsiveness and violent behavior to control her environment. For whatever reasons they might be occurring, the fact remained that they were inappropriate, inefficient ways to cope, and my responsibility was to help her change them into something more beneficial. Unfortunately, to do that, I had to begin by imposing my will over hers.

But it looked awful. And unaccountable. Because how did I explain "Well, this is what I sense about the situation," when "sense" could in no way be proven?

Julie lowered her head. "I'm really sorry, Torey. I know I let you down. But I was so scared we were hurting her. She was struggling so hard."

"It was forceful, but we weren't hurting her. It was physical, but we – you and I – were in control of what we were doing, so we weren't going to hurt her. That's the difference between what we were doing and what Venus was doing. At no time was I going to cross the line and hurt her, but she didn't have the same controls. That's why I needed you to hold her legs. Because I didn't want her to hurt herself. Or one of us."

Julie didn't respond immediately. She kept her head down, but I could see a frown playing itself out across her features.

"I know you're not going to want me to say this," she said when she finally did look up, "but I don't think what you're doing is right. I'm still really uncomfortable with this, because I just don't agree it's the way to do it."

"What do you think we should do?"

"I don't know. Just not that. We're scaring her so much," Julie said. "It's hard for me to see that's right."

"Yes, I think we are scaring her. To be honest, it scares me. But . . . sometimes we need to get in and do hard things. I have to have control in here, Julie. I have to be the one who sets the boundaries, not any of the children. Up until now Venus has been using these behaviors to control her world, and they haven't led to a happy life for her. It's my task to help her find other ways of doing things. But I can't do that until I've gained control of the situation. And to do that, I'm going to have to get down and dirty."

"Why can't you just wait? Just give her time to adjust to being in your class? Golly, we're only in the second week of school here, Torey. Can't you give her time? I mean, most of these kids come out of violent homes already. How can you justify using violence against them in the classroom?"

"I don't think it was violence. I was restraining her. It was controlled. I was simply setting the limits."

Julie nodded in a faint, unconvinced way.

A pause.

Julie let out a long, heavy sigh. "Okay, yeah. You're the one who's trained in all this. You've got the experience. I'm nobody really. Just an aide…" Another sigh. "But I still feel really uncomfortable with this 'means justifying the ends' kind of approach. Know what I mean?" She looked up at me. "I'm not kidding, Torey. This girl comes out of a nightmare home situation. I know, because I've been at this school for a while and I've seen what she and her siblings live like. I can't believe it's right for us to be horrible to her too. Ever."

"I don't think it did fall under being 'horrible to her,'" I said, "but I take your point." There was a pause. "I guess the only thing left to say is that in the future, it'd probably be better if you told me ahead of time when you don't want to do something rather than give up halfway through it. That way I'd cope better."

"Yeah, I'm just really sorry, Torey. It's a principles issue. I hope you understand."

The awful thing was that I did understand. And in my heart of hearts I agreed with Julie. In an ideal world people in my position should never have to force their will on children like Venus. But then in an ideal world there would be no children like Venus. In this pathetic, ignoble, real world we were stuck in, however, I could see no other way to bring order out of chaos. Before anything could be done to help Venus – or the boys either, for that matter – limits had to be set to achieve the secure environment necessary for growth. These were unhappy, out-of-control children, which was why they'd been placed in this room to begin with. They had to be certain I was more powerful than any of their worst urges or most horrible feelings, that I would not cave in, give up, or in any other way abandon them to those things in themselves they could not control. Only with that security could they then risk change.

The academic necessity of doing this, however, and the gritty reality of putting it into action were quite different things. Moreover, there was always the agonizingly fine line between the right amount of force and too much. And the fact that each child was different. And each circumstance. There was never a formula.

In my heart of hearts I dearly wanted to be the kind of person Julie believed in, the kind who could change the world simply by being loving enough. I felt it was crucial to keep such ideals alive, to keep believing that good would triumph over evil, that love could conquer anything, that no one was hopeless, because while the world might, in reality, not be that way, its only chance of changing was if we believed it could.

Consequently, I ended the day on a low note, going home more bothered by my encounter with Julie than by my encounter with Venus. This was such a hard position for me to defend. The truth was, I was on Julie's side, not mine.

Chapter Seven

The next morning Venus did not come to school.

At recess time I went down to the main office to phone her house.

"Hullo?" answered a thick, sleepy sounding voice.

I said who I was and why I was phoning. Was Venus there?

"Huh? What? Dunno," the voice at the other end replied. Then the line went dead.

I dialed again. Again, the same sluggish, sleepy voice. I couldn't actually tell if it was male or female. Female, I guessed, but not Wanda.

Once more I explained I was Venus's teacher and I was concerned because Venus was not at school. I said we'd had a disagreement the previous day and I was worried that Venus might still be upset. "Is this Venus's mother?" I asked.

The person at the other end was incoherent. Drunk possibly. Whatever, I couldn't make sense of the call.

As a consequence, I decided to visit Venus's house after school. Normally I didn't do this without giving the parents ample warning, but I was more than a little concerned about having allowed her to leave the school premises the day before in the state she was, and I wanted to see for myself that Venus was all right. Moreover, I wanted to make it perfectly plain to whomever was in charge at her house that unless she was ill, Venus had to attend school. This wasn't a choice Venus or Wanda could make. It was the law.

Julie came with me. Venus and her family lived about five blocks from the school down one of the seedy side streets between the railroad and the meat-packing plant. Although it was now known as an area of crime and drugs, a century earlier when the town had been founded, it had been laid out with broad sidewalks and boulevards planted with elm and cottonwood trees. The elms had long since succumbed to disease and been cut down, but the cottonwoods had thrived, heaving up the decaying sidewalks and casting the whole area into dense shade. Most of the houses had been built between the two world wars. None of them were large houses, but most had porches and broad lawns. Now, however, the porches were broken-down and un-painted. Many houses had boarded-up windows, and the lawns, unwatered and too shaded by the big trees, were worn largely to dirt.

Venus's home was not a house but a trailer set back on an empty lot. It was old and fitted permanently to a concrete foundation. The screen door was hanging open, and a man sat on the doorstep. I parked the car and got out.

He was a skinny, small-built man, probably two or three inches shorter than I was. His hair was that nondescript color somewhere between dark blond and light brown and it was rather wavy, rumpled almost, as if he hadn't bothered to brush it when he got up. He had a thick growth of stubble and a very hairy chest showing through his unbuttoned shirt. He sat, smoking a cigarette and watching us come up the path to the front door.

"Hello, I'm Venus's teacher from school."

"Well, hi," he said in a distinctly lascivious manner that made me very grateful for having Julie along.

"Is Venus here?"

He considered this a moment, as if it were a difficult question, then smiled. "Could be. You want a seat?"

"*Is* she?"

A slow, rather insolent shrug. "I reckon."

"Venus didn't come to school today. I'm concerned about her. It's very important that Venus come every day, unless she's ill. So, is she here?"

"Why? You want to see her?" he asked, but before I could respond, he leaned back and called over his shoulder, "Teri? Someone here about Venus. Teri?"

There was no response.

The man smiled at me in a casual way.

"Are you Venus's father?"

"You think all these black bastards are mine?"

A woman, perhaps in her late thirties, appeared in the doorway behind him. She had shoulder-length hair, corn rowed neatly into small braids, and looked as if she just woke up, despite it's being three-thirty in the afternoon. She blinked against the late summer sunlight. "Who are you?"

I explained again who I was and why I was there.

"Oh fuck," the woman said wearily. "Wanda?" she shouted over her shoulder. "Wanda, what the fuck you done? Didn't you take Venus to school again?"

Wanda stumbled to the doorway.

The woman turned. "What you done, you lamebrain. Why didn't you take her to school today?"

"Beautiful child," Wanda said and smiled gently.

"Yeah, I'll 'beautiful child' you one of these days. Why didn't you take her to school?"

"Her no go school," Wanda replied plaintively.

"Yes, her do go school, you big fucking idiot. How many times you got to be told? You're good for nothing." The woman raised her arm as if to hit Wanda, but she didn't. Wanda scurried off. The woman turned back to me. "Look, I'm sorry. It won't happen again."

"Are you Venus's mother?"

"Yeah." She ran her hands through her hair, pushing the braids back. She was a rather pretty woman in a tired sort of way.

"Could I talk with you a moment about Venus?"

"Why? What's she done?"

"She hasn't done anything. I was just wondering . . . could we chat a moment? I was hoping you could fill me in a little on her background."

The woman rubbed her face in a weary fashion and backed aside. "Yeah, come on in, if you want."

I stepped gingerly by the man, still sitting in the doorway. Julie, who was wearing a skirt, pressed it to her legs as she edged by. The man grinned up at us.

Inside there were two teenage girls and a boy sprawled over the furniture in front of the TV. Beyond, there was a built-in table with bench seats on either side. Wanda sat on one. She was doing nothing but staring at her hands.

"Get out of here, you guys," the woman said. "Turn off that fucking box. I told you half an hour ago to turn that off."

"Shut up, bitch," the boy said. He must have been about twelve or thirteen.

The woman raised her foot and kicked his leg none too gently. "Get moving."

He muttered crossly, got up, and went outside.

"Teri?" the man called from the doorway. "Get me another beer while you're at it."

"Get it yourself," she replied.

"Frenchie? Hey, Frenchie, get me a beer."

I didn't know which one was Frenchie, as there was no response from any of the people in the room.

"Wanda?" he called. "Wanda, get me a beer."

Lumbering out of her seat, Wanda plodded to the

refrigerator. She yanked the door open so hard that cans of beer tumbled out and went rolling across the floor. Teri swore at her. So did the man.

Heaving a discouraged sigh, Teri flopped down on the couch. She gestured for Julie and me to sit. "Just don't tell me you come about problems," she said wearily, "'cause there's nothing I can do. I got too many problems to deal with already. You can see that just looking around. So please don't say you're here about problems."

I could sense she was telling the truth there, that she really didn't have the resources to cope with much more. I felt sympathy for her then.

"Is Venus here?" I asked.

"Dunno," Teri said. She was obviously tired. She rubbed her hand over her face again.

"Do you suppose we could find out?" I asked. "I'd like to see Venus."

Teri lifted her head and scanned around the trailer, as if perhaps she'd overlooked the child. Then she turned her head and looked back at Wanda. "Wanda? Where's Venus?"

Wanda ambled out of her seat. She wandered down the narrow corridor and into one of the rooms at the end of the trailer. Several moments passed in expectant silence. Julie and I had our necks craned to see where Wanda had gone. Teri leaned forward and removed a cigarette from the pack on the coffee table. She lit it and took a long, slow drag, giving a relieved-sounding sigh at the end.

Wanda meandered out of the back room carrying something. As she came up to us, I could see it was the plastic doll, wrapped in a receiving blanket. It had been dressed in old baby clothes. Wanda smiled shyly at me and cuddled the doll. "Beautiful child," she said and smiled again.

"*Wanda*," Teri cried in exasperation when she saw the doll. "*Venus*, you asshole. I said go get Venus, not your fucking doll."

But Wanda never did get Venus. Indeed, we never managed to see Venus at all. Instead, Wanda wandered off with her doll into another part of the trailer and never returned, while I was distracted by the realization that Wanda needed intervention every bit as much as Venus.

Venus returned the next day as if nothing had ever happened, so I decided to pick up where I left off. During the time before school, I'd rearranged the classroom furniture to give me a small, cubiclelike space screened off from the rest of the room. This way I could work alone with Venus without constant interference from the boys.

That afternoon, after getting the boys settled with their folders and leaving Julie in charge, I took Venus around the corner of the file cabinet and into my little cubicle. I'd added a small table and two chairs. I sat her in one chair and positioned the other on the opposite side of the table. I sat down.

I got the feeling of a faint sense of alarm from Venus when I took her into this private area, but it was just a sense. Nothing about her facial expression changed much, and she sat without a lot of encouragement, but there was a slight glance around the small area and a springy lightness to her shoulders that I was coming to recognize as the precursor to movement. She didn't move, however. Within a minute or two, she'd settled down to stonelike stillness.

Opening the package of M&Ms, I took out a small handful and held them out. "Remember these? We had these day before yesterday. Remember?"

To look down at the candies in my hand, she only moved her eyes.

I let the M&Ms spill onto the table between us with a satisfying clatter. Bright and colorful, they lay scattered across the tabletop. I left them like that for several moments and did nothing, hoping Venus might be tempted enough to take one of her own volition or at least register an interest in them.

Not so.

"Candy," I said. "Do you like candy? Most children do."

She stared at me, her face immobile as wood.

"We eat them," I said. I put one in my mouth. "Mmmm. Really sweet. Chocolate-y."

She kept staring and I got the feeling that she thought I'd gone stark raving mad. This made me smile and eventually laugh.

"Here, you have one," I said. I picked up a red M&M and put it between her lips. It hung there, so I took a finger and pushed it the rest of the way into her mouth.

Nothing.

"Can you taste it?"

Nothing.

"Try chewing it."

Venus just sat.

"Chew." I reached over and moved her chin with my hand while making exaggerated chewing movements myself. I was reminded, as I did this, of a scene from a *Star Trek* program where a member of the starship crew was trying to teach the fine art of eating to a woman who had spent most of her life as a sort of living machine. Not so unlike Venus.

This didn't seem to have an effect, so we both just sat. The chocolate would melt in her mouth eventually and she would taste it whether she wanted to or not. I watched her, waiting to see her swallow.

Eventually she did.

"Nice?" I asked. "Do you want another?" I reached over and shoved a green M&M between her lips.

Venus and I spent forty minutes doing that. During this time I pushed a total of twenty-two M&Ms into her mouth. Nothing changed over the course of that whole time. She just stared at me as I pushed the candy into her mouth, waited for it to melt, waited for her to swallow, and pushed the next one in. She never looked down at the candies, never appeared to chew them, never tried to get them more quickly, never even acknowledged they were there at all.

All this time I kept up a quiet patter, largely about the

taste of the candy and the sensation of eating them, but Venus responded to my words no more than she did to the M&Ms.

When the bell rang to signal the end of the school day, I got up, put the candy away, and brought Venus around the corner of the cubicle to join the other children.

Wanda was at the door to take Venus home. Julie charged by, trying to keep up with the boys as they raced for their buses. I beckoned to Wanda.

"Will you come talk to me a minute, Wanda?"

"No talk to strangers."

"Have you been told that?" I asked. "Yes, that's a sensible rule, isn't it? But I'm not a stranger. I'm Venus's teacher. I've been to your house. Remember? I came and saw you the other day after school."

Wanda was carrying the baby doll wrapped in the receiving blanket again. She held it close to her chest.

"I'd like to talk to you about Venus. Won't you come in and sit down?"

"No go stranger house."

"Here. Would you like some M&Ms?" I asked. It was dirty of me, because I was probably undoing all the efforts to keep Wanda safe from strangers, but it did the trick. Wanda ambled into the room happily as I poured the candies on the tabletop.

"Is that your dolly?" I asked as Wanda sat down.

"Beautiful child," she said and caressed the molded plastic hair.

"Yes. You like to take care of your doll, don't you?"

"Beautiful child. Her no go to school."

"No, your dolly doesn't go to school, does she? But what about Venus? Venus goes to school, doesn't she?"

"Beautiful child." Wanda caressed the doll again.

"Can you talk to me about Venus? What does Venus do when she isn't at school?"

"Beautiful child."

"Here, have some more M&Ms."

Unlike her sister, Wanda had no inhibitions about eating. She stuffed the candy into her mouth by the handful and chomped messily.

"When I came to your place the other day, where was Venus then? I didn't see her. Remember, you tried to find her. Where was Venus?"

"Her no go to school."

"No, I know that. But what does she do at home? Can you tell me?"

"Eat."

"Venus eats?"

"Eat!" Wanda said more insistently, and I realized she meant she wanted more candy. The package was almost empty. I poured what was left onto the table. Wanda scrabbled it up with both hands. I looked beyond her to Venus, who stood beside the doorway. She wasn't watching us. She was just staring into space.

"Go home now," Wanda said when the candy was gone.

"Wait," I said.

"Go home now." She got up. "Beautiful child. Go home, beautiful child," she called to Venus. Before I could stop her, she was to the door and out with Venus in front of her.

It was only after she'd left that I discovered the doll in its receiving blanket, forgotten on the floor.

Chapter Eight

I had one activity I'd always done with all my classes. Indeed, I'd used it occasionally in therapy with individual children as well. I'm sure it has some proper, formal name and probably proper, formal rules, but my version grew out of desperation one rained-in recess many years back when I was a student teacher. The children couldn't go outside to play and were wild with pent-up energy, so I decided to take them on an imaginary journey. We all sat down in a circle on the floor and closed our eyes. Then I told them to look inward, to envisage a deep-sea diving bell, because I was going to take them on an adventure trip under the sea.

This worked fantastically. I had the children first imagine their diving bell – what it looked like, what was in it, how it felt and smelled – then they imagined the descent down deep into the water. Then we started looking for things and I asked different ones to describe what they saw. If their descriptions were sparse, I queried gently to make a more complete picture. No one had to contribute but everyone did.

We stayed in the circle, our eyes closed, and wandered around under the sea for about fifteen minutes. When we finally emerged back into the classroom, the children were delighted. We made pictures of it to put on the wall in the hallway and talked about our trip for a long time afterward. Indeed, for many it became the single best memory they had of my student teaching.

From then on, I made imaginary journeys regularly. As I became more experienced, I knew more about what I could do on the journeys. If the children needed to relax and calm down, we visited quiet places and spent a lot of our time listening and feeling the atmosphere. If the children needed a change of scenery, as during that rainy recess, we went somewhere exotic. If the children needed cheering up, we visited a circus or a zoo or a carnival. Once we had an imaginary birthday party. At Christmastime we went to the North Pole. I found it a particularly useful activity with attention-deficit children, who often had a hard time calming themselves down. The act of sitting together on the floor with our eyes closed seemed to help them block out enough other stimuli so they could focus well.

Thus, this seemed like it would be a useful technique for my Chipmunks. I felt Jesse, in particular, would benefit.

Because he suffered from Tourette's syndrome, he was often jerking and twitching involuntarily. It also caused him to make sudden noises. He didn't shout out obscenities, the Tourette's tic popularized in the media, which is actually rather rare; however, he did make a sharp yelping sound, rather like a startled bark, and he did this quite a lot. He also had a noisy, stylized sniff that went along with his facial tic, and this produced a piggy kind of noise. All considered, the others were tolerant about these tics, or at least they didn't single out the tics as a reason to fight with him. Nonetheless, the tics were disruptive and occasionally alarming, if you didn't expect them.

So I felt the guided journeys might be of benefit to Jesse, because his tics always became worse under stress. I was hoping that the journeys might provide a relaxing alternative in his day that would calm the noise and motion a little bit.

I also hoped they would help Billy. My goal for him was that he develop awareness of his thoughts *before* he did something, so that he had a better chance of intervening. At the moment, Billy just *did* and then coped with the aftermath. I was sure he wasn't even conscious there were any "before" thoughts affecting his actions, so constructive use of imaginary journeys seemed like a good place to start helping him develop an understanding of thoughts as something you produced yourself and could control.

Thus, Monday after morning recess, I said, "Okay, gang,

we're going to do something different. Once you have your shoes off and in the box, I want you to come over here and sit down in a circle on the floor."

This elicited excitement. Though somewhat uncontrolled and chaotic, this group was also enthusiastic, which made them fun to work with when they weren't killing one another.

"Okay, I want you sitting, but get comfortable. Shane, keep your hands to yourself, please. Venus, sit down." I had to rise up again and direct Venus into place. "Zane? Sit. No, *sit*.

"Everybody ready? Now, we're going to take a journey. Right here. Right now. And since we're Chipmunks, I think we should visit the woods. Ready?"

All the boys nodded.

"Close your eyes then. Not tight. Just gently, so you're comfortable. Keep them closed. Get yourself comfy." I closed my eyes too at the beginning and leaned forward, forearms on my knees. "Now, we're off. We're walking toward the woods. Can you see? Look ahead." I opened my eyes and checked on everyone. "No, Zane, keep your eyes shut. Look ahead inside your mind. There's the woods. See the trees? Everybody look in their minds. See if you can see the woods ahead. Can you?"

"Yeah!" Billy said enthusiastically.

"See if you can tell what kind of trees they are. What kind of trees are in your woods? Does anybody know?"

"Yeah," said Billy immediately. "Pine trees!"

"You're seeing pine trees. Does everyone see pine trees? Or does someone see something different in their woods?"

"I see the kind that's got big flat leaves," Shane said.

"Okay. Good. Pine trees and the kind of trees that have flat leaves. The kind that lose their leaves. We call them 'deciduous trees.' So, look at your trees carefully. What kinds of trees are in your woods?"

"I see trees with leaves *and* pine trees," Jesse said. "My forest has got them both."

"Yeah, me too," Billy said, not wanting his imaginary woods to be without something someone else saw.

"Are they tall trees?" I asked. "Have they got thick trunks? Look around? Do you see any young trees there too?"

"Mine are *big*!" Billy cried.

"Can you put your arm around one of them, Billy? Everybody. Go up to one of your trees and try to reach around it. Feel the bark. Feel it with your fingers. But put your face against the tree too. You're trying to stretch your arms all the way around. Feel what it feels like."

I opened my eyes again slightly to see the boys, all of them with their hands stretched out in the air, reaching to feel imaginary trees. I peeked over at Venus. She too had her eyes shut tight. She didn't have her hands up in the air like the boys did, but her fingers were splayed out on her knees and twitching slightly, as if possibly she was feeling for an imaginary tree of her own.

"Mine's got knobbly bark!" Billy cried with unexpected loudness.

"Quietly, Billy," I said. "You'll scare away the animals."

"Knobbly bark," he whispered.

"Yeah, mine too. I can feel it on my cheek," Jesse said.

"What about you, Zane? What does your tree feel like?"

"It's a pine tree. It's rough."

"Can you smell it?"

He nodded and smiled slightly, his eyes still closed. "Yeah."

"I can smell mine!" cried Billy, still a little loud.

"Shut up, Billy, you'll scare the animals away," Jesse said.

"Oh look," I said. "Something's moving through the trees over there. What is it? Look carefully. Over there in the distance. Going through the trees. Do you see it too?"

"A deer!" Billy positively shouted.

"You stupid pisser!" Jesse cried. "You keep hollering. You scared the deer away!" And before I knew what was coming, Jesse punched Billy in the mouth.

This, of course, rather rudely pulled us all out of our imaginary visit to the woods. Not expecting to be hit, Billy burst into tears. Jesse got up and stomped off, twitching and yelping. Zane and Shane were on their feet, shouting, "That's not fair! They wrecked our time. We weren't done! They wrecked it! They ought to go in the quiet chair!"

I felt sorry for Billy, innocent victim of his own enthusiasm, because I knew he hadn't meant to wreck things. He had simply been enjoying himself and, as ever, had lost control. I gave him a cuddle and rubbed his chin. And while I could hardly condone what Jesse had done, I didn't want to punish him. He too had simply been caught up in the imaginary journey. So I walked over and put an arm around him afterward, saying I was sorry Billy had disturbed things for him and I understood how it made him feel angry but reminding him for the millionth time that I couldn't allow hitting and please would he try to remember that?

Shane and Zane stood forlornly. "Can we do it again? It wasn't fair. They wrecked it. Please, can we do it again?" Zane asked.

"Yes, we will. But not just now," I said. "We'll do it tomorrow at the same time."

"Noooo," Shane moaned. "I want to do it now. It's not fair."

"I know. You feel disappointed. Tomorrow we'll do it again."

"Pleeeeeeeese?"

"Tomorrow."

"This afternoon. Okay?" Zane begged. "Pleeeeeeeese?"

"We can't this afternoon. Julie comes then and we're getting a new girl, so we need to do other things. Tomorrow after morning recess."

The twins stomped off, disgruntled, to their tables.

I turned to look for Venus. And there she was, still sitting cross-legged on the floor, her eyes still tight shut. I regarded her. Why was she like that? Again, my first instinct was to believe she couldn't hear us and thus had not realized we'd stopped the activity. But then, if she couldn't hear, she wouldn't have known we'd *started* the activity. Or what we were doing during the activity. So why was she still sitting with her eyes closed? Did some part of her brain not register that we'd stopped? Or not want to register we'd stopped? Or was it just plain resistance?

Coming over, I squatted down directly in front of her. "Venus?"

No response.

I was a little reluctant to touch her, in case she wasn't expecting it. "Open your eyes, Venus. We're done with the imaginary journey. We're doing something else now."

Slowly, she opened her eyes.

I smiled. "You stayed a little longer in the woods than the rest of us, huh?"

She looked at me.

I looked back at her.

Her expression was so enigmatic that she could have been an alien child sitting there.

That day the part-time students were due to start coming. Up until that point we hadn't been much of a cohesive group, as chaos had always been too close at hand. However, the arrival of "them other kids," as the boys chose to call them, brought out the team spirit.

"They ain't gonna be Chipmunks, are they?" Shane asked during morning discussion as I prepared them for the arrival of our first new student.

"*No*!" Billy cried. "No, Teacher, they *can't* be Chipmunks. Okay? Please? 'Cause just us guys get to be Chipmunks."

"What do you think about that, Jesse?"

"Yeah, just us guys who live here."

"All right then," I replied.

"I think we ought to have a special signal," Billy said. "You know, something that makes us *know* we're Chipmunks." It was said as if this were some elite society we were speaking of. "Something to help us keep our spirits up when we got all these other geezers in here to put up with."

"Let's go 'Chip, chip, chip, chip, chip,'" Zane suggested.

"Don't you think that might get a little noisy?" I asked.

Of course, this meant all the boys had to do it.

"And not too discreet."

"What's discreet mean?" Billy asked.

"Discreet means when you keep something kind of private and don't make a big show of it," I said. "Something like a hand signal might work better."

The conversation pursued this vein for several minutes with the boys trying out various movements and gestures that they thought could serve as this special signal. I watched Venus as they talked. She was sitting at her table, as were the boys sitting each at their individual tables, as we'd not yet progressed to the point of being able to sit peaceably next to one another. Given my big, booming voice I had no trouble being heard when the kids were scattered all over the room, and the boys' personalities were all so loud and expansive that the distance among them still helped more than it hindered. They could jump up, swing their arms around, and be their usual, lively selves without crashing into anyone else. In this respect, the distance was useful for Venus too, as she did not explode unpredictably simply because someone had inadvertently invaded her space. However, it also made it easier for her to isolate herself. I could tell she was completely tuned out of this conversation. Leaning slightly forward, arms crossed on the tabletop, eyes blank and unfocused, she was as motionless as the furniture itself. And, indeed, that's how the boys responded to her. Venus, for all intents and purposes, was not there.

"Well, what I think," Zane said, "is that we should wiggle our feet. Like this. 'Cause we're the ones who don't got no shoes on. If you don't got shoes on, you're a Chipmunk, huh? And so you can wiggle your toes."

"Hey, way cool!" Billy cried, whipping off a grubby sock and sticking his bare foot up on the table with a thud. He wiggled his toes.

"Billy, remove it," I said sharply.

Billy didn't take his foot down but instead burst into a spontaneous rendition of a children's ditty, "Stuck my head in a little skunk's hole! Little skunk said, 'Well, bless my soul! Take it out! Take it out! Take it out!'" Zane and Shane chimed in with him, "REMOVE IT!"

One of the children coming to me for extra support was a little girl named Gwen, although everyone called her Gwennie. Gwennie was eight, a very attractive little girl with shiny, straight, bobbed blonde hair and unexpectedly dark eyes. She had originally been diagnosed as having

HFA, which stood for high-functioning autism. Like many autistic-type children, Gwennie was a bright child, doing well academically. Her reading skills were excellent and her math skills were good. However, social skills were another matter altogether, because Gwennie took everything literally and at face value. She could not interpret the nuances of speech, of other people's facial expressions or their behavior, nor could she understand how to adjust her own behavior to that of those around her. As a consequence, she was unpopular with the children in her class because she often said blunt, hurtful things or barged in on games or activities.

The social inadequacy was further hampered by her interests. Intensely pursued special interests are common in perfectly normal children of this age group and seem to be part of a healthy developmental process. Hence, the typical "collecting" stage, where acquiring trading cards or toys becomes a fascination for most school-age children, and for some, at least momentarily, a real fixation. As is typical for children with autistic tendencies, Gwennie raised these childish obsessions to a whole different level. For example, she collected pencils. While pencils themselves weren't an unusual object of desire and a lot of the kids collected them, particularly the pretty, shiny ones or those with vivid designs or strangely shaped erasers, Gwennie was fascinated by plain old standard-issue yellow ones. She routinely carried about twenty of them around with her at any given time, and despite the fact that they all looked just alike to the rest of us, Gwennie knew each of these pencils individually. She liked to feel and examine them regularly and to lay them out on the tabletop and then line them up in ascending order from the longest to the shortest. Every time she went into a new classroom, she insisted on knowing if there were any other yellow pencils in there and couldn't settle down until she found out if there were and if so, how many and how well used. Each time she saw one, her little eyes just lit up.

This all paled, however, compared to Gwennie's *big* obsession: foreign countries. Gwennie had acquired an encyclopedic knowledge on this subject and loved nothing better than telling you about the geography of Indonesia or the population statistics of Belgium. The problem was, this was *all* she really wanted to talk about. When I first found out she was due to spend time in our room, I was curious because her academic skills were so good. After half an hour of listening to her, however, I quickly came to suspect it was not so much a matter of giving Gwennie the benefits of my room as it was giving Gwennie's teacher the benefits of a break from her. We all soon discovered just how tiring she could be.

She came through the door Tuesday just after lunch.

"Hello, Gwennie," I said. "Here, I'll show you where you're going to sit."

"The total land area of Sweden is four-hundred-forty-nine-thousand, nine-hundred-sixty-four square kilometers. Its capital city is Stockholm and Stockholm is also the largest city. Sweden is bordered by Norway on the north and Finland on the east. It is one of the five Scandinavian countries. The others are Finland, Norway, Denmark, and Iceland. The people are chiefly of Germanic ethnicity with a few ethnic Finns. The other major cities are Gothenburg, Uppsala, Sundsvall, Östersund."

"Okay, Gwennie, thank you. Would you sit here, please?"

"Have you been to Sweden?"

"No. Here's your folder."

"Have you been to France? France has five-hundred-forty-three-thousand, nine-hundred-sixty-five square kilometers and the capital city is Paris. About thirty-four percent of French land is cultivated."

"Hooo," Billy said softly under his breath, "this one's cuckoo."

Jesse raised one socked foot and wiggled his toes.

As Gwennie was going to come three afternoons a week, I decided that here would be an ideal partner for Venus. She and Gwennie could work on social skills together, which even I realized was pretty much of a long shot, as both girls were virtually at nil in this department. But I felt that having two was better than my working individually with them, as they could model for each other in a way I never could.

The first day I sat the two girls down together, which, of course, meant maneuvering Venus into position like a doll, and corralling Gwennie, who was trying to tell Jesse about

South Korea. I chose just about as basic an activity as I could. I had cut out pictures from magazines and pasted them onto index cards. Each showed a person with a very definite facial expression – smiling, laughing, crying, frowning – and I'd collected about four examples of each.

"Can you tell me how this girl feels?" I asked Gwennie and showed her a picture of a girl beaming at a little puppy.

Gwennie looked at the picture.

"How does she feel? Look at her face. See what her lips are doing? What does that tell you?"

"Do you know the capital of Belize?"

"Gwennie, we aren't talking about countries just now. Look at the picture, please. What is this expression? It's a smile, isn't it? What does a smile tell us about this little girl? What does it tell us she is feeling?"

"Most people in Belize are Roman Catholics. Are you a Roman Catholic?"

"Gwennie, we aren't talking about that just now. Look at the picture, please. What does this girl's smile tell us about the way she is feeling?"

Gwennie leaned forward and studied the picture intently.

"What does this picture tell you?"

Gwennie looked up, her eyes wide. "Maybe this girl's Finnish?"

Of course, doing this activity with Venus was even more fun. I showed her the same picture I had showed to Gwennie. "Look. See this girl?"

Venus stared blankly at my face.

"Down here, Venus." I reached over and gently tipped her head down enough to see the card with the picture on it. "Look. She has a puppy in her arms. And look at her face. See. See how her lips go up. She's smiling. She sees that puppy and she obviously likes holding him, because look how much she is smiling at him. Can you make a smile for me?"

Venus stared blankly at me.

"Here. Like this." I made an obvious smile with my own lips. "Can you do that?"

"I can do that," Gwennie interjected.

"Good girl. Look at Gwennie. She can smile. How are you feeling when you smile?"

"Ill," Gwennie replied.

"You're feeling ill?" I asked with surprise.

"How are you feeling? Ill," Gwennie said and smiled expectantly, and I realized she was simply parroting back a response she had heard somewhere before. This was conversation as far as she was concerned. Each question had a specific, invariable answer.

"Can you make a smile like that, Venus?"

No response.

"Here. Like this," Gwennie said and made an exaggerated smile. She leaned toward Venus.

Whether Venus was about to go into attack mode or not, I couldn't discern, but she shifted in her seat when Gwennie had suddenly moved toward her.

"Not too close. Venus feels nervous when someone gets unexpectedly close," I said and put an arm out to separate the two girls.

"Is she an Eskimo?"

"No."

"Eskimos live in the Arctic. Their proper name is Inuit. It means 'real people.' They speak more than six different languages."

"No, Venus is American, just like you. Only she doesn't always feel like talking."

"Perhaps she is a Carmelite nun," Gwennie responded earnestly.

Chapter Nine

The next afternoon started off badly. Billy got into a fight with a child from another class during the lunch break and was banished to the principal's office. Bob gave Billy the expected lecture and then made him sit in one of the "principal's chairs," which were lined up in the hall outside Bob's office. This was where the "bad kids" sat until Bob told them they could return to their classroom. Billy was incensed. As ever, he couldn't see how anything that had happened was his fault, and when he came back to my room after the bell rang, his face was red with indignant anger, his voice on the edge of tears at the unfairness of it all. *Everybody* hated him. *Everybody* treated him unfairly. It was this stupid school and why did he have to come here anyway? He wanted to go home *right then*. He wanted his brother. He wanted to go to school where his brother was, because then people wouldn't keep picking on him.

Fortunately, Julie was there, so she could take the other kids, because I wanted to spend time alone with Billy. My gut feeling was that what he really needed was sympathy and a cuddle, and I knew if I was nice to him, it would make him cry. I wanted to spare him the humiliation of bawling in front of the others, particularly Jesse, who didn't have a lot of patience with Billy anyhow.

This would have worked out, if I hadn't forgotten about Gwennie. I was in the hallway with Billy when she came up the stairs. "Hi," she said cheerfully. "How come he's crying?"

"None of your business!" Billy snapped back.

"How come he's crying? What happened? Did he fall down? I fell down. Yesterday. Look. I was on my bike and my bike fell over." She showed us two scraped knees.

"Make her go away," Billy pleaded.

"I got a Raleigh bike. It came from England. England is one of – "

"Gwennie, could you just go on into the classroom, please? I'm talking to Billy just now."

"Yeah, it's private!" Billy said.

Gwennie didn't move. She just stared at us. "What's wrong with him?" she asked me, as if Billy weren't even there. "Has he got something the matter?"

"Yeah, you!" Billy cried and swung an arm out at her.

Gwennie wasn't as out of it as she appeared because she

quite gracefully stepped back out of his swing. And just stood there.

"Gwennie, please. Julie's waiting for you."

It was no use. I gave up, opened the door, and took both Gwennie and Billy into the classroom.

Julie was only just coping. Shane and Zane had gotten into an argument about who was supposed to use the cassette recorder first and Jesse barked his nervousness.

"I remember being a baby," Gwennie suddenly announced. "I remember my mother putting me in a little chair outside."

"That's nice," I said hurriedly. "Now could you find your chair in here, please? You too, Billy, time to start your folder. You find your chair as well."

"Oh? When did my chair get lost?" he queried.

"I mean, sit down in it."

"I was sitting in my little chair and I saw a bird," Gwennie said. "A bobolink. Bobolinks live in the Great Plains. Some live in Canada. The capital of Canada is Ottawa. Canada's a very big country – "

"*Gwennie.*" I pointed sternly to her chair. That's when I noticed Venus was not at her table.

"Where's Venus?" I asked Julie.

Julie, looking decidedly harassed, glanced around quickly. "I think she went to the bathroom. She *was* here. I'm sure she was here."

I went over to the window. There was Venus, lounging on top of her wall. I had no idea if she had ever come in from lunch or not. "We can't have this," I said. "The amount of time that kid misses because no one notices she isn't here. I'll go get her."

"No," Julie said with unexpected feeling. "*I'll* go get her."

I could hear the unspoken plea not to be left alone in charge of the others. Over the previous few days, I was becoming increasingly aware that I was expecting a bit too much of Julie. While she was experienced in the classroom, she was not a teacher and had no pretensions to be. Obviously, my room had come as a shock after her experiences as a support person to Casey, who was hardworking, sweet-tempered, and confined to a wheelchair.

So while Julie went down to the playground to charm Venus off her wall, I got everyone started on their work. Or at least she tried to charm Venus. Minutes passed. Five, ten. I glanced out the window and Julie was still down there, standing beside the wall, talking up to Venus, who appeared to be ignoring her completely.

About twenty minutes later, Julie returned. She didn't say anything, but the look of defeat said it all.

"I'll go get her," I said. "Everybody here is busy. They can do an activity of their choice, when they're done with their folders. If you run into problems, call Bob up."

I think when I said that I knew I wasn't coming back up myself, at least not for a long time.

Down in the empty playground, I crossed to where Venus was sitting on the wall. "Venus, it's time for class. When you hear the bell ring, it's time to come in."

No response whatsoever. She was in her glamour-queen pose, reclined back with her arms behind her, supporting her weight, head back, eyes closed, one leg up, one leg outstretched along the wall, long hair tumbling down.

"Venus?" I stood below her. The wall was about six feet high, so it was really a very inconvenient height to bring her down from.

She totally ignored me.

"Venus? Do you hear me? It's time to go in. It's time for class."

I knew I'd crossed the Rubicon. By coming out onto the playground myself to get her, I'd played into her game. The only way to make it my game was to ensure she went back with me. I couldn't back down now and give up. At the same time, I knew whatever I did had to be well gauged. If I reached for her and missed or did not get enough of a grip, she would be over the wall onto the other side and off, the way she had done the other time.

I stood a moment longer, trying to figure out the best way to tackle the problem. It was difficult because the wall was taller than I was and Venus, of course, was on top of it. I didn't want to lose her but I didn't want to hurt her either. Nor myself.

Was she aware of me? This was the question that always lurked in the back of my mind. How much awareness was in this incredibly inert child? On the one hand, I felt much of it had to be within her control on some level. There was the definite feel of a power struggle to much of her behavior, certainly during moments like this. She didn't *want* to come in and she was accustomed to not having to do what she didn't want. Like a possum playing dead, if she remained motionless long enough, she was left alone. On the other hand, it was such *total* unresponsiveness. This gave it the feel of something physical, something so globally wrong that it was beyond her control, like brain damage or hearing loss or a very low IQ. And because I didn't know, because I hadn't encountered a child like Venus before, I was left feeling scared of doing the wrong thing.

But inaction never accomplished anything. With one sudden move, I jumped up and grabbed hold of her leg with one hand and her dress with the other. She hadn't been expecting that. I quickly pulled her off balance and she came down off the wall and into my arms.

Venus sprang to life then. She shrieked blue murder and fought furiously against my grip.

I held on. I tried to sit down to keep her from kicking me, because, of course, being outside, she had her shoes on.

Venus screamed and screamed and screamed. Teachers and children came to the windows of their classrooms. Indeed, I saw someone come out of the house across the street and peer over their fence.

I wrapped my arms around her in a tight bear hug and sat down. Venus came down with a thud into my lap. She kicked and screamed and struggled.

Bob galloped out of the building. "Do you need help?"

"Hold on to her legs. I just want to get her controlled."

Bob grabbed Venus's legs and pinned them to the asphalt.

"Calm down," I said in a soft voice to her ear.

Venus screamed and struggled harder. She disliked Bob holding her legs intensely and directed most of her energy there.

"Calm down," I said again. "I'll let go when you're calm."

She continued to fight fiercely. Minutes ticked by. She still screamed in a high-pitched, frantic manner.

Minutes. Minutes. Minutes. It was hard to hang on to her. Bob grimly kept hold of her legs. My arms hurt with the tension of keeping her against me. How much worse it must have been for her.

Everyone could hear us. There was an embarrassment factor I hadn't expected. Normally this was the kind of gritty activity that went on behind closed doors.

I kept talking to her, almost whispering in an effort to get her attention. "Calm down. Quiet. Quiet now. I'll let go when you're quiet." Over and over and over again.

A small eternity spun itself out over the playground. I had no idea how long we were there because I couldn't raise my arm to see my watch, but I was afraid we were going to run into recess. Would the other teachers think to take their children to a different part of the playground? I dreaded the idea of other children surrounding us, watching. Once started, I felt the need to see this through to its conclusion, particularly after the last time with Julie, when Venus had managed to fight long enough to win her freedom.

This was a power struggle I needed to win, if I wanted Venus to start playing the game my way.

Venus went hoarse with her screaming.

"Calm down," I said for the hundredth time.

Then suddenly she screamed, "Let go!"

Bob and I exchanged surprised glances.

"Calm down. I'll let go when you're calm."

"No! No, no, *no*!"

"Yes. No screaming. Quiet voice."

"No! Let go!"

So, I thought, she *can* talk.

About twenty minutes passed before Venus actually did start to calm down. Exhaustion was taking over by then. She'd almost lost her voice. Her muscles quivered beneath my grasp. Indeed, mine were quivery too.

"Let go!" she cried one last time.

"Quiet voice," I said.

"Let go." It was said softly, tearfully.

So, I did. I loosened my grip and stood up. Bob let go of Venus's legs. I lifted her to her feet but still kept hold of her wrist because I expected her to bolt.

"Wow," Bob murmured as he dusted off the pants of his suit. "It's been a while since I did that."

Venus was still crying, but they were child's tears.

Kneeling on the asphalt, I pulled Venus against me in a hug. She cried and cried and cried.

Finally I picked Venus up in my arms and carried her into the building. We started up the stairs but when I hit the first flight, I didn't go on up. Instead, I took her down the hall to the teachers' lounge. As I hoped, the room was empty. I went in and closed the door behind me. I set her down. Indeed, for the first time, I risked letting go of her altogether.

"Why don't you sit there," I said and directed her toward the sofa. Venus did as she was told. I took money out of my pocket and put it in the pop machine. "I'll bet you're thirsty after all that, hey? Do you like Coke?"

Venus was watching me. I thought perhaps there was the slightest hint of a nod. Perhaps not. Perhaps it was only wishful thinking on my part. I picked the can out of the tray and opened it.

"Here."

For the first time Venus responded of her own accord. She reached out and took the Coke from me and drank deeply of it.

"That was hard work, wasn't it?" I said and sat down across from her. "I'll bet you're tired. I am."

She watched me closely.

"Let's not have to do this again, okay? Next time the bell rings, please come in. The bell says 'Time for school.' So you need to come into the building when you hear it ring. That's the better way. I didn't like having to do it this way."

Venus lowered her eyes. She regarded the can of Coke for a long moment. Then she leaned forward and placed it on the coffee table. For that brief moment she looked like any kid. Then she sat back, let out a long, slow sigh, and the shade lowered again. I could see it happening. It was almost a physical thing passing over her. Venus went blank. Moving that Coke can was the last spontaneous movement she made for the rest of the afternoon.

Chapter Ten

As exhausting and traumatic as the day had been, I went home that night in a buoyant mood. Suddenly, there seemed possibility. Venus *could* talk. Venus *could* respond. Now all that was left was finding a way of drawing her out, of making her *want* to communicate with us.

But what way was this going to be?

I spent the whole evening preoccupied with this question. I cast about my apartment, looking for something to stimulate her, some idea that might work. Pulling out drawers from my file cabinet that contained teaching materials and work from students in years gone by, I forgot about having supper as I sat on the floor and went through folder after folder, looking for inspiration.

Two separate memories kept intruding as I searched. One was of the very first child I had ever worked with.

Her name was Mary and she was four at the time. I was a college student, working as an aide in a preschool program for disadvantaged children. Mary was my first experience of elective mutism, where the individual, usually a child, is able to speak normally but refuses to do so for psychological reasons. In Mary's case she had been badly traumatized by what I now suspect was sexual abuse, although this was back in the days before such things were generally recognized. Whatever the etiology, she was terrified of men and spent much of her time at school hiding under the piano. I was charged with the job of developing a relationship with Mary. Like Venus, Mary had been very unresponsive too, although not to the degree Venus was. She had also refused all the staff's usual methods of involving her in classroom activities. I was inexperienced and idealistic, so I'd never considered the possibility that Mary was too damaged or had too low an IQ to respond. I'd crawled down on my hands and knees under the piano day after day, talking to her even though she never talked back, reading to her when I finally ran out of words. It was a long, slow process over many months, but in the end Mary did form a relationship with me and eventually she did start talking again. I mulled back over the memory, reliving those long-ago moments spent under that piano that even now stood out in my mind for its unusual color – it had been splatter painted, a zillion white points of paint on a dark turquoise back-ground, like snowflakes against the winter twilight.

That was my memory: Mary's wary eyes staring out from the turquoise-colored darkness. I had been made to feel really good about succeeding with Mary. The staff had been supportive throughout and very congratulatory when Mary finally started talking and joining in. No doubt, such a positive outcome and such positive feedback put me on the path to my future career. But I remembered feeling just a bit guilty about all the attention. Why? Because truth was, I had *done* nothing. I had used no special techniques, no special training, no deep insights. I'd simply spent time with her. Made it clear I was happy to spend time with her, even if we weren't doing much, even if I had many other things that were important too. And that was all it took to help Mary.

The other memory that kept intruding over that evening was of a close friend of mine whose son had suffered a severe head injury at six as a result of being hit by a car. I remembered her using a soft-bristled baby brush to brush his arms and legs as he lay comatose in the hospital bed. I couldn't quite remember what the theory behind this was, something elaborate about realigning the nerve endings that I didn't quite believe, but the idea of waking him back up to life by softly stimulating him in this way had made sense to me.

Over the course of the evening, the two memories started to integrate. I'd read to Venus. I wasn't able, of course, to spend one-to-one time with her like I had with Mary, at least not during the school day, so I was going to have to do it outside class. But that was okay. I'd frequently worked extra time with students. And I'd make it tactile. I wasn't quite sure how. Brushing her arms with a baby brush seemed a little over the top. Or at least a little strange, because I didn't suspect she had a brain injury. But I had a very strong feeling that Venus needed this kind of tactile input. Remote as she was, either physically, up on her wall, or emotionally, sitting in my classroom, I sensed she was "out of touch" in the real sense of the word, in the literal sense of the phrase.

I started looking through my bookshelves for children's books. I chose a few. Then as I was taking down folders from a higher shelf, a comic fell. I picked it up. *She-Ra, Princess of Power*.

I wasn't quite sure how I'd acquired this particular comic. Probably taken from some child in a former class and forgotten about. She-Ra was the sister of He-Man, who was some toy manufacturer's massively popular marketing dream in the early 1980s. Stimulated by a cartoon called *The Masters of the Universe*, these toys may not have actually ruled the universe, but for several years they'd come darned close in my classroom. Ever present in the form of comics, Saturday morning cartoons, and small plastic toys, He-Man, his companions, and his assortment of arch enemies had dominated my boys' free time, generated a million recess games, and provoked a mania of obsessive collecting and trading.

To me He-Man had seemed a pale imitation of the old-time superheroes, like Superman and Batman, copied shamelessly right down to the cowardly secret identity. Moreover, the skills of the marketing men targeting their prey irritated me. Nonetheless, while He-Man was rather one-dimensional, I found he and the other characters engaging and decent enough, and there was no denying how much the little boys in my classroom loved following the adventures or acting them out on the playground. As a consequence, I'd lived peaceably with He-Man when he was at the height of his popularity and had become as conversant in the details of his life and that of his followers and their arch enemy, Skeletor, as any gossip columnist following the private lives of the stars.

On the other hand, I'd remained rather more dismissive of She-Ra, He-Man's sister, as she seemed a little too transparent an effort to cash in on little girls, given that the toy manufacturers had already captured the hearts, minds, and pocket money of little boys. An exact replica of her brother in female form – secret identity, arch enemies, and superpower in the form of a magic sword – She-Ra had never really caught on in my classes the way He-Man had anyway. My girls had all been "My Little Pony" addicts in that era.

I opened the comic and paged through it. There was a momentary sense of nostalgia as I saw the old, familiar *Masters of the Universe* names. These characters had once been such a part of daily life and now I hadn't brought them to mind in years. The memories filled me with the sensation of warm sun – that smell of sun on linoleum, that baking feel of sun through glass, all, I suppose, because the year *Masters of the Universe* was at its height was also the year I taught in a classroom with huge windows facing west. So, maybe it was simply a sense of old times' sake that made me put the comic in with the books I was going to bring to Venus.

Gwennie, we were discovering, was very badly bothered by sudden noises. This was particularly unfortunate because of Jesse's sudden, frequent barklike sounds. Gwennie, in response, would clamp her hands over her ears.

"Tell that boy to stop," she demanded one afternoon.

"I'm sorry it's bothering you, Gwennie," I said, "but it isn't a noise Jesse can help making."

She couldn't screen it out. Hands over her ears, she rocked back and forth.

"Julie?" I asked. "Could you take Gwennie out in the hallway to work? Maybe for now that'll help."

I went to work with Jesse while Julie and Gwennie went out of the room. Jesse seemed to be going through a stressful period, because his twitches and noises had become much worse over the previous few days. I was making a mental note to phone his grandmother and find out how things were at home when an explosion of sound came from the hallway. Getting up, I went out to see.

Gwennie was having a full-blown tantrum. I didn't know what had set it off. Possibly she'd simply had too much sensory input and couldn't keep herself together any longer. Whatever, she had thrown herself down on the floor, kicking and screaming like a two-year-old.

"Get her up," I said to Julie. "Bring her inside."

Julie hovered, either uncertain or unwilling to grab hold of her.

I stepped in and grabbed Gwennie's arm. "Come on, sweetie. We can't do this here. It makes too much noise."

She didn't want to be touched. I'd discovered Gwennie was very sensitive to most stimuli, whether auditory, visual, or kinesthetic and today she'd clearly just had it, but I needed to move her out of the hallway because her screaming would disrupt other classes. Even as it was, I could hear classroom doors closing up and down the hall. So I half-pulled, half-dragged her into the room and over across to the reading corner.

"You sit here for a while. Look, here's the picture book of Germany. Remember this one, Gwennie? When you're feeling better, you can have quiet time and look at it for a while."

She was too out of control to care, so I left her screaming on the rug.

Gwennie wasn't inclined to tantrums, but when she had one, it was a doozy. She was in a rather awkward position – on her knees with her bottom up but bent forward so that her forehead was on the floor rather like the Muslim prayer position – and she had her hands clasped over her head. She screamed and screamed.

The kids all hated it, understandably, and several of them sat with their hands over their ears. Julie clearly hated it too. She moved nervously around. "Shouldn't we be doing something for her?" she asked. "Should I try to hold her?"

I shook my head. "No, I think she's had too much stimulation. She was probably already wound up when she arrived and couldn't cope with the added noise in here." Some children with autistic-type problems often find sensory stimuli more intense than average – noises sound louder; smells are stronger. Same for touch. So I didn't think she'd want to be touched at that point. She just needed to let off steam. "Why don't you work with Zane instead?" I suggested. "You could do math flash cards."

After recess we were going to do cooking. This was an activity that I often used in my classrooms, since it could be used to teach math and reading, as well as patience, something few of my children had enough of. The added benefit was that virtually all the children enjoyed cooking. It was a freer and friendlier form of learning, and food is a powerful motivator.

I didn't think I'd better try anything too elaborate with this bunch, at least not during these early days, so I baked some cupcakes at home and brought them in. All we were going to do was make the icing. Then the children would ice their cupcake and decorate it. We planned to view all the finished results and then, of course, eat them!

I thought it went relatively well, given this particular

group and their normal behavior. Zane did smash one cupcake in anger when he couldn't get the icing to go on the way he wanted. And Jesse did push one into Billy's face, and they fell to fighting on the floor, but then Jesse and Billy would probably have fallen to fighting at some point, whatever we chose to do. I helped Gwennie back into the group. She was still feeling a little fragile and did not want anyone to be anywhere near her or even *look* at her cupcake, but she did manage to get icing onto it before slinking off into the reading corner to devour it. Julie was assigned to Venus, and this, of course, was its own usual hassle. Venus had to be guided to the table, her hand lifted to take the icing knife, her other hand guided to take the cupcake.

"No," I said, noticing Julie struggling. "Don't let her get away with moving back. Make her join. Stand behind her so she can't back off. Then just take her hand and do it."

I wasn't sure whether, after coping unsuccessfully with Gwennie, Julie was afraid that she might set Venus off or whether she disagreed with forcing Venus to participate, but she seemed very hesitant. It was hard to know with Julie. She was hesitant about everything that involved pushing the children to do something. She was not an initiator. Nor, I discovered, was she very good at standing her own ground in the face of noisy opposition from one of the kids. But we were coping. While our styles were very different, I was so grateful for Julie's help in the classroom that I could live with the difference. With children like Venus and Gwennie, who needed instant one-to-one attention on occasion, it was invaluable having another adult present.

We survived cooking, and for the most part the kids loved the activity. When the afternoon came to an end, I was quite pleased. It had been a tiring day, but despite the various upsets, I felt like I'd stayed on top of everything and we'd ended the day in a reasonably cheerful, upbeat mood. I took the kids down to their buses and returned to the room.

While I was down at the buses, Julie had endeavored to clean up the room in the aftermath of the cooking activity. She had the back sink full of soapy water and dirty dishes.

"Hey, don't bother with that," I said. "We'll just put them in that cardboard box over there and I'll take everything home and put them in the dishwasher."

It was an innocent remark, made because I didn't want to see her working so hard on something that didn't really need doing. I was well aware by that point that Julie, like Gwennie, had just about had it with the day. And as with Gwennie, an innocent remark proved to be the straw that broke the camel's back.

There was an extended moment when the muscles of Julie's face pulled tight and she stood, frozen, all her concentration focused on keeping control. It was one of those odd slow-motion moments, because it felt long even though I knew it was short. I was aware of her expression, aware of what was happening, but not able to react fast enough to do anything helpful. Julie threw the paper towel down into the sink and left the room.

I went after her.

She didn't go far. She stood just outside the door, taking deep, noisy inhalations to keep herself from crying.

"Hey, kiddo," I said and that proved too much for her. She dropped her head and dissolved into tears.

I reached out and put an arm around her shoulders. "Come on back in the room."

Back at the table in the middle, where we usually did our after-school work, Julie flopped down. I lifted over the box of tissues and then sat down myself across from her.

"I can't do this," she said. This made her cry in earnest again. She'd had her elbow on the table, hand bracing her cheek, but she opened her hand to cover her face and turned slightly away from me.

"No, I think you're doing fine," I said softly. "It was just a bad day."

Julie shook her head. "No, I can't do this. I thought I could. I thought I'd like it, but I *hate* it."

"It was just a bad day," I said.

"They're *all* bad days for me, Torey. I can't do this. I can't be what you expect of me."

"No, I'm not expecting, Julie. You're doing well. I'm happy with how you are in here."

"You *are* expecting. Maybe you don't know you are. But you are. You expect me to be as good as you. You expect me to *be* you. And I can't be."

I'd been aware there were problems. I knew Julie found the daily rough-and-tumble a little too rough and tumbly sometimes. And true, I was aware of relying on her more than she was really trained for. But I had no awareness of expecting her to "be me," as she put it. This took me a bit aback because these sounded very much like the words that come right before "I quit."

"What do I do that makes you feel this way?"

"You want me to *be* you."

"In what way?"

She snuffled and wiped her eyes with her fingers. "You want me to think like you. You want me to do things your way. If I don't, if I fail ... I feel scared to fail because then I know you're going to be thinking, 'If she'd done it my way...'"

"That's not really what I'm thinking at all, Julie. If you fail, what I'm going to be thinking is: 'How can we get this sorted out?'"

Julie didn't respond. She wiped her eyes again.

Unfortunately, as I considered what Julie said, I realized it was partly true. I did find her permissive attitude toward the children out of sync with my philosophy, and when she got herself into trouble I was sometimes aware of thinking that maybe now she'd see the value of my approach. So, yes, there probably was an element of that. But they were normal kinds of thoughts, natural thoughts that come up whenever there are differing points of view. There'd never been any intentional control freakery involved.

The awful aspect of this discussion was that Julie was not saying she found it hard to cope with the kids. She was saying she found it hard to cope with me. This made me feel guilty and unexpectedly defensive.

"What do you think would help?" I asked.

"Nothing," she said pessimistically. This brought the tears back. She struggled with them a moment, the muscles of her face taut.

Watching her, I was distracted yet again by the thought of how young she looked. She could have been fifteen or sixteen from her appearance. I was overcome with an urge to ask her how old she was, which was hardly appropriate at the moment, but it led me to ponder how difficult it must be to establish any type of credible authority when you looked like a teenager. With kids or adults. It also occurred to me that such youthfulness brought out a maternal response in me. I wanted to give her a hug and tell her I'd make it better. I didn't really want to say maybe she was more right than I was and we'd try it her way.

"This is a *lot* different from working for Casey Muldrow," she said in a very heartfelt way.

"Yes, I'm sure it is. And I'm sorry for my part in this. I've been expecting too much out of you," I said. "I shouldn't have done it."

"It's not your fault. It's me. I thought this would be fun. I thought it'd be an interesting challenge, because I thought I was ready for something more challenging..." Her words trailed off.

"I've been acting like this is your field and you're fully trained," I said. "Which is my mistake, not yours. You're doing all right. I'm happy with what you're doing. I know it looks like Chaos City in here most days, but, really, we're doing well. The boys are coming together."

She dropped her head down and braced it on her hand.

"And, listen, I'm aware we have different philosophies," I said. "We have different approaches. That's not a bad thing. Certainly it's something I can live with, so I don't mean to make you feel that you should change."

Julie reached over for a tissue, took it, blew her nose. "Yeah. Okay," she said. She gave a long sigh and then shrugged. "I guess it's just been a bad day."

I nodded.

"I didn't mean to lose it. That's probably the last thing you need. First the kids, then me."

"Don't worry about it," I said.

"Yeah, well. It probably is just me." She rose from the table. "Anyway, I think I'm going to go home. I've had it for today."

"Okay."

I really would have preferred she stayed. She was still clearly upset, and I knew she'd be in tears again once she got to her car or wherever. I would have preferred us to have talked until everything was hashed out between us and we ended up with, if not agreement, then at least a companionable understanding of our differences. I had to accept, however, that I was probably not someone she wanted comfort from, at least not at that moment. Indeed, I was probably who she wanted to get away from.

Julie picked up her things and left. I sat glumly.

Oh well. At least she hadn't mentioned quitting.

Chapter Eleven

Hell broke out two days later. It was over the lunch hour, and I actually wasn't at school at the time. I had a friend teaching at another school nearby and it was her birthday, so I'd popped out to join her for a celebratory double cheeseburger at Burger King. I was only gone thirty minutes of my forty-five-minute lunch hour, but when I pulled my car back into the parking lot, I was greeted by the sight of an ambulance and a great furor on the playground. Given the rush of people toward me when I got out of my car, I had no trouble discerning one of my kids was involved. And, of course, it took no great genius to guess it was Venus.

The details leading up to the event still weren't clear, but apparently Venus had gone into one of her rages and taken after a little boy in the first grade. He fled to the climbing bars for safety with Venus in hot pursuit. In his haste, he missed one of the bars, fell off, broke his arm, and hit his head.

To say the school staff were in an uproar was a vast understatement. Complacent as Bob normally was, on this occasion he had gone absolutely ballistic. It came from fear mostly, I think, because the little boy was from a fairly well-to-do family – the kind to know lawyers personally – and Bob's first thoughts were of a lawsuit.

"That child has to go!" he was crying. "We can not keep her here. She's dangerous. She's going to kill somebody sooner or later and she just can't be here."

The playground aides were in a panic. The little boy's first-grade teacher was angry to the point of shouting at me, as if my being off the school grounds was the sole reason this had happened and I was personally responsible. I should have been *controlling* her, the teacher yelled.

Venus had been taken inside. She was still screaming. I could hear her through the doors, through the partition of the office, through the walls. I moved past the people on the playground to go in to her, but Bob put a hand out and touched my arm.

"No," he said. "Don't bother."

I looked at him.

"Just leave her. Go on up to your room."

"What do you mean?"

"She's not going back into your class. She's done here.

We've called her mother," Bob said. "So just go up to the kids you've got."

"But – "

He shook his head. "No. This was an incident too far. She can go on homeschooling or … I don't know. Frankly, I don't care. As long as she's out of here." His eyes met mine. There was a small pause and then he shrugged. "Anyway, your kids are all upstairs waiting, so it's best if you just go on up."

I was in a state of shock. It had all happened so fast. Before lunch Venus was part of the class. After lunch she was gone.

The boys were sitting wide-eyed. Julie hadn't even made an effort to occupy them. Probably she couldn't have, if she'd tried, as the hubbub down on the playground was too much to ignore.

"Man, what did I tell you!" Billy shouted as I came through the door. "Said Psycho was gonna kill somebody someday, huh? I said that, didn't I? I was right."

"Billy, sit down, please," I replied and took off my coat. "Everybody. Find your seats."

"Mine's not lost," Billy piped up.

I shot him the evil eye. "I'm not having a good day. It would not take much for me to feel *very* angry, Billy."

Billy pulled his head down between his shoulders.

"So, what's going to happen?" Jesse asked.

I knew he meant Venus.

"Okay. Look, guys. Come here. Pull your chairs over into

a circle right here. Because I know you've probably got lots of feelings about what just happened out there and lots of questions. So, let's have a talk about it, okay?"

Just then, Gwennie arrived.

"Gwennie, you too," I said. "We're going to start the afternoon with a discussion instead of what we normally do."

"Yeah, we're going to discuss how Psycho Girl killed some poor kid in the first grade," Billy added.

For this group they were pretty cooperative. I didn't make the circle too close, so as not to infringe on anyone's personal space, but I did get them to put their chairs in a semicircle in the middle of the room – the first time I'd tried such a thing with them – and no one immediately committed mayhem. I put Julie between Billy and Jesse. Indeed, I sat on the other side of Billy with the hopes that between Julie and me, we could keep him halfway restrained. Gwennie did not like this change in her routine. She was the hardest to settle.

"Gwennie, sit down, please."

She sat, but within two seconds she was on her feet again.

"Gwennie, sit down, please."

"It's time to do programs. Time to do my folder."

"Today we're doing it a little differently. Then we'll do folders. Sit down, please."

She sat, but within two seconds she was again on her feet.

"Geez, sit down, would you?" Billy squawked.

"Who says you're the boss?" Shane muttered and half rose out of his chair.

I sliced my hand through the air meaningfully. Shane sat immediately. Gwennie eyed me a long moment, but then she sat too.

"Okay, good. Thank you. Now," I said, "I know what just happened is scary."

"It's not scary! It's exciting!" Billy shouted and shot off his chair, punching his fists like a boxer. "Psycho Girl Kills a First-Grade Baby! Pow! Bang!"

"Shut *up*!" Jesse screamed and in a second he was off his chair and onto Billy, knocking him to the floor, pummeling him. "Shut up, shut up, shut up, you dickhead blabbermouth! I wanna *stop* hearing your voice all the time!"

At this degeneration into fisticuffs, Julie's shoulders sagged. She looked at me, and there was defeat in her expression. I have to admit, I was sort of short of spirit myself at that point.

"Boys!" I didn't bother to get off my chair. For just that moment I felt, well, if they wanted to slug it out . . . "Boys!"

The two grappled a minute or more on the floor but my lack of intervention seemed to perplex them. There was hesitation. Billy glanced in my direction. Jesse took advantage of Billy's moment of inattention to pin him to the floor.

"Are you quite finished?" I asked.

Jesse was sitting astride Billy's back. Billy started to cry when he found he couldn't get up.

"I said, are you *quite* finished?"

Jesse looked over. He nodded and started to rise. "I just wanted him to shut up," Jesse replied.

"Yes, I know how you feel," I said, "but that's not how you do it."

Billy was indignant. "You're suppose to be protecting me," he snuffled. "Not letting some bad-ass black kid beat me up."

"She's supposed to be shutting you up for once," Jesse retorted.

"Sit down. Billy, sit in your chair and be quiet. Jesse, you too."

Both boys did as they were told. Now, how long did I have before the next outburst? Thirty seconds?

"Who saw what happened out on the playground?" I asked.

"Me," said Shane.

"Me too," Zane said.

"I did! I did! I did! Call on me, Teacher!" Billy was jumping up out of his chair, waving his hand about six inches from my eyes.

Jesse was eyeing Billy. I eyed Jesse. "Did you see, Jesse?"

He nodded.

"What happened?"

"That girl – "

"She has a name, Jesse. She's been part of our class every day since school started, so let's call her by her name."

"Doesn't matter anyway," Billy interjected, "'cause she ain't coming back. I heard Mr. Christianson say. Said she's gonna have to go on homebound. I went on homebound. Last year. It sucks. 'Cause like you can't do anything except stay at home. And my brother said I was lucky. He *wanted* to stay at home all the time."

"Jesse?" I asked, craning around Billy who was out of his chair and standing right in front of me.

He shrugged. "Just what she always does. Kinda walking around on the playground looking mean. And then this kid comes up. Guess he must of bumped her or something. Dunno. Wasn't watching. And then she just got chasing him and kept chasing him till he got up to the top of the monkey bars and then she pulled him off. Like I said. She was just doing what she always does. Beating kids up."

"Well, me, I'm *glad* she's gone," Billy said with feeling. "I'm glad Mr. Christianson's making her go away. 'Cause she *was* psycho, even if you said she wasn't. I didn't like her in our class."

"Would you want someone to talk about you like that, Billy, if you had to go away?" I asked.

"Well, if I was psycho like her, yeah. I wouldn't mind. She was *bad*, Teacher. You were pretending she was ordinary all the time, but you weren't a kid. If you were a kid, you would have knew she was *bad*."

After school, I was putting away things from my briefcase and came across the children's books and the She-Ra comic I'd brought in for Venus. So, that's it, I thought. End of that. I felt sad. It had ended before it'd even had a chance to get started. But that's how it went sometimes. I put the two books on the reading shelf for the other children. The comic? I could see no point in keeping it. The character was out-of-date and not too exciting to start with. None of the kids would be interested. I leaned forward and pitched it toward the trash can sitting beside my desk. It fell in with a thump.

So, we picked up and carried on without Venus.

School had been in session almost eight weeks by this point, so I concentrated on bringing this little band of renegades closer together – mainly, if truth be known, so that I could get shoes back on them before the cold weather set in, because we were still at the stage of needing to remove shoes every time they came into the class.

I found a sense of unity was one of the most crucial aspects of my type of milieu and a key to my success in working with these sorts of children. For many of them, particularly those who came with histories of disruptive, antisocial behavior, it was their first experience of "belonging," of being part of any kind of positive, cohesive group. Once they felt this sense of belonging, the children often behaved better and demonstrated higher self-esteem than I could have inspired on my own. So I felt it was important to achieve this "group identity." The challenge each autumn was how.

In the normal course of things, eight weeks was more than enough time to "settle a class in." During this period the children became accustomed to me and to the limits I set, to my forms of discipline, my expectations and the kind of work I gave out, and they became used to the dynamics of the group and how each person in it functioned. So by the end of this time, I expected all the kids to have a sense of the class as "us," to feel a part of it and to find safety and security in knowing its rules.

However, with this group it wasn't quite as simple as it had been in other years. Eight weeks in and we were still without shoes, still sitting in tables at opposite corners of the room, and still routinely degenerating into fistfights. The Chipmunk society was a small help. The boys had developed a good sense of "us" in contrast to the other kids who spent time in our room – including, unfortunately, Gwennie, who spent enough time with us to be a part of the main class – but they had it only as in "us" versus "them," which wasn't really the idea. They liked wiggling their toes at one another, but they did it more to express antisocial feelings toward the part-time kids than as a show of unity.

Consequently, I arrived one morning with a big wooden box that I had used in previous classrooms. In those days, it had been the Kobold's Box, and I often made up stories for the kids about the "Kobold," a little invisible gremlin who lived in our classroom and watched out for good behavior. When he saw someone behaving well, he wrote a little note describing the kindness and put it in the Kobold's Box. But because the Kobold soon got writer's cramp from so much good behavior, he needed help. So I asked for the children themselves to be on the lookout for kind behavior and when they saw it, to write notes and put them in the Kobold's Box. This seemed a little cheesy for my rough-and-tumble group, so I told them it was the "Chipmunk Spy" box.

"We're going to do something different," I said during morning discussion. "We're going to see who's the best secret agent in this group."

"You mean like James Bond!" Billy shouted. This called for instantly jumping out of his seat and up on top of the table. He pointed his finger like a gun and made shooting noises. Of course, this meant the other boys had to join in.

I stood there and said nothing. This would eventually annoy them into sitting back down to find out what I was going to say next.

So I explained the plan to them. At the beginning of the week, they would draw names to find out who their intended "victim" was. Then, each day they had to do something nice for that person – a good deed – *but*, and this was a big "but," they were secret agents! So, they had to do it secretly, so the other person didn't know it was them. And at the end of the week, we'd try to guess who our secret agent was.

I explained that each day the secret agent would have to come to me to confirm he had *done* a good deed. Then he'd write down what he had done for his "victim" and put it in the box. I said at the end of the week I'd read each of them out. To add a bit of gusto to the proceedings, I told them we'd have treats on Friday while we were doing the box, and the people who had managed to do a good deed *every* day for their "victim" would get a spy badge. I also suggested that if they wanted to be extra clever at being a secret agent, they could do good deeds for other people too, and that way they'd throw their "victim" "off the scent."

It wasn't as straightforward as doing the Kobold's Box. Indeed, all this "secret agent" business was rather complex, but that, I suspect, was what appealed to the boys. They were of the age to want to be in gangs and clubs, but they didn't have the social skills to smooth the way. So, activities that involved lots of rules to be learned and challenges to master were very popular.

"What about Gwennie?" Jesse suddenly asked.

"What about Gwennie?" I replied.

"Is she going to get included?"

"What do you think?" I asked.

"Well, she's not going to do it. If she's someone's secret agent, they won't get no nice things done for them."

"But she's part of the group," I said.

"Just in the afternoons," Shane said. "So she ain't a Chipmunk. Not really. We never said nothing about no girl Chipmunks."

"What about Venus? She was a girl," I said. "She was a Chipmunk."

"Venus ain't here no more. She don't count," Shane said.

"Besides," Billy added, "if we counted Gwennie, it'd be an odd number. This is only going to work if there's an even number of us."

"But it would be Friday afternoon when we do the box and have treats. Gwennie is here on Friday afternoons," I said. "It wouldn't be fair not to include her."

"But she won't do it," Zane said. "She'd forget. That person wouldn't get no secret stuff done to them."

I raised my eyebrows in an exaggerated expression of perplexity. "Perhaps we better not do it, if we can't include Gwennie. Perhaps it was a bad idea."

"No, no, wait," Billy cried. "We want to do it."

"What do you think we should do then?" I asked.

The boys looked at one another. Billy shrugged. Jesse shrugged. This made the twins shrug in unison.

I stood, silent, and waited.

"Just leave her out," Shane said finally.

"I can't do that. We have to come up with something that includes everybody."

Shane shrugged again. Again, there was a complete round of shrugs.

"Maybe you could do Gwennie's part," Jesse said at last.

"Yeah!" Billy cried. "Good idea, Jesse! Teacher can do Gwennie's part."

"Would that work?" I asked.

"Yeah," Shane said. Zane nodded.

"Okay," I said. "Whoever Gwennie's person is, I'll give her a hand."

"Oooh, cool!" Billy cried. "A secret agent teacher!"

Chapter Twelve

The week before Halloween, we had a visit from Ben Avery, the school psychologist. As part of a district-wide assessment and placement program, he was giving achievement tests, plus the WISC IQ test to all special education students in restricted placements, which included the children in my class. So this meant Ben was with us for four days.

For the most part, I wasn't in favor of all this testing. The accuracy was affected by so many things, such as cultural differences or socioeconomic factors, that they seemed a waste of time. I would have much preferred someone of Ben's caliber contributing to the classroom environment for four days rather than closeting himself away with standardized tests. But it wasn't my choice. So, one by one, he took the kids away.

The first two days were spent on Shane and Zane and the results were, sadly, pretty much what I expected. Shane scored an IQ of 71 and Zane a score of 69 – both right on the borderline of mental retardation. Both had severe reading problems. Indeed, Zane was still at the "prereading" stage of identifying shapes and letters. Shane was only just beginning to recognize the alphabet and a few simple words. Their math was a little better, but only just. Ben spent a lot of time with me afterward, discussing the wisdom of changing them over to a class for mildly mentally handicapped children, because he thought this might meet their needs better. Except for their difficult behavior.

In the end I felt they were better staying with me. Jesse and Billy, who both came out of seriously deprived socioeconomic backgrounds, were not doing much better academically, so Shane and Zane were not dragging down what I could do in the class.

The next day was Jesse's turn and he, in fact, did better than I'd expected. He scored a full-scale IQ of 109, which was average. This was in contrast to his reading skills. The reading achievement test put him at a low first-grade level, which was close to where he was working in class. Ben's other tests revealed serious weaknesses in auditory processing and visual integration, so Ben and I talked a long time that afternoon about learning disabilities and about how Jesse's Tourette's syndrome might be affecting his academic skills. I thought I would try to concentrate more on finding ways to make learning easier for Jesse. I'd done quite a lot of work with learning disabilities early in my career, so I decided to go home and check what materials I might have to help me assess what kind of learner he was and which of his senses were stronger. That way I hoped to bring his academic skills up closer to his ability level.

As usual, Billy turned out to be the goat among the sheep.

"You're not going to believe this," Ben said when he came into my room after school the next day.

Julie and I were sitting at one of the tables, making lesson plans. We both looked up.

Ben pitched Billy's WISC test, Frisbee-style, toward us. It spun in smooth circles the six or more feet until I caught it between my hands. I turned the paper over and lay it on the table.

Verbal score: 145

Performance score: 142

Full scale IQ: 142

"You're kidding," I said when I saw it.

"Knowing Billy, he probably cheated," Julie said.

"Well, I didn't see any crib notes up his sleeve," Ben replied. "Nothing written on his palm saying 'The definition of *catacomb* is…'"

"*Catacomb*?" both Julie and I said in unison.

"This *can't* be our Billy," Julie said. "I don't think he's ever completed a worksheet since he arrived."

Ben said, "This kid has definitely hidden his talents."

I was thinking more along the lines of alien abduction.

Pulling the WISC score sheet over in front of me, I read it. A big surprise, certainly. Especially from a boy who was behind in everything and had never shown any academic inclinations whatsoever. But . . . the more I thought about it . . . it *did* explain a lot. We just hadn't noticed it, because that wasn't what we were looking for.

The days passed. Then the weeks. Halloween came and it was celebrated with gusto in our room. Everyone wore their costumes, except for Gwennie, who hated it all. Shane came as Spiderman and Zane came as what I suppose one would call Spiderman II, as he had exactly the same costume. Jesse's grandmother had made him a rather sweet black-and-white dog costume, and he arrived with long, floppy black ears attached to a headband and a shiny black nose painted over his own nose. I thought he was supposed to be the cartoon character Snoopy and praised his idea only to be told indignantly, no, he was "just a dog." Billy opted for typecasting and came dressed as a red devil.

Wild as the kids still were, I didn't dare have a proper Halloween party, like other classes were having. Instead, I made up little goody bags of candy and we had cookies and punch right after the afternoon recess. Even so, it was more chaos than fun. Because the kids were overexcited by the change in routine, there were lots of fights, crying, shouting, screaming, and "quiet chair" time, and Gwennie threw up on the rug in the reading corner because she ate too much candy. Nonetheless, I was glad we did it. We would have felt we'd missed out, if we hadn't.

Then came November with its long, gray, overcast days and cold, gusty winds.

Venus never really left my mind during all this time. I kept checking the wall along the playground, half expecting to see her there. And half hoping. But I didn't. She had vanished as completely as if she'd been nothing more than a mirage I'd seen, when I'd arrived at school that first day.

Two of her brothers continued to attend the school. They were both in upper grades and both receiving extensive learning support, so I'd dawdled a bit in the teachers' lounge when the learning support teacher, Mary McKenna, was there. I didn't know Mary very well. She hadn't been part of the district team when I'd been an itinerant learning support teacher. She was an older woman who gave the impression of being competent and efficient and she was friendly enough, but not openly so. Consequently, I found it hard to drop questions about Venus naturally into conversation with her. Moreover, I was self-conscious when Bob was in the room, because Bob knew immediately what I was doing.

"Mary doesn't have Venus," Bob said to me out in the hallway after overhearing me one afternoon.

"No, I know, I was just – "

"Venus has a special homebound teacher. Someone from district eight. Homebound is all she does."

I nodded.

There was a pause.

"I was just wondering how she was doing. Wondering if her brothers had maybe said anything … I was just … I mean, have you heard any news?"

Bob shook his head.

"Nothing about how she's getting on? If she's talking? Or … anything?"

Bob shook his head again.

Then he clapped my shoulder in a reassuring, almost fatherly way. "Well, we weren't ever going to get very far with her anyway."

"How do you mean?" I asked.

He shrugged. "Too slow. Too many family problems. You know."

"Life's crapped on her, so we really shouldn't worry about her?"

"No, I mean we win some, we lose some. You have to take that attitude with some kids. Some things you can't change; so, when it goes out of your hands, you just have to believe it was for the best."

I smiled faintly at the irony. "We've come a long way, haven't we – you and I – from where we started."

Bob knew instantly I was referring back to those heady, idealistic days together early in our careers when there were no hopeless kids.

"Are you saying, 'Have I grown up?'" he asked. "Because if so, Torey, yes. I have. I've been around long enough now to know – to really comprehend – that you *do* win some and you lose some. And you have to go with those you win and, sadly, let go of those you lose."

I nodded.

"It's sad, I know. But it's also life."

I couldn't refute him on that. There had been kids I couldn't help; ones I'd had to give up on. There'd been plenty of them. And I, too, had had to reconcile the better world I wanted with the real world I had. Nonetheless, I still didn't like being forced to give up on ones I hadn't yet given up on myself.

Another pause wandered into the conversation and stayed. Bob started to turn away to go back to his office.

"Beautiful child," I murmured.

"Huh?" Bob turned back toward me.

"I said, 'beautiful child.' Thinking of the irony of it. That's what Wanda always calls her. 'Beautiful child.' When, in fact, Venus is one of the least beautiful children I've ever seen. Nothing. That kid has nothing beautiful going for her. But all the time, Wanda calls her 'beautiful child.'"

"Well, to Wanda, she probably is," Bob replied.

He hesitated a moment.

"You know the truth about them, don't you?" he said.

I looked up.

"It's off the record, but it's true. At least that's what Social Services say."

"What?"

"Teri isn't Venus's mother. It's actually Wanda. Teri's last partner, the one before the greasy character she's got now, he knocked Wanda up."

"Oh geez." It made horrible sense.

Bob pursed his lips. "This guy didn't even get done for it. Knocked up a retarded thirteen-year-old and then he just waltzed off."

"Oh geez."

Bob made a small, defeated sound. "Beautiful child, indeed."

My head was going off like a popcorn popper by the time I got back to my classroom. Suddenly many other things were making sense. If Venus *was* Wanda's child, what if Wanda had been left with primary care of Venus in her infancy and early childhood? Even if Venus's IQ was not affected, what kind of environment would she have been brought up in? It would be very questionable that someone of Wanda's limited abilities could provide adequate stimulation for a baby and certainly not adequate care. I remembered Wanda with her baby doll, held carelessly, loved one moment, then forgotten and left behind the next, when something else distracted her. What if Venus had spent her early years treated like this? There may have been very little stimulation – especially verbal stimulation. Perhaps she was left alone in a crib or playpen until Wanda remembered her. Perhaps she had cried so long that it finally occurred to her that crying did no good, that one simply waited, immobile, like the babies in Third World orphanages with their blank faces and still bodies. What if the only time the other family members interacted with her was to clout her into silence, hence she learned that defense was the best offense? So she attacked before anyone could attack her.

All supposition on my part, but it fell into place like some horrible jigsaw puzzle.

The Chipmunk Spy idea wasn't what one would call successful.

The first problem was that Shane and Zane had such poor reading skills that they could do none of this by themselves. They had to have Julie help them read who their "victims" were, which made it hard to keep things secret, and they needed help writing out notes to put in the spy box.

Then there was the small matter of the boys liking the *idea* of being a spy and, even more, liking the idea of treats on Friday afternoon, but no one actually liking the idea of doing good deeds.

I could tell things weren't working out on the very first day. I kept saying, "Have you done your good deed today?" And everybody nodded and said, "Yes." So I reminded them that they had to get Julie or me to confirm it and the only one who had was Jesse. He was secret spy to Zane, and his good deed had been to pick up Zane's worksheet paper, which he found on the floor, and put it back on Zane's table. Not exactly a gold-hearted act, but it was a start.

On Tuesday, Jesse again came to me. This time he said he'd lent Zane the colored markers during art. I hesitated to point out that I had *told* him to share the markers because he had hogged the whole box on his desk, and when I did, all the boys had taken some, not just Zane.

I also saw Billy put a note in the box. "Billy," I said, "be sure to confirm your good deed with Julie or me, so we know you did it."

"I did it," he replied indignantly. "Don't you trust me? Fucking place, we got no trust here. How do you expect us to do anything if you never trust us?"

I put a finger to my lip. "Watch your words, please."

"See? You don't even trust me to talk."

Given his brilliant mood, I didn't persist with interrogating him about good deeds.

Friday came. The evening before I'd made gingerbread men – great big ones with each child's name on them – and I brought them in for the spy box treat. I also made a very snazzy "spy badge" for the winner.

Everyone got extremely excited when they saw the gingerbread men. All morning the boys drooled over them, identifying which one had their name on it. Indeed, the gingerbread men proved so much of a distraction in the morning that I had to hide them in the cupboard.

When the end of the day arrived, I had everyone sit down at their tables. I put the gingerbread men on my desk and then made a big deal of bringing the spy box over to the middle table and opening it up. "What do you think we're going to find?" I asked with overexaggerated anticipation. Billy was getting into a fervor already. He wanted to short-circuit all this talk and go straight for the gingerbread men.

I opened the box. There was only a handful of notes inside. Nine, to be exact. The five I had written on Gwennie's behalf for Shane, who was her person. Jesse's two notes for Zane, and two entirely blank pieces of paper.

"Ah," I said. "Not much in here."

I read out the ones I'd done on Gwennie's behalf for Shane.

"I got the most! I got the most!" Shane cried. "Where's my treat?"

"That's not actually the way it works," I said. "We get the treats for having *done* the good deeds. But there haven't been very many done."

"But I got the most!" Shane yelled. "I want my treat."

"Hold on a minute. You didn't *write* any, Shane."

Shane burst into tears. "But I *won*."

"I didn't understand it. I didn't understand what we were doing," Zane piped up.

"What about me?" Jesse cried. "I done the most good deeds. I get a treat. I should get all of them. And the badge too. That's mine. I won it fair and square."

"You did *two*. And what's this blank piece of paper? Billy? Why did you put that in here?"

"Teacher!" Billy shrieked in response and pointed. "Look what she's doing!"

I whirled around to see Gwennie, standing by my desk where I had set the gingerbread men. She was biting the legs off each one, fast as she could.

"*Teacher*!!!!!" Billy screamed, and before I could stop him, he was out of his seat, shooting toward Gwennie.

I intercepted him but could not catch all the boys. Julie bolted into the fray too, but it was too late.

Jesse picked up the single whole cookie that remained, which happened to say Zane on it.

"That's mine!" Zane shrieked and ran toward him.

"I won. And I'm not eating anything with that girl's cooties on it," Jesse replied and crammed the whole cookie into his mouth with a massive shoving motion.

Within seconds everyone was in one big writhing, fighting, crying tangle on the floor.

I pulled them apart. At least I tried to. Jesse was choking over his cookie, because he'd been knocked to the floor before he'd had time to swallow. Gwennie was shrieking in the usual high-pitched banshee wail she gave out when she went on overload. Billy was fighting so hard that he was literally foaming at the mouth. The twins just screamed and lashed out at everyone. About half of what was left of the gingerbread men had been ground underfoot.

Between Julie and me, we managed to get them apart, to their feet, and into their chairs.

"Sit!" I said, using my most ferocious teacher's voice.

Begrudgingly, everyone stayed in their chairs.

"Now cross your arms and put your heads down on your

desks. The bell rings in just under five minutes, so you stay that way until then."

Everyone, even Gwennie, followed those instructions. Except, of course, Billy.

"You too," I said, giving him the evil eye.

"Can't," he replied with just the faintest hint of defiance.

"And why's that, might I ask?"

"Because you said put your head down on your desk and I don't have a desk." He spread his hands wide, palms upward, like he was the most innocent kid in the world. "Just got this table."

"*Now*, Billy."

There was a long look between us. Finally, Billy crossed his arms on the tabletop and lay his head on them. "Fucking school," he muttered as he did so.

Thus ended the Chipmunk Spy Club.

Chapter Thirteen

There was no denying that my usual techniques for getting control of a class and making a cohesive group from it were not working with this bunch. All the boys had hyperactivity and attention problems; all were impulsive and aggressive. Gwennie, with her intolerance of sudden noise or movement, added her own brand of chaos to the afternoons.

Initially I'd looked forward to Gwennie, because I'd been told her autism had only involved social issues, that she was otherwise capable of working successfully in a classroom situation. And, of course, I'd foreseen pairing her with Venus. But in practice I found Gwennie operated much further down the autistic continuum than I'd expected. She was easily overstimulated, easily frustrated, and had very, very little tolerance of disruption to routine. This made her a rather bad fit with Billy, Jesse, Zane, and Shane, who regularly made mincemeat out of any routine and were totally incapable of conducting anything at a noise level much below that of a jackhammer.

Zane and Shane presented their own special problems. Although they came from a warm, supportive home, their parents, who had adopted the boys when they were less than a year old, were already in their midforties when the boys had arrived. They were lovely people and they clearly adored these two boys, but they were not well equipped to deal with Zane and Shane's serious problems. Neither parent was well educated nor energetic nor particularly young at heart, so I frequently had the mother on the phone. Often she was in tears of despair over something or another they had done before school. Many of the disasters were of the sort any pair of young boys could have gotten up to – irritating and usually very messy, but not really dysfunctional behavior – but she found it very hard to cope, usually because the boys did not remember the consequences of their actions. The same things happened over and over and over again, in spite of all her efforts.

And goodness knows, when Shane and Zane *did* behave in a difficult manner, they could be very difficult indeed. The primary effect of FAS is mental retardation, and in that respect the boys had gotten off relatively lightly with a borderline IQ. However, FAS also often causes several behavior problems, among them the triplet bugbears of all special education classrooms – impulsivity, hyperactivity, and poor concentration – as well as some specialized problems. The biggest one with Shane and Zane, which is typical of many FAS children, was an inability to learn from experience. Indeed, memory in all forms was very poor for the boys. They had to be taught things again and again and again, and each time it was like starting over. This meant it was hard for them to "learn the rules" of behavior in the classroom. Moreover, there seemed to be a connector missing between remembering things and understanding how to make use of them. Even if they *knew* the rules, i.e., could recite them, they still could not apply them. Consequently, I was coming to realize that a lot of the behavior problems I was having with Shane and Zane were a result of their inability to understand the consequences of their actions.

Another big problem area for us was that neither of them had any real concept of ownership. If they saw something in the classroom or on the playground they liked, they'd just take it. This wasn't stealing to them. They simply did not understand it belonged to someone else and to use it, you had to ask. This, of course, made them very unpopular, both inside our class and out. Indeed, friendship was a concept quite beyond either of the boys.

Jesse was the only student in the group who had anything approaching a normal level of activity or concentration, but his tics interfered badly with his learning ability. Stress caused the tics to become more frequent or pronounced, and he had a wide variety – grimacing, jerking his head, sniffing. When he was upset, he often tended to make a fist and repetitively hit the side of his head at just above the temple area. And when concentrating, he was inclined to repeat words over and over. These were usually harmless phrases such as "Oh man. Oh man. Oh man." Or "Gotta concentrate. Gotta concentrate." This did get wearing, and the other boys, distractible as they all were, found it hard to attend to their own matters when Jesse was muttering. But his very worst, more intrusive tic was the barking – sudden, loud, almost explosive – and Gwennie, in particular, couldn't cope at all when he was doing that.

In addition to the tics, Jesse also had fairly serious learning disabilities. I think until Ben had come to do the testing, we had not appreciated how much of his academic difficulty was due to this, but in the time since Ben had assessed him, I had spent a lot of time trying to discern where his learning problems lay. They revolved mainly around reading and spelling. He had difficulty decoding words and also difficulty comprehending them, once he had ascertained what they were. As with Gwennie, I found that Jesse had a hard time learning in a noisy classroom. He couldn't discriminate sounds well when there was background noise, so that words like *there* and *chair* often sounded alike for him. This made learning in our environment more of a challenge.

And then, of course, there was Billy. Since the clear indication on the assessment that Billy was gifted, I had made a real effort to engage him productively in class, despite his poor academics and appalling behavior. Not an easy task! Billy did not want to sit. Billy did not want to work. Billy did not want to do reading or math or anything else he was *supposed* to do. All Billy really wanted to do was talk! And fight.

I tried to channel this within the confines of our classroom setup. I thought perhaps if I *arranged* for Billy to do some talking, maybe he wouldn't want to do so much off-task talking. So I gave him small study projects with the idea that he could "report" to the class the things he learned. This might have worked if I could have gotten Billy to sit still long enough to read anything or write down any notes, or if the others could have been tied to their chairs to listen.

The sad truth with Billy was that no one had told *him* that he was a gifted child and thereby should be interested in doing all the clever, creative little things I was arranging for him. No, Billy persisted in being Billy, no matter what I came up with: loud, rambunctious, overenthusiastic, and with the attention span of a gnat.

Into this mix came my ongoing problems with Julie. If there was such a thing as "taking a hard line on permissiveness," Julie was a proponent. She felt children should be loved, encouraged, and rewarded and everything else they did ignored. Period. No other discipline. And as the weeks passed, it became clear that she took an increasingly serious stand on this belief. It was rather like sharing the room with a militant pacifist. Common sense told you that it was an oxymoron, fighting for peace, but it was also very difficult being forced to justify the opposite: let's fight for violence.

The practical outcome of this was that we had very different ways of responding to situations in the classroom. If one of the children misbehaved, Julie's reaction was "Let's talk about *why* you threw that book down." My reaction was, "Pick it up." If one of the children got out of his seat and tore around the room, Julie's inclination was to say nothing and praise the ones who were still in their seats. This might have worked, had the one up out of his seat not gotten up in order to beat the other ones over their heads. Or had there *been* any other ones in their seats. Most of the time, if one got up, they were all up, careering around the classroom in attack mode.

Given that most days my boys were intent on either killing one another or reenacting some version of *Lord of the Flies*, Julie became easily overcome in situations where fighting broke out. It wasn't very practical to ignore fighting or, in the heat of the moment, ask them why they were doing it. But she wasn't happy raising her voice or ordering people off to the quiet chairs, my two usual reactions. And she was even less happy throwing herself into the fray to pry the boys apart. The best she managed was to try and grab one and hug him, speaking softly over and over about how important it was that we not hurt one another. Meanwhile, his opponents were off locating weapons of mass destruction.

I had two big problems with all of this. First, I genuinely

liked Julie as a person. I liked her sense of humor, her industriousness, her personality. And I *wanted* her to like me. So it was hard to have to take on the role of the bad guy, always pointing out the drawbacks to her approach, forever saying how it was *much* more helpful if we presented a united front. Moreover, I didn't like the position I was having to defend. In previous schools, I'd always been the liberal one, the open-minded one, the least restrictive. I hated suddenly being cast as the conservative. It jarred my self-image. Second, our differences made me feel self-conscious in the classroom. As the weeks went on, I knew I was going to have to structure the environment more strictly to get on top of my little guys' behavior, but I put it off and put it off, largely because I hated having to tell Julie she was going to have to do it too.

But, in the end, it came...

After twelve weeks of struggling with this class without any noticeable improvement in behavior, without any secure sense that I was in control, I decided that I needed to go with a more well-defined approach. I wasn't a great proponent of behavior modification, but it has its uses and here seemed to be one of them. So, I set out to design a program to bring order out of chaos.

At home I took four separate pieces of white poster board and, using construction paper, I made a traffic light out of each one. I wrote the boys' names on them and inserted small brads at the three points on the traffic light where the red, yellow, and green lights should be to let me hang things there. Then I made up a bunch of circles from index cards with one color on each one of them: red, yellow, or green. And finally, I made up a big grid chart with the days of the week labeled across the top.

The next morning in the classroom, I explained what was going to happen. Everybody started out with their traffic light on green. If I had to give a warning to someone about their behavior, I would take off the green circle and stick on a yellow. If I had to send someone to the quiet chair or in any other way discipline their behavior, the yellow circle went to red for the length of the time-out. I stuck the grid chart up on the bulletin board, then I held up a packet of sticker stars. I assigned each boy a particular color of star. If someone could go a given work period on green – through math period, for instance, or reading period – he got a star to put on the grid chart. Five stars together – an entire day on green – and he got *this*. I held up a Hershey bar. When we had a total of fifty stars of any color, we'd have a class party.

The boys cheered at the sight of the candy. Billy thought it was all a Very Good Idea. Jesse looked a little confused. It went right over Shane's and Zane's heads, I could tell, but they knew their colors, so I hoped they'd catch on soon enough once the program was under way. And as I feared, Julie hated it.

"Behavior *modification*?" she asked, picking up one of the Hershey bars as if it were a cattle prod. "They were doing this with Casey when I first came, but I got him off it. I hate behavior mod."

"I'm not a big fan myself," I said.

"It's dehumanizing. It's treating the kids like animals."

I hesitated to point out that at the moment mine were behaving like animals.

"Bribing them to behave. With *candy*. I mean, couldn't we at least use raisins or something? Something vaguely healthy?"

"I'm not sure raisins would cut it," I said. "I want control first. Then health."

"Yeah," she said. And her tone reflected that she thought I'd pretty much said it all with that statement.

The first week of the program was hell. No two ways about that. Mostly it was administrative hell, because I had to carry the damned little colored circles around with me and dash to the traffic lights to stick them up unerringly whenever behavior changed. And I was forever forgetting to dole out sticker stars – and discovering quickly that I had to be *very* alert to who actually *had* managed to go a whole period on green behavior, as Shane and Zane often forgot what was going on, so missed their stars, while Billy was forever trying to fudge the system.

It was not perfect. There was no sudden change in behavior. There was no class party that Friday, as I'd hoped. Indeed, I'd only managed to pass out two Hershey bars in five days, both to Jesse. But slowly, slowly the boys did seem to be paying just a little attention to their behavior and to the behavior of the class as a whole. Troublesome as the whole plan was to administrate, having such concrete, visual reminders of the need to behave did seem to make a difference. So, we took a few mouse steps toward becoming a group.

The other thing I decided to actively do was teach "values" to the class. I didn't normally do this sort of thing. In most of my previous classes, we had had "morning discussion," where I brought the children together in a circle before lessons began and we discussed various topics. It was usually a combination show-and-tell and troubleshooting session, where kids could voice things that were important to them, air worries, complain and discuss predetermined "topics," such as appropriate behavior in a given situation. This had always worked well and been a mainstay of my teaching technique. But not this year. In part this happened because we had the other resource students coming and going through the day, including first thing in the morning, and so there was not a good time for discussion without interruption. However, the main reason was that they were a very small group, so one difficult member easily disrupted everyone, and even without disruption it was hard to keep this group sitting down that long and paying attention. They were not bonded, not interested, and not willing. The times I'd tried morning discussion, it had always ended in a shambles, usually with a fistfight or my sending most of them off to quiet chairs. So, I'd dropped the activity initially. However, as time passed, I felt more and more of a need to have some space during the school day to help the boys understand more appropriate behavior and to explore and practice it through conversation, role-playing, and art.

We started very simply. It was after recess in the last half hour of the day when the boys were at their tables.

"Each day, we're going to take some time and talk about some words," I said. "Today we're going to talk about *bad*. Has anybody ever called you a 'bad boy' or 'bad girl'?"

"Have they *ever*!" Billy shouted out.

"Like all the time with you, Billy," Jesse added.

I put a finger to my lips. "You'll get your turn in a minute. So, Billy, what kinds of things have people said to you?"

"Bad boy! You don't sit still!" he said. "Bad boy! You don't do your work. Bad boy! You got everything messy."

"Good. Okay. What about you, Jesse. Has anybody ever called you a bad boy?"

Jesse shrugged. "Maybe."

"What about you, Shane?"

He nodded. "Zane peed the bed last night and Mama said, 'Bad boy, you done that.'"

"Did not!" Zane cried and shot to his feet.

I waved a yellow traffic circle frantically. "Yo, Zane. Think again. You don't want to go to yellow, do you?"

He paused, looking at me.

"You want to get a star at the end of this period, don't you?"

He nodded slowly. "But I didn't pee the bed. *He* did."

"Okay. Can you sit back down in your chair?"

"I know another one," Billy interjected. "Lying. You lie and someone always says that's bad."

"That's right. What about you, Gwennie? Has someone ever said 'bad girl' to you?" I asked.

Gwennie was staring out the window. Julie had been meandering around the room – "patrolling," as we called it – and she approached Gwennie's table. Gently she reached out to reorient Gwennie's head, but Gwennie pulled back before Julie could touch her, so I knew she was more present than she gave the impression of being.

"Gwennie?" I asked again. "Can you join us in the conversation too?"

"I know another one," Billy shouted out. "You're bad if you don't pay attention!"

"Thank you, Billy, but could you wait your turn, please? Give the others a chance to talk. Gwennie?"

She shrugged.

A pause.

I waited.

"It's snowing in Sweden right now," she said softly.

"Gwennie, right here." I pointed to my eyes. "Look up here."

"You don't pay attention," she said. "Bad girl. You never pay attention. You're a really bad girl."

"Thank you for sharing, Gwennie. So, what do we know about *bad*? *Bad* is just a little word, but it can pack a big punch."

"Ouch!" Billy cried out, clutched his right eye, and fell off his chair onto the floor. "Ooooh, owie!!!" He writhed.

I leaped to my feet, concerned. "What's the matter? What happened?"

Billy peeled back his hands slowly and grinned. "I just got punched in the eye by *bad*. Little word, but, boy, does it pack a punch!"

With a sigh, I waved a yellow traffic disk in front of him. "Here. You go hang it on your traffic light yourself."

Chapter Fourteen

Mid-December, Bob stopped by my room first thing in the morning. I was sitting at my desk, assembling the children's folders when he came in.

"You know Venus?" he started.

I looked up.

"I think we're getting her back."

I was delighted to hear this news. "Really? What's changed?"

"Not for the good, I'm afraid. There's been some ... the family's going through some traumas. One of the older kids was arrested for dealing drugs. Apparently he was doing it at home and there's a question of which other kids are involved. Stan Moorhouse – you know Stan, don't you? – from the district administrator's office, called me last night and said that Social Services got hold of him, and they think maybe it is better if Venus is not at home all the time. They're concerned about this. And apparently they're concerned about this Danny guy that lives with them, because he's the one who's been looking after the kids. Teri works at night, so she's usually sleeping. He's the one keeping track of Wanda and Venus and whoever else is home. They were saying that even though there is no evidence he's involved in any of this, if we can provide an alternative for Venus here, it would be preferable to homebound at this time."

"Well, I'm happy to have her back. But what about the violence problem on the playground? Are we going to be able to pick up from there?" I asked. "Or are we risking problems with the regular kids?"

"Stan Moorhouse says the district could supply her with an aide for lunchtime. It's cheaper than a homebound tutor, and it should help those problems. We have to arrange something ourselves for recess. It may mean giving you a different recess period." He slipped that one in fast, hoping, I think, that it'd miss my notice.

I wrinkled my nose.

"Anyway, we'll see."

So, as quickly as she had disappeared, Venus returned. The following Monday, two weeks before Christmas vacation, Bob led her through the classroom door.

"Oh no! Psycho's back!" Billy shouted melodramatically.

Quick as a fox, I had that yellow traffic disk out of my shirt pocket. I waved it meaningfully in the air.

"No fair! School's not even started yet! No fair! I'm not on yellow. Not yet!" Billy shrieked.

"Then zip your mouth," I said and gestured.

"Zip it? Zip it? But I haven't got a z – "

I waved the disk again. *Very* meaningfully.

Venus looked a little shabbier than I'd remembered. Rubber bands that had once bound her dreadlocks were now deeply embedded in her long hair along with toast crumbs and what looked to be jam. The clothes she had on, a pair of black pants and a red tartan plaid top, were clearly not her own. Overwashed, faded, and pilled, they were two or three sizes too big for her thin body – donation clothes that no one had bothered to try to make look like anything else. On her feet were mismatched socks and a pair of pink Barbie sneakers with the plastic edging split and falling away.

"Hello, Lovey. I'm glad you're back. Here. We saved your table for you." I led her to her old place at the table in back of Zane's.

Not much had changed. Venus sat down, stared after me as I passed out work folders and started math period. She didn't open her folder. She didn't even lower her head.

"Is she going to get a traffic light too?" Billy asked. "You gonna do her the red, green, and yellow thing? What you gonna do with Psycho?"

"What are you going to do with Billy?" I asked.

This didn't deflect him. "She ought to get a traffic light. Then you can give her reds for not working. *I* get reds for not working."

I lifted up the yellow warning disk. "I'll ask again. What are *you* going to do with Billy right now?"

A long moment passed between us. Billy glared. "It's not fair," he muttered. "I can't say *anything*. It's a dictatorship in here."

"You can call it a dictatorship in here, if you want. And it might not seem fair, but it's the way it works. So, let's see if you can stay on green the *whole* period. Okay?"

I sat down beside Venus. I had no idea where she was in math. I'm quite sure none of us did. Taking a box of colored wooden shapes, I lay three out on the table: a blue cylinder, a red cube, and a green cone. I lay three corresponding cards with pictures of the items on the table. "Can you show me which one matches this one?" I asked her.

No response.

"This one does, doesn't it? See? Red. Red. Square shape. Square shape. This picture matches that cube there, doesn't it?" I picked the cube up and put it on the card. "Now, which one matches this card?"

No response.

"This one. See, it is blue. And the picture is blue. Same shape. See the same shapes?" I picked up the cylinder and lay it on that card. "Now, how about the last one. Can you show me which matches it?"

Not much of a challenge there, but Venus was not going to respond.

"Here, let me help you." I reached over and took hold of her arm just above the wrist. Beneath my fingers I could feel muscles suddenly tightening. Was I going to set her off? That possibility had flashed through my mind before I touched her, but it didn't happen. She simply stiffened so that I could not move her hand.

I pushed my chair back. "We're going to do something. Here, stand up."

She didn't stand of her own volition, of course, but I got her to her feet easily enough.

"Out here. Away from the table. We're going to do some exercises." I remained seated but pulled Venus over in front of me. I took hold of both her hands. "Okay, here we go. Shoulders." I placed her hands on her shoulders. "Hips." I pulled her hands down to her hips. "Knees." I moved her hands down to her knees, not an easy task, as she did not initially bend enough to do it. "Toes." I couldn't get her down to her toes. "Here. I'll show you. Shoulders, hips, knees, toes. See? See how I'm doing it?" I touched my hands to my own shoulders, hips, knees, and toes, although I remained sitting in the chair. "Now you're going to do it." I took hold of her hands in each of mine. "Shoulders. Hips. Knees. And… " I tugged her gently down. "Good. Toes." I let go of her. Venus stayed in the hunkered-down position, touching her toes.

I reached down and took her hands again. "We're going to do it over." I pulled her back to a standing position. "We're going to do it over and over, so you don't feel stiff. Here we go. Shoulders. Hips. Knees. Toes. Shoulders. Hips. Knees. Toes. Good. Now, back up. Toes. Knees. Hips. Shoulders. Down again. Shoulders. Hips. Knees. Toes." I had to pull her through every single motion.

"Hey, do that with me!" Shane cried and was out of his chair, running over.

"Okay. Here," I said, quickly getting out of my chair to intercept him before he got too close to Venus. "We'll all do it. Everybody up." I stood behind Shane, took hold of his hands, and led him through the exercise the way I'd been doing it with Venus. "Shoulders, hips, knees, toes."

"Me too!" Zane said. "Do it with me now!"

"I get a turn!" Jesse cried.

"Well, *I* get a turn then," Billy added. "Even if I was the *only* one to stay in my seat the whole time without ever getting up without asking, so that I should be the *only one* still on green."

I grinned at him. "Okay. So you earned an extra star for that."

A brief moment of spontaneous joy followed. I pulled each one of the boys through the simple exercise in turn and they loved it. I did it repeatedly, alternating children, faster and faster, up, down, up again to see if I could trick them until we were all laughing and out of breath. Except, of course, Venus, who just stood and stared.

The school district had hired a special aide to supervise Venus for the forty-five minutes over the lunch hour. She was a trained behavioral aide, which seemed like overkill to me, given that she did nothing except stand outside on the playground with the sole purpose of watching Venus, who normally did nothing except stand or sit on her wall. I was rather hoping she might actually be there to interact with Venus, but not so.

I didn't want my group to lose their recess time with the rest of the kids because of Venus, so I told Bob that between Julie and me, we would take responsibility for supervising her during the two breaks, which were each twenty minutes. This meant, of course, that we each had to give up one of the two breaks ourselves, but it was a small sacrifice compared to making the children spend their recesses in isolation. Anyway, I hoped it wouldn't last forever.

Julie covered the morning recess, as she often went out on the playground with Casey Muldrow. I took the afternoons. We didn't do any more than just stay out on the playground with the aides, ready to intervene at a moment's notice. And for the most part, there was no problem. Whether Venus was aware there was someone on full-time duty hawking over her or whether she was in slightly better control of her behavior, I didn't know, but we had no real trouble. She snarled a few times; we intervened, reminded others of Venus's need for space, reminded Venus it wasn't appropriate to snarl and no one was intending to hurt her, then we retreated back again. Most of the time, however, she stayed far distant from the other kids, usually doing no more than leaning against "her" wall at the edge of the playground.

On the third day, I did something different. When the recess bell rang, I said, "Let's stay here."

Venus looked at me blankly.

I helped the boys with their shoes and their outer clothes and opened the door so that they could thunder down the stairs with the third-grade class next door. Then I went back. Venus was still standing, just where she'd been.

"We've got twenty minutes. That isn't very long. But I thought we'd read a story instead of going outside to stand by the wall."

I picked out Arnold Lobel's *Frog and Toad Are Friends*, a longtime favorite of mine. It was an easy-reader children's book with large, well-spaced print and an engaging series of rather humorous little stories about the eponymous Frog and Toad.

"Come here. Let's sit down and I'll read you this. I'll bet you haven't heard these stories."

Venus stared at me.

"Come here."

No response.

I'd already seated myself in the reading corner. I stood back up and went to her. "Come on." I put a hand behind her back and directed her over to the reading corner. I sat down again. "Here, sit down."

She stood.

"Come on." I rose back up on my knees, grabbed hold of her, and pulled her down in my lap. I wrapped one arm around her and drew her in close against me. With the other, I held up the book and began to read. I'd never previously tried holding Venus in an affectionate way on my lap, and it was a challenge. She sat very stiffly. It was like holding a manikin.

The book took less than ten minutes to read. All the time, Venus sat, every muscle tensed. I didn't have the sense that she would dash away if I let go of her, but likewise I didn't have the sense that she was particularly enjoying this. There was an expectancy to her stiffness, as if she were waiting for something to happen. It crossed my mind then that perhaps she had never had anyone read to her the way I was doing now. An incredible thought, but sadly possible.

Not wanting to disturb our détente by getting up to locate a second book, I opened *Frog and Toad* again. There was one particularly funny little story where Frog is unwell and Toad tries to think up a story to tell him. Toad goes through the most outrageous efforts to think of a story, and most children find this very funny. So, I read it again, this time with more gusto and some sound effects.

"Isn't Toad funny?" I said. "Look, he's standing on his head to make himself think of a story. Isn't that silly?"

No response.

"Maybe he thinks when all the blood rushes to his head, a story will too. Silly Toad. Now look what he's doing. Look at that. He's pouring a glass of water on his head. Do you think that will help him think of a story to tell Frog?"

No response.

"No, I don't think so either. It'd just make his head wet. Now what's he doing? Look at this picture."

No response.

"Silly Toad! He's hitting his head against the wall to make himself think of a story. Would you do that?"

No response.

"No, I wouldn't either. Why?"

No response.

"Yes, you're exactly right. It'd hurt your head, wouldn't it? You'd get a great big bump right there, wouldn't you?" I touched her forehead.

No response.

The bell rang, signaling the end of recess.

"Whoops, that's us. Gwennie and the boys will be back any minute. But we had fun, didn't we?" I said as I lifted her back to her feet.

No response.

So, that became the pattern of our days. Working on the assumption that, as Wanda's daughter, Venus was a severely neglected child who had not experienced much interaction, I endeavored to create a series of stimulating events that would be hard to ignore, even if she did not respond. "In your face" events, as Bob called them. And I tried to keep them regular and repetitive so that she would know what to expect.

Thus, before every lesson – every *single* lesson – I did the shoulders, hips, knees, toes exercise with her. I included the boys, who seemed to profit more visibly from this extra bit of activity inserted regularly into the day than Venus did. They liked the five minutes of jumping around, loved the predictability of its happening every hour, and adored having me choose one of them to pull through the exercises the way I did Venus. But I could only pull them through in the afternoons, when Julie was there to pull Venus through, because she simply would not *ever* do them on her own.

Indeed, I made a conscious effort to use touch in many ways with her. I did talk this over extensively with Bob first, largely because we were just beginning to move into the era of child abuse awareness when physical contact between teachers and students was becoming an issue. But Bob, being of much the same way of thinking as I was, was happy with the approach and understood the value of tactile communication with a child like Venus.

I had three quite separate goals in using touch in this instance. First, as the simple but very effective communication tool it was. Warm, caring touches – pats on the back, quick hugs, a reassuring hand on the shoulder – could communicate more effectively than words that I was aware of her presence, liked having her there, and did not in any way find her disgusting or unpleasant. Second, as a demonstration that touch could be positive, warm, and nonsexual, which was an important distinction to make with children for whom physical or sexual abuse was a possibility. And third, just as pure tactile stimulation. Approaching Venus's almost catatonic state from the point of view that she had been vastly understimulated as a baby and young child, I felt it was important to use all senses available to me to "wake her up."

The other thing I did was read to her. Every day during the afternoon recess. After exhausting Frog and Toad and their various adventures through two or three books, we went on to the rather more sophisticated adventures of Russell Hoban's Frances, a very human little girl in the guise of a small badger. There are several of these books and the stories are longer and more complex, so I went over them slowly, reading and rereading, talking about all the details of the stories. Having not met a child, girl *or* boy, who did not identify with Frances's feelings and her juvenile logic, I hoped they would also work their magic on Venus.

About the same time, music made an appearance in the classroom as one of those serendipitous, spur-of-the-moment ideas.

I'm not among the world's most talented when it comes to music. I can carry a tune and I have a good enough ear for pitch. However, I am also almost completely bereft of any sense of rhythm, and I have a singularly bad problem remembering lyrics. Consequently, I was not naturally attracted to teaching music in the classroom, probably because I was often no better at it than the children, and in some instances, worse! However, it occurred to me that music would be another important way we could provide positive stimulation for Venus. And ... when I considered it, here was another way for the boys to let off energy. So, I thought, what the heck. I *could* sing. And the boys loved singing, whether they could do it or not.

So, I made a conscious decision there in December, heart of the Christmas music season, that we'd make music a part of every day. I had to plan this rather strategically, as we now had the other learning-support children coming in regularly for twenty or thirty minutes here and there, and it seemed unfair to cut into their time in the room. This meant music had to be a "movable feast," appearing whenever I could squeeze it in. We started with singing. Anytime I could manage it. "If You're Happy and You Know It" was an old favorite. And "B-I-N-G-O," which the boys loved because of its shouting. But I included some old-timers, such as "High Hopes," "In the Cool, Cool, Cool of the Evening," "Little Arrows," and "If You Want to Swing on a Star," because they were funny, could be mimed, and stood up well to being sung with gusto. But mainly because *I could remember the words*! And, of course, as it was the Christmas season, this gave us lots of Christmas songs to work with. Indeed, "Jingle Bells" almost became our theme song we sang it so much.

The music thing caught on *very* quickly. We started singing every time someone made it through a whole period with their traffic light on green. Billy turned out to be quite talented at altering the words of songs, so he was always coming up with a new version of an old familiar. They were usually dopey words but fun, and everyone liked hearing their name in a song. I found it was a good way to get everyone changed from one activity to another, so I often started us singing when it was time to get ready for lunch or the like. Better yet, it proved a foolproof way of distracting everyone's attention away from doing something they shouldn't, particularly those times when people were starting to get a bit testy with one another. If I said "Let's sing," almost everyone wanted to. Even if the testy person did not join in, the others always would, and the mood would change. Within a short time, we were singing so often, it felt like living inside an operetta. Right down to the slightly surreal quality when people unexpectedly burst into song.

Venus herself never participated in any of this, although Julie or I often chose her as a "dance partner," if we did actions. But she didn't ignore us either. I often saw her watching the boys intently as they sang out familiar words and danced and mimed. And Venus wasn't the only one not ignoring us. One lunchtime, I opened the classroom door to let the boys out to join the other classes going down to lunch. We'd been singing "Little Arrows" while we were waiting for the bell to ring. While it was a rather dippy little love song, the boys simply loved miming arrows zinging back and forth, and it had just the kind of gutsy tune that worked best for us, so, when the door opened, they all burst out singing the chorus of "Little arrows in your clothing, Little arrows in your hair. When you're in love you'll find those little arrows everywhere," and disappeared down the stairwell.

Pam, who taught third grade in the room next to me, was standing in her doorway, and she shook her head good-naturedly when she caught my eye.

"I probably shouldn't let them out doing that," I said. "Somebody downstairs has already complained about all the noise in the hallway!" I laughed.

"You guys are so happy in there, aren't you?" Pam said.

"It's crowd control actually."

"No. I hear you, Torey. You guys are *always* singing. *All* the time."

It suddenly occurred to me that we might well be disturbing Pam's class. The building was old and the walls were thick, so not much penetrated, but she was right. "All the time" did describe it.

"I'm sorry," I said. "I hope we're not too noisy."

"No. I think it's great. My bunch would think I was nuts, if I tried to sing all the time. But your little guys ... they're just so enthusiastic about everything. I think you're lucky to have such a happy class."

I smiled in surprise. I hadn't thought of it that way. I hadn't seen happiness sneaking up on us like that.

Chapter Fifteen

In our own ersatz–von Trapp family way, we finally started coming together as a class. It mattered to the boys that we sang; it made us "fun," and it made them want to be included. It gave us a group identity. We were no longer "the resource room." We were the class that was always singing. Unfortunately, as this happened, it highlighted a different problem – the ongoing discord between Julie and me. In this instance, it was because Julie steadfastly refused to join in all the goofy singing. She couldn't sing, she said. I laughed it off the first few times, joking that I was hardly Maria Callas, and Shane and Zane wouldn't have known a tune if it had been spoon-fed to them by Rodgers and Hammerstein. So *good* singing didn't really come into it. Being able to carry a tune was no prerequisite to joining this sing-a-thon. We were just having fun. Then Julie became a little more emphatic, explaining that, in fact, she *hated* singing, *especially* group singing. Kids had teased her about her inability to sing when she was little and she still felt sensitive.

I could understand this and I didn't want to make her feel bad, so I ignored her refusal to take part from that point on. The boys, however, kept pestering her. I'd say, "It doesn't matter. In this class we let people make these choices for themselves." But it did matter. Singing had become synonymous with wanting to join us. We were bonding over this, becoming the group we had never previously managed to be. When Julie refused to participate, it cast her in the role of an outsider. The subtext then became that I was excluding her. By using something she was not good at, something she disliked, to bond us, I was implying I didn't want her. This wasn't true, of course. The whole singing business had literally just happened. Certainly, it was never something I would have planned to use because I wasn't very musical myself, but as chance would have it, the boys were, and this just jelled for us. But Julie didn't see it that way. We had gone beyond things being an issue of my way and her way to a point where she occasionally voiced the feeling that I was *planning* these differences. I was attempting to keep her from being part of us.

This left me deeply dismayed. I disliked the subtle tension that was always present in the room when we both were there. I disliked the sense that I couldn't depend on Julie to back me up when things got difficult. I disliked most of all her thinking that any of our discord was intentional, because it never was.

What had gone wrong between us?

I never quite understood what had caused our problems. Was it just a personality clash? Something that didn't work in the context of my classroom? A deeper problem? I didn't know. I kept watching, kept thinking, kept trying to analyze what I sensed. My problem was that while I was quite a good analytical thinker when it came to concrete things, I was a much more intuitive thinker at the abstract level. I could "sense" when something wasn't right, but I had a hard time identifying it. This made it difficult to go to Bob and tell him about the situation because what could I say? She was being too nice in the classroom?

And that, of all the things, was the difference between us that was driving me nuts. I hated the cliché, but this woman really did have the patience of a saint. Perhaps it particularly irritated me because I'd always considered patience to be *my* strength. With many children I had been successful solving difficult problems largely because I simply could be very, very patient and wait things out without feeling frustrated or irritated. Admittedly, it was more of a personality trait than a cultivated virtue, but nonetheless I'd always been rather proud of it. Yet my patience was not even in the same league as Julie's. She seemed capable of tolerating *anything* without becoming upset or annoyed. One part of me found it almost offensive that she greeted every mishap in the classroom with relentless calm. Another part of me, however, was green with envy for something I knew I could never do.

Things finally came to a head on the last day before we broke up for winter vacation.

When Billy arrived that morning, he was clutching a brightly wrapped blob of a gift.

"This is for you, Teacher. I bought it myself."

"How thoughtful, Billy," I said and set it on my desk. "Thank you so much. I'll really look forward to opening this."

"Open it now," he said.

"Don't you think I should wait until Christmas?"

"No! Open it now. I want to watch you open it. I want you to see what it is!"

The other children were starting to arrive and they gathered around my desk. Smiling, I undid the ribbon. The irregular-shaped package had been literally mummified in Scotch tape, so I picked up the scissors and carefully cut through the wrapping.

Inside was a statue of a gray cat about a foot high made from glazed pottery. "How beautiful, Billy. Thank you so much."

Billy was grinning ear to ear. "I bought that myself. I paid my own money for it. Know how much it cost?" He didn't wait for a reply. "One dollar and ninety-nine cents. I bought it at the Dollar Store. Everything there is supposed to only cost a dollar. But this was one of their *expensive* gifts. And I got it myself with my own money."

"Well, thank you so much, Billy. I like cats a lot, so I'm pleased to have such a nice cat statue. When I get home, I'll find a special place to set it up."

"Yeah, I thought that," he said. He picked up the cat statue and caressed it lovingly. "I thought 'Teacher'd like this.'" He looked up. "I really did think that. I was thinking of you."

I leaned down and gave him a hug. "You are a thoughtful boy, Billy," I said. "I've always known that."

Looking enormously pleased, he smiled and hugged me back.

I set the cat statue on my desk and went off to start the day.

Our class was having a Christmas party that afternoon, which was courting disaster because of the change in routine. Shane and Zane seemed particularly badly affected by the day's excitement. Both boys found it very hard to control themselves in anything other than a very structured, predictable setting.

We had worked a lot on helping them deal with this inflexibility. For instance, we'd made up words to some of our favorite songs that helped to remind them to stop, take a breath, think, then act. We regularly played games like freeze, where the class would be doing something and I'd call out "freeze," and everyone would have to freeze in the position of whatever they were doing, take a deep breath, and hold it until I said "thaw." We also had special "quiet music" that I put on when things became too stimulating and a special "quiet place," where Shane and Zane could sit down and collect their thoughts to help them stay in control, that didn't have the association with punishment that the quiet chair did. Even so, they could become very, very naughty if their routine changed much.

That morning had been fairly chaotic, but it was helped by the fact that we had none of the part-time students there, as it was the last day before vacation. So I'd been able to give them my full attention and structure the time with a lot of low-key activities.

Over the lunch hour, however, the treats arrived. Jesse's grandmother brought in cupcakes. Shane and Zane's mother stopped by with a huge tray of cookies cut out in the shape of Christmas trees. Julie arrived and helped me set up the party table. Although the rest of the school was having a Christmas party all afternoon, we were only going to have our party during the time following recess, as that was when Santa Claus was due to arrive in our room. Even with this shortened party time, however, it was impossible from lunchtime on to ignore the fact that Something Exciting was going to take place. When Shane and Zane took all the goodies in, they just went gaga.

The first upset happened even before the bell rang.

"Look what Shane's done," Jesse called out.

I was in the process of hanging out my attendance slip and closing the door. I turned to see Shane holding a fat red marking pen. He had colored all the skin on his left hand and up the arm of his shirt.

"Oh dear," Julie said in an amicable voice. "Did you forget markers are for paper, not for people? Come here, Shane. Let's wash it off."

I got started with the afternoon's activities.

Julie washed Shane's hand as best she could. There weren't enough paper towels at the sink, so she went to the cupboard to get a new pack. Shane was splashing water by hitting the flat of his hand on the bottom of the sink. He looked up at me as he did it, a beady little expression in his eyes because he knew I was watching, and then stuck his finger against the faucet. Water sprayed everywhere.

Julie turned to see the mess. "Oops," she said calmly. "Water on the floor. Someone might slip. Here, let's take towels and wipe it up."

She took paper towels and bent over the spilled water. Shane just took towels. Being meant for a paper towel dispenser, they were loaded into the pack in an interfolded manner, so one towel lifted up the edge of the next towel. He experimented with pulling them apart rapidly, which meant they flew off in all directions in rather graceful arcs.

I didn't want to undermine Julie's authority by intervening, but I kept a close eye on the proceedings. Noticing him doing this, Julie rose back to her feet. "Towels are for wiping things with, Shane. Here." She gave him a towel. "Please help." She knelt back down to finish wiping up the water.

Shane wasn't falling for that one. Instead, he started hitting her over the head with the towel. It didn't hurt, of course, but he was persistent. She ignored him at first until he started swishing the paper towel against her eyes so that she couldn't see.

"Towels are for wiping, Shane. Will you help?"

Shane continued to hit her with the paper towel.

She rose up and took his hand. "Come back over to your table. You have your folder there. Let's see if there is a nice picture of Santa for you to color. That would be fun, wouldn't it?"

I watched all this, hypersensitive to how I would have handled it differently. For one thing, I would have raised my voice. Not shouted. But I would have used my voice, as well as my words, to make it very apparent that I considered coloring yourself with a marker, spraying water all over the floor, and then throwing a bunch of paper towels around ... not acceptable classroom activities. Then I would have ensured *he* mopped up the floor, and if he hadn't cooperated, I would have had him in the quiet chair until he felt inclined to do it.

Yet, thinking all that, I felt slightly guilty. I could justify my method as giving Shane a clearer message of how to behave, but the truth was, I would have also done it because I was annoyed with him. I didn't *like* that kind of behavior. My reaction would have been – at least in part – personal. But was that right? I was here to *help* him. These were special children with heavy burdens. Julie stayed so child-oriented, so relentlessly cheerful in her efforts to interact with them in a humane, compassionate way that encouraged good self-esteem. And here was me, reacting out of: "Don't do that because I don't like it."

The afternoon went from bad to worse. For once the traffic light system failed me. They had been going from yellow to red on and off all morning, but by afternoon, everyone was permanently on red and no one cared. Jesse, overexcited, could not control his tics. He barked and flinched and grimaced. When not doing that, he fought. He and Shane biffed it out over a pencil. He and Billy went two rounds on the rug in the reading corner before I managed to pry them apart and get them into separate quiet chairs. Gwennie was also jumpy. She hated Jesse's barking and sat for long stretches of time with her hands up over her head, trying to shut it out. And when we weren't looking, she dived into the Christmas goodies, stuffing candy and cookies into her mouth with both hands. Shane and Zane were a nightmare of truly outrageous activities. Shane pulled things off the bulletin board. He kicked over chairs. He tried to break one of the back windows by hitting it repeatedly with a block. Zane unzipped his pants and peed on my chair. Venus was the only one not to cause trouble and that's because she was absent that day.

The centerpiece of the half-hour party after recess was the arrival of Santa Claus, who was, of course, really Bob. He was visiting each room in the school with a sack of goodies and arriving in our room last, since we were having the shortest party. Most of the children in regular classrooms were getting small bags of candy, but the Lions Club was sponsoring our class throughout that year, so they had provided gifts for each of the children in the room, including Gwennie, even though she was only part-time.

As I was welcoming Santa, Shane and Zane were both up out of their seats and running around. I nodded to Julie to corral them and get them back where they belonged.

Shane, zooming by my desk, picked up the gray cat statue that Billy had given me.

"Put that back, you little fucker! That's not yours!" Billy shouted. He was out of his seat.

Santa put down his sack and grabbed Billy by the arm.

"Jingle bells, Jingle bells," I started. "Come on, everyone! Jingle all the way. Oh what fun..."

Santa had joined in, singing heartily and still gripping Billy. Billy started to sing, even though he was still glaring at Shane. So did Jesse. Gwennie kept her head down, her hands over her ears.

Julie crossed over to Shane, took the cat statue from his hands, and put it back on the desk.

I started to clap as I sang. Coming up to Zane I clapped cheerfully in front of him. He joined me, clapping and singing. Then finally Shane started to clap too.

I marched. I clapped and sang "Jingle Bells" until everyone, including Santa Claus, was marching around the room, clapping and singing too. Finally we ended up in the reading corner.

Santa went back to the door to retrieve his bag. Five or six minutes of relative peace followed while Santa gave out the presents and the boys whooped with excitement at tearing off the wrapping paper. This distraction gave Gwennie enough time to elude us and start stuffing her face over at the party table. I don't know how many cookies she had eaten when I noticed her present, lying still wrapped on the floor. Grabbing her by the shoulder, I led her back to the reading corner.

We had all the children sit down on the rug in the reading corner while Julie and I passed out cookies, cupcakes, and punch. Santa pulled over a little chair and sat down to read "The Night Before Christmas" to the children while they ate.

A tiny moment of peace reigned.

Then, just as he got to the "Now Dasher! Now Dancer!" bit, there was a soft burble and Gwennie started to vomit. It just ran out of her like a fountain, down the front of her dress, into her lap, across her shoes, and over the rug. The boys leaped up in surprise. Gwennie started to cry.

"There, there," Julie crooned, taking hold of her shoulders. "It's just throw-up. Don't cry, honey. Did it scare you? Don't worry. It's just throw-up."

It's *not* just "throw-up," I was thinking irritably. It's a great big horrible smelly mess that's wrecked the one peaceful moment in our Christmas party, and if Gwennie wouldn't stuff her face so, it wouldn't happen. I hated myself for having such thoughts, because I knew Gwennie could not help being sick, but I *did* think it. But, damn it, it *was* more than "just throw-up." I felt sorry for Gwennie, but I also felt sorry for the boys, the rug, and Santa, who had vomit on his costume-shop Santa boots. And me.

I moved the boys over to the other side of the room, called in the janitor, handed Santa a couple of paper towels to wipe off his boots, and put the remaining cookies out of reach. Julie took Gwennie down to the girls' rest room to clean her up.

We only had five minutes of the day left by the time Julie and Gwennie returned. Santa was gone and the janitor was there by then, so I decided to call it a day. I told the kids to get their coats on and we'd spend the rest of the time on the playground.

That's when I turned around to see Shane picking up the gray cat statue again. He wasn't doing it maliciously. Clearly he just wanted to look at it, but he picked it up and started toward me with it, probably to show me something about it. But the lace on his left shoe was untied. He stepped on it and stumbled. He didn't fall, but the cat statue slipped from his hands and fell to the floor. It hit with a dull crash and broke into countless pieces.

Billy instantly burst into tears. He didn't get angry. He didn't go into his usual attack mode when something went wrong. He didn't even move. His face just drew down and he started to bawl. My heart melted for him.

Startled by the crash, Shane started to cry too.

In an instant, Julie was there, her arms around Shane.

"Did that scare you? It was just an accident. Don't cry, sweetheart. It doesn't matter. Accidents happen."

I'm embarrassed to admit it, but at that moment, I just lost it.

"It *does* matter!" I said. "Billy bought that. It was his gift to me. It *does* matter it got broken!"

Realizing I was very angry, Shane started to cry in earnest.

Billy rushed to join me. "You stupid motherfucker! You broke my cat. I'm gonna *kill* you!"

This brought me quickly to my senses. "No, you're not," I said. I put my hands on his shoulder. "I'm really, really sorry for what happened, but I don't want you to get into trouble on top of it. Go get your coat on, so you can go on the playground." I looked at Shane. "I want you in the quiet chair."

"I didn't mean to." Shane was sobbing.

"I'm sure you didn't, but you shouldn't have been touching it. It wasn't yours."

He didn't question me. He went over and sat down.

"I'll stay with him until the bell rings," Julie said.

I nodded. Turning, I took the other children downstairs to the playground.

Quite frankly, I felt like crying myself. Certainly I didn't feel like going back upstairs to sort all this out between Julie and me, which is what I knew I had to do once the children had gone home. So once everyone was bid good-bye and put in their respective cars or buses, I reluctantly returned to the classroom.

Julie was on the far side of the room, straightening up things in the aftermath of the janitor, who had shifted the tables around in order to clean the floor in the reading corner.

"Sit down," I said. "We need to talk this over."

"It's just been a bad day," Julie said. "I'm sorry if things didn't go like we planned."

"No, it's more than that. We need to thrash this out between us."

Julie came over and pulled out the chair across the table from me. She sat down. I did too.

"I know we have different philosophies. I can respect that," I said. "In fact, in many ways I'm very impressed by you. You have many admirable qualities. But what's going on in here, what you're doing in here ... like with Shane ... this is a kind of ... emotional lying, Julie. You aren't responding honestly to these situations."

"What do you mean?" There was a vaguely defensive tone.

"I mean, you're behaving the same way toward him when he's splashing water or throwing paper towels as you do when he's sitting down and doing his work. You use the same loving, peaceful voice. But you can't be *feeling* loving, peaceful emotions then. Not when he's hitting you with a paper towel when he should be helping wipe up the water."

"Yes, I do," she replied calmly.

I looked at her.

A silence crept in.

"Yes, I do," she said again, perhaps a little more quietly this time. "Because I should be loving and peaceful. That's *good*, Torey. That's the way we should be."

"Not all the time."

"Why ever not?" she asked.

"Because it isn't honest. People don't feel loving and peaceful all the time. People feel annoyed or angry or tired or upset sometimes, and these are all part of us too, and while it is important to be in control of these emotions so that they don't hurt anyone, that's not the same as behaving as if they aren't there. And it isn't wrong that they're there. We're telling emotional lies when we act as if we don't have these feelings."

Julie just sat.

"That's not good. It isn't giving the children the tools to learn how to control these feelings themselves. Instead, it's making them think we're different from what they are. Relentlessly cheerful people aren't real."

Julie sighed. "You're the only person who's ever made me feel that being cheerful is wrong," she said.

"There's a deeper level to this too," I said. "It has to do with right and wrong. I know it's important to show acceptance and tolerance, to make people feel good about themselves, but the plain truth remains: if we don't actively teach right and wrong, children don't learn it. It's our responsibility to teach the children how they *should* behave. Not everything they do is right. They need to be actively shown the difference between right and wrong behavior and shown ways to behave better that will eventually allow them to grow into happier, more fulfilled people."

"Which is your opinion," Julie responded.

"Yes, my opinion. And it's also my opinion that this is the way to good self-esteem. We feel better about ourselves when we behave in ways that make others respond positively toward us. We feel better about ourselves when we have a sense of being in control of ourselves. Self-esteem doesn't come about by people always telling you good things about yourself. How would all these good words even carry any weight, unless you knew the same people would also tell you not-good things about yourself when the need arose? Self-esteem isn't passive. It's active. It comes from mastering your world, from being competent and in control. And how can you achieve those things if people do not help you learn the behaviors involved?"

"But who are we to say what those are?" Julie countered. "I'm not comfortable making all these value judgments. What *is* right and wrong, Torey? I'm not God, so how do I know? And I'm not willing to set myself up as God. There are too many narrow-minded people in this country already as it is, and I'm not going to be one of them. I don't think that's our place. Values should be taught in church. Not in school."

"Values should be taught everywhere."

"Yes, but whose? We don't have the right to judge these things," Julie replied. "This is a diverse school. We have different cultures here. Different ethnic backgrounds. Different religions. Different socioeconomic levels. This matters, Torey, and we can't make value judgments for people whose lives are different from ours. I'm not African–American. I'm not Latino. Yet most of the kids in this school come out of those cultures. I'm not living below the poverty line. I'm not developmentally delayed. Yet most of the kids in our class are from one of those groups."

I hesitated. Again, I was aware of having to fight the opposite side to what I normally did and, again, I felt uncomfortable with this. "There are still some basic values," I said. "Basic values that have nothing to do with what color you are or what language you speak," I said, "or how high your IQ is or how much money you have. Human values. One of them says everyone has rights. So anytime you are doing something that takes away someone else's rights, that's wrong."

Very cautiously, Julie nodded. "Okay," she said slowly. "I'll agree with that."

"So Shane grabs up the gift Billy gave to me and he drops it. And when you say to him, 'Shane, it doesn't matter, that was just an accident' – yes, it *was* just an accident and I realize he had no intention of dropping the statue when he picked it up. So we shouldn't get disproportionately angry. He was behaving like a kid – but it was *still* wrong that he did that. It did not belong to him. He'd already been warned off it before. To say it was 'just an accident' and 'he didn't mean to' when he broke it might be good for his feelings, but it isn't good for his morals. Dropping that statue interfered with *my* rights, as owner of the statue, because now I don't have it anymore. And it interfered with Billy's rights. Billy spent *his* money. It was *his* gift. It was his heart behind it. It isn't right to hurt Billy just because Shane 'didn't mean to do it.'"

"But he *didn't* mean to do it. And it *did* happen. Getting mad at Shane wouldn't unbreak the statue," Julie said. "So why should we damage his self-esteem too? This little boy has so many problems already. He couldn't help it, so why make him feel worse?"

"Because it *was wrong*."

"I don't think it was," she said.

"And because it was emotionally dishonest. We didn't actually feel inside like it didn't matter."

"It wasn't to me."

Silence then.

I regarded her across the table. Finally she shrugged and moved to get up. "I'm sorry, Torey. I wish I could agree with you, because I can tell you think it is important. But the truth is, I don't."

Chapter Sixteen

And then it was January.

I continued my reading with Venus during the afternoon recess periods. I chose to stay with the same few books – Arnold Lobel's Frog and Toad books and Russell Hoban's Frances series on the idea that familiarity would be a good way to go. There was still little indication of the level of Venus's intellectual functioning, and given her family history, I knew she, like the twins, might well be in the "educable" range – shorthand for mildly retarded. If we worked with the same ones, then there was a better chance that she would understand and appreciate the stories. Moreover, familiarity allowed her to anticipate the action in the stories. They were all humorous, so I hoped that as she came to anticipate what was going to happen next, this might evoke a smile or some other indication that I was actually engaging her.

Truth was, I knew I was engaging her already. The signs, however, were very, very subtle. For instance, she now hung back at recess period. When the recess bell rang at the end of an activity, Venus paused. She didn't actually go over to the reading corner yet. No response that open. But she didn't allow herself to be blindly herded to the door by the others either. And she was always checking my eyes, checking the inclination of my body. When I turned to go to the reading corner, she turned herself, and although she waited for me to call her over, she did respond then. She would cross the room now to join me.

Indeed, what pleased me more was that I noticed her doing the same thing at the morning recess. Even though I didn't read to her then and she always went out on the playground with Julie, there was now that moment of hanging back. My sense was that she was *hoping* I might read to her, that she was waiting to see if it was possible. But we were talking subtle here. Very, very subtle behavior changes. If I hadn't been paying such acute attention to her, I'm sure I wouldn't have noticed anything but a blank face and immobile body.

In mid-January, I thought I would try to elevate us to the next level of communication. Instead of picking out one of the books, as I usually did, and commencing to read, this time I chose two. One Frog and Toad book. One Frances book. I held them out.

"Which story shall we read today?"

Venus regarded me.

"You choose. This one? Or this one?"

No response.

I waited. Sitting down on my knees, I lay the two books in front of me. "Come down here," I said quietly.

Unexpectedly, she did. She knelt down opposite me.

"Which book shall we read today? The Frances one? Let's see. It's called *Bread and Jam for Frances*. That's a funny one. Remember? We read it last week. Or shall we read *Frog and Toad Together*? I like that one too."

No response.

I waited. A minute, two minutes passed. And two minutes feels like eternity in such a silence.

I pondered the best course of action. More waiting? Or choosing for her? I did not want to make this confrontational but I also did not want to run over any embryonic efforts to cooperate by solving the situation myself.

I saw her arm move. Very, very slightly. She didn't even lift her hand off her knee, but her arm twitched. So, I interpreted it, assuming even a wrong interpretation still put the onus of choice on her.

"That one?" I said, lifting the Frances book. "You want this one?"

Her eyes met mine.

I nodded cheerfully. "This one? Yes, I like this one too."

So, this became our game. Each day I gave her a choice of books. Each day I asked her which one she wanted. Each day we waited and waited for a response until finally she did something – incline her head, twitch her arm – *anything* that I could take as an answer. I couldn't exactly dignify it so much as to say Venus was *choosing* the books, but I did have the sense that she was making an effort.

This went on, day after day, without variation.

Then ... the first breakthrough.

We had gone through the whole palaver of choosing which book. The drawback to this activity was that it always cut quite badly into the twenty minutes we had during the recess period for reading together. On this day, it had taken almost seven minutes to choose *Best Friends for Frances*, so I settled down to read it.

As had become our custom, I took Venus on my lap. I felt this was an important part of the process. Working on the theory that she had been a very severely deprived child in terms of attention and stimulation, I always tried to provide her with tactile stimulation when I could – holding her, hugging her, laying my hand on her shoulder, catching her attention by touching her face. I often ran my free hand up and down her forearm as I read. As with my friend who gently brushed her brain-damaged son, I felt the regular, rhythmic sensation would provide valuable stimulation for a contrary brain.

This had been a distracting day for me. Along with the fact that it had taken quite a while to choose the story, so we were a bit short of time, I was further distracted by the fact that it had snowed heavily outside and I could hear some of the children on the playground hitting windows with snowballs. They weren't my windows and I assumed the playground staff would be on top of it, but I kept hearing them, kept pausing. Finally, I put my free hand down on the floor and rose a little ways up on my knees, lifting both of us up in the process, so that I could see over the edge of the window. But I couldn't get a good enough view. So, muttering something about "naughty children," I went back to reading about Frances the badger and her friendship woes.

Several minutes into the story, I unexpectedly felt Venus's hand on my wrist. When I'd risen to try and see out the window, I'd taken my free hand down. Now, very gently, she reached down and lifted my hand back up, placing it on her other arm.

"You like that?" I said quietly. "You want me to put my arms around you while I read?"

There was the most imperceptible of nods.

"Okay," I said and continued reading.

That was it. That was all the interaction I had for that day. But I couldn't have been more pleased.

And thus it started.

After almost five months in my classroom, Venus very slowly began to respond. This was, by no means, a miracle breakthrough. She still did not talk. She still did not do anything at all in class. But during the twenty minutes we were together over the afternoon recess, a very subtle form of communication started up between us.

The next day when I presented her with the choice of two books, she hesitated in the way she always did and I waited in the way I always did. But then very, very slowly she raised her right hand an inch or two away from her body and put her index finger slightly forward. It was impossible to tell which book she was indicating, but it was clear for the first time she *was* indicating.

"That one?" I said, holding up the Frog and Toad book.

An almost imperceptible nod.

For a week or so we went on like this. I don't think she was actually choosing a book, per se. She was simply lifting a finger. But I was willing to accept any effort at communication.

Then, about ten days later we progressed again.

"This book?" I said after she had moved her index finger.

There was a long pause, and she did not give her imperceptible nod.

I waited.

No response.

"This book?" I asked again.

Very, very, *very* slowly she lifted her hand and leaned slightly forward to tap the other book.

"Ah, you want the Frances story? Good. I'm glad to know. Yes, of course, I'll read that."

Venus nodded. Indeed, she nodded a second time more obviously. Then she came willingly onto my lap.

Coming back from our winter break, Julie and I had picked up pretty much where we left off. Nothing more was said about the disagreement on the last day of school.

This lent a small, continual undercurrent of tension to the classroom. Julie made it apparent that she did not feel she was doing anything wrong. This made me self-conscious about whether we were having real problems or whether this was simply *my* problem. In the end, I decided to seek Bob's advice.

I explained the situation – that Julie and I had a difference of philosophy that we just didn't seem able to reconcile – and asked him what he thought I should do about it.

Bob was surprised. I didn't have a history of colleague problems. I was occasionally regarded with mild suspicion, largely because I was unconventional, noisy, and inclined to speak my thoughts fairly unedited, but I found it easy to get along with people and I'd always had good relationships with the other staff. Moreover, he was surprised to find that, of all people, it was Julie I was having trouble with. Julie was so personable, so self-effacing and sweet. And she had an impeccable record for the time she'd been at the school.

"I wish you had come to talk to me about this earlier," he said when I finished explaining. "If it's actually compromising the atmosphere in the classroom, we should have sorted it out by now."

"I think *compromising* is the wrong word."

Bob regarded me.

I paused. "Well, yes. Maybe 'compromising' isn't the wrong word. I suppose it has. It's taken such a long time to bring this group together. I mean, geez. There's only *five* kids. I think if I'd felt Julie was behind me … And now … if only she would *support* me."

"Support you how? How, specifically, do you feel she isn't supporting you?"

I considered.

The frank truth was that by steadfastly refusing to join in our zillion silly songs every day she wasn't supporting me. But I felt so stupid for saying that. Nothing in Julie's job contract had specified she should *sing*. Yet, by not joining in, she kept herself apart from us. That made her feel like an outsider, as if *we* were excluding her, while it made *me* feel like she was excluding us. This emphasized the division between us. I found this hard to tell Bob because it made me sound petty. How could singing a bunch of children's songs become so important?

But it was. The songs had become our group identity.

Haltingly, I tried to explain this to Bob.

"It doesn't have to do with how *well* she can sing. I'm no great shakes myself. Musicality has nothing to do with it. It's the refusal to join in, to be part of us."

"Well, you might be asking just a *little* bit too much, Torey," Bob replied gently. "I can think of quite a few adults who would be too self-conscious to go around bursting into song. Even if it was just in front of a bunch of kids."

"Yes, I know. But that's not what I'm saying really. It's the joining-in part. Not the singing. I mean, she wouldn't *have* to sing. I guess that's what I'm trying to say. She's not simply 'not participating.' She's refusing to participate. There's a qualitative difference. After all these months of not being able to bring this class together, I've finally hit on something that works. If she wanted to be supportive, she could clap the rhythm or hum or dance with the kids or do something to indicate that she *agrees*, that she's *glad* we've come together as a class."

Bob scratched his head thoughtfully. "I can see this one coming," he said with a humorous edge to his voice. "Calling Julie in here and saying, 'Well, if you can't sing along in Torey's class, would you please hum or dance, please?'"

We both laughed.

"No, seriously," Bob said, "I do hear where you're coming from on this. It still surprises me. I will admit that. But then Julie's only responsibility up to this point has been for Casey Muldrow."

"And what about the philosophy issue? How should I handle that?" I asked.

Bob sighed.

"To be perfectly honest, I find it creepy," I said. "I try not to. But it's like being with a Stepford wife. Julie just does *not* respond to anything negatively. She is relentlessly positive, like everything is on the same plane. I keep thinking, How can you use the same tone of voice to say, 'Oops you just dropped the fishbowl and killed all the fish' as you use to say, 'I love you'? And she keeps thinking it's right."

A pause.

"And then I think, 'This isn't human. How much rage are you swallowing?' 'How terrible will it be when it comes out?' 'Will you be a really scary person then?'"

"Do you think the children feel this way?" Bob asked.

"I dunno. They seem to relate to her all right. They play her up. She isn't very good with discipline and they know it, so they can get really obnoxious. But maybe it's only me who thinks she's scary. Maybe I'm sensitized by this point."

And then silence.

"So, what shall we do?" Bob asked. "How do you want me to handle this?"

"Get me another aide?" I said quietly, more as a wish than a question.

"I don't think that's possible. Not if she's not doing anything really wrong."

"No, I realize that. But she's not any happier about all this than I am, I'm sure. If she could have a quieter, more predictable classroom and I could have a plain, old, ordinary person. Not a saint..."

Bob smiled. "What if I just talk to her, for a start? Get everything out in the open. See where she stands. See if she can alter her behavior a little. And maybe you can alter yours."

"As in?"

"As in being a little more tolerant of a different approach."

I nodded.

"From the sounds of things, I can hear where you're coming from on this. And I have faith in whatever methods you are using. So, it does sound like Julie has some problems and I will talk to her about them. But there are a million ways of interacting with people. If she isn't actually hurting the children, if she isn't upsetting them or interfering with their progress, then we may simply have to accept that this is a way different from our own, but it isn't wrong. And so we'll need to adjust too."

Chapter Seventeen

Since Venus had returned at the beginning of December, her behavior on the playground had been more controlled. This was due in part to the fact that she was being so closely supervised. She still had her own aide at lunchtime. Julie watched her at morning recess, and I kept her in at afternoon recess. So there was much less chance of her attacking other children. But even so, there seemed to be fewer problems generally. Although there had been some minor scuffles, we didn't have a serious run-in until early February.

On this particular occasion, Venus simply seemed to be having a very bad day. She had had a small run-in before school. Wanda had trudged up the many stairs to the classroom slowly, huffing and puffing, her ever-increasing weight making the climb hard work. Venus was coming up behind her when one of the twins, frustrated by Wanda's slow speed, had pushed on by. This enraged Venus, who let out a howl and took after him, but he had a head start. He shot into the classroom and I managed to snag Venus at the doorway. I plopped her in the quiet chair. Within a few minutes she had collected herself enough to sink back into her normal stupor, so that was the end of it.

Midway through math we had another incident, this time with Billy. I didn't know what started it, but I suspect it was something totally insignificant, like Billy's brushing against her. Venus roared to life and socked him on the side of the head before I could intervene. So back to the quiet chair.

Then at recess she again had a flare-up. This time Julie interceded before it went too far and Venus retreated to leaning against her wall, even though it was snow covered. She returned to the classroom soggy and silent when the bell rang and resumed her place at the table.

At lunchtime I was just finishing my soup and sandwich in the teachers' lounge when I heard Venus's familiar scream filtering up from the playground. Pam, who was sitting across from me, raised her eyes to meet mine.

"Here we go," I muttered and rose from my chair.

Looking out the window, I saw a crowd gathered over by the spiral slide. From there I couldn't tell who all was involved, but I knew I better go down. So I packed up what remained of my meal, set it on the side table, and left the room.

Bob was already on the playground by the time I got there,

as were two other teachers, Julie, and, of course, the aide who was responsible for Venus. It was hard to tell what had happened. No one knew exactly what had set Venus off, but she had taken offense at something that a third-grade girl had done and had chased the girl all the way across the playground until the girl had started to climb up the slide to get away from her. Apparently then Venus had grabbed hold of the girl's legs and tried to pull her off. She hadn't managed. The aide who was supervising her had caught up with her by this point, but the third-grader was still screaming bloody murder and Venus was screaming even louder. And fighting harder. She thrashed fiercely, struggling to break the grip of the three adults who held her.

My biggest concern was less Venus herself at that moment than that someone was going to say how inappropriate it was having this girl at school and suggest she be returned to homebound education. Excluding her had happened so quickly on the previous occasion that I was fearful of a repeat. So my focus was solely on getting her off the playground.

"I'll take her," I said when I reached the group. "I'll take her upstairs."

I grabbed Venus under the arms and flung her up over my shoulder like a sack of potatoes. I don't know if it was my sudden movement or if the position itself had an effect, but when I did it, she immediately stopped struggling. She was still screaming, still crying, but she didn't fight. Clutching her tightly, I headed off for the school building.

Venus sobbed noisily.

I plodded up the stairs, one after the other, and cursed quietly about being on the top floor. She was a child of seven, and so not tiny. It felt like climbing the Matterhorn. At the top, I opened the door into the unlit classroom and set her down.

She was still sobbing in the strangulated half-screaming way that was her trademark.

I took a moment to catch my breath. My intention had been to put her in the quiet chair, but I didn't. Instead, I came down on one knee to be at her height.

"You're really having a bad day, aren't you? Things aren't going right for you."

Venus regarded me through her tears. She wasn't perhaps quite as blank as usual, but nothing gave me the impression she would respond to me either.

"I know the children make you mad sometimes. I know they get on your nerves and you feel very angry. But it is important to handle these feelings in a different way, because I want you to stay in my class. Here. With me. But you have to handle your angry feelings differently. If you can't, Mr. Christianson will say you need to go on homebound again. Then you will have to stay home all the time."

There was a flicker of expression on her face. Just enough that I knew what I'd said registered. And that she didn't want to go back on homebound.

"Did things go wrong before you came to school today?" I asked.

She had stopped crying altogether, although her dark eyes still welled with tears.

Taking a tissue, I reached over to wipe her wet cheeks. She flinched back slightly.

"I'm not going to hurt you. Here. To make you feel better." I tried again.

Venus was watching me very, very carefully as I lifted the tissue and gently wiped her face. I put my other hand on her shoulder.

I smiled. "You would rather be in here, wouldn't you?" I asked. "With us. You don't want to be on homebound. You want to come to school, don't you?"

She nodded. Very, very, very faintly. I wouldn't have seen it, if I hadn't been watching her so closely. But it was a nod. It was a willing gesture.

I smiled more broadly. "You know what would happen, if you didn't go to school?" I asked and let a teasing note come into my voice.

She didn't respond except to keep her eyes on me.

"You might grow up to be a mule!" I laughed and then I started to sing one of our favorite songs in the class, indeed, one that I'd used for years in working with children: "Would You Like to Swing on a Star."

"A mule is an animal with long, funny ears." I waggled my hands beside my head. "He kicks up at anything he hears."

This did get a reaction out of Venus. Her eyes went wide in surprise.

I reached down and took her hands. "Here. Step up here. Put your feet on top of mine. We're going to dance."

Venus clearly did not expect me to say this. She looked up, startled, then down at her feet.

"Come on," I said. I bent down and lifted one of her feet onto my shoe. I straightened up and took her hands. "Put the other one on my other foot."

Cautiously, Venus lifted her other foot and stepped up on top of my shoe.

I continued singing and started waltzing us around the room.

It was a surreal moment, dancing around the unlit classroom with Venus standing on my shoes while I sang an unaccompanied, slightly off-key version of a 1950s pop song.

I hadn't planned this. Indeed, I hadn't had even the briefest thought of it beforehand. There had been no "Maybe this will be better for her than the quiet chair," or "Maybe this will shock a response from her." There was only that moment of simple connection when I'd said "Do you want to come to school?" and I thought of the words of the song. Then spontaneity took over. Even I was somewhat surprised to discover myself whirling around the room.

We continued. I sang all the verses of the song and we kept dancing. I sang it again. Around and around the room we went.

Originally I was holding her hands in my hands, but as

we progressed, I changed. I kept holding her left hand in my right hand, but with my left hand, I clasped her close against me so that I could move more fluidly. I was a lousy dancer. No two ways about that. I had no idea if this was a waltz rhythm or not, but it didn't matter, as this was definitely not waltz music. So we went here and there with no rhythm at all. But it didn't matter. When I looked down, Venus looked up to me. And she smiled. It was only a little smile with lips tight, but there was no denying. It *was* a smile.

Suddenly, the light went on.

"What *are* you doing?"

I stopped abruptly and turned my head. There was Julie in the doorway.

"It's almost one o'clock," she said, gesturing toward the clock, as if she realized she was interrupting something private and needed to explain her presence.

I smiled back. "We were dancing."

"So I see. And I thought you'd come up to visit the quiet chair." Julie had a wry smile on her face. "Never do know what production's playing up here, do we?" She grinned at Venus as she went past.

But it was lost on Venus. She had retreated into unresponsive silence.

When afternoon recess came and Julie took the other children out, I went over to the reading corner. Venus followed voluntarily, as she had done for some days now.

"Would you like to pick a book?" I said. Thus far we had

still been working with the two sets of stories about Frog and Toad and about Frances and I had been giving her a choice between two each day. But this afternoon I didn't pick up any of them.

Venus stopped dead at the edge of the rug in the reading corner when I said that.

"You pick today," I said. The books we usually used were lying on top of the low bookshelf within easy reach.

No response.

I waited.

No response.

Venus edged a little closer to me. We were perhaps three feet apart when she started. Her steps were minuscule, a few inches at a time, but she came closer. Not toward the books and the bookshelf, but closer to me.

I waited.

We had only twenty minutes, and we used up about ten of them in this agonizingly slow process of crossing the rug. I tried to show no impatience. Indeed, I didn't feel any, so it wasn't hard. The natural consequences of running out of time would speak more clearly than I could. I just stood and waited.

By this point, Venus had edged right up to me. She looked up at me. It was a long, searching look, the meaning behind it enigmatic, but it wasn't blank as usual. Then very, very cautiously she lifted one foot. It hung there, suspended in midair for thirty or forty seconds, before she very, very slowly lowered it on top of my shoe.

"Ah," I said in sudden understanding. "You want to dance again? You don't want to read, you want to dance."

Her eyes still on my face, she gave a small, quick nod.

So we danced. I sang "Would You Like to Swing on a Star" again and swung her around on my feet. Off across the room again, back and forth, holding her left hand with my right, wrapping my other hand around her back to hold her close enough against me so that I could move fluidly. She pressed her face so tightly into the wool of my sweater that I could feel the warmth of her breath through the material.

The next day when morning recess came, the bell rang and the boys shot off for their coats. I went out in the hall to supervise the whooping excitement as my children clattered down the stairs after Pam's. When I turned to shut the classroom door before going down to the teachers' lounge, I saw Venus was still inside the classroom.

"Hey ho, recess time," I said from the doorway.

She crossed over.

"Quick, quick. Get your coat. Julie will be waiting for you. She'll be saying 'Where's Venus this morning?'"

Venus stopped.

"Come on. Quick, quick."

She looked up at me and I could sense the expectancy.

I smiled warmly. "You're not in a hurry today, I see."

Very carefully, she lifted one foot and lay it on my shoe. She was farther away from me than before, so it required a bit of deft stretching. Resting it ever so lightly, she looked up.

I grinned. "I see. You don't *want* to go outside today. You want to dance."

A slight, slight nod.

"I see. Hmmm."

Venus was watching my face very carefully.

"Can you use the words?" I asked. "Can you say: 'I want to dance'?"

A pause. She was still watching me intently, her dark eyes searching my face. "Dance," she murmured so softly it was nothing more than a breath.

And so we did.

Chapter Eighteen

Of all the children, the one I felt most concerned about was Jesse. Despite the testing earlier in the year, which substantiated Jesse's normal IQ, he remained academically low functioning. He could not read even the most basic sight vocabulary. Indeed, his skills were little better than Shane's or Zane's, who were both younger and more severely challenged intellectually and behaviorally.

His Tourette's syndrome created numerous problems in this department. The tics interfered with his concentration and flooded his mind with obsessive thoughts. In particular, he was inclined to get sidetracked repeating words, either out loud or mentally, and this required extra time to do everything. In addition it seemed to incline him to a general restlessness that made it hard for him to sit down. Even when he was concentrating, he fidgeted constantly.

But mostly he didn't sit down. Two minutes with bottom applied to chair was about as long as he lasted before he was up. Often he didn't wander. He just had to get up, move around, and reseat himself, which, of course, was very disruptive to his work. This restlessness also seemed to feed into a more general tendency toward aggression and irritability. Partly this was caused by the other kids becoming distracted by his movement and reacting, but partly, it seemed to be a sort of global irritability that Jesse felt toward almost everything. I think this was connected to the Tourette's and to Jesse's frustration at trying to control the tics enough to get through the demands of the day. Whatever, it took a terrible toll on his schoolwork.

I attempted to deal with this by responding to the positive things Jesse did and ignoring as much as possible the tics and their consequences. The other children were remarkably good about accepting Jesse's various noises and actions without too much ado. As inclined to fighting as they were, it was seldom personal. Most of the aggression in the classroom seemed to come more out of each individual's inability to control his own impulses rather than any particular animosity toward others, and hence, the children could be surprisingly understanding and diplomatic. Indeed, Billy sometimes even intervened on Jesse's behalf on the playground when children from other classes teased him about his tics.

In an effort to address Jesse's reading problems, I resorted to an old favorite of mine – the homemade game. There is a children's board game called Candy Land that involves progressing along a long snaking path made up of different colored squares, and the players move forward by drawing cards from a pile and then moving their playing piece to the matching square on the path. When I'd first started teaching, I'd discovered that replacing the colored cards with math problems that the children then had to match to the right answer on the path made a good, quite enjoyable game. This led me to see what a wonderfully adaptable game Candy Land was in general, and I'd created many other variations along the way. In this case, I thought I would adapt it for Jesse, using simple sight words like *was* and *what* and *saw*, things he was always encountering and always confusing.

One of the pluses about Candy Land is that in the real game there are "wild cards" that can advance the player dramatically forward – or backward – in the game, depending on when they are drawn, and this added element of chance always lent excitement for the players. When I designed my own games, I added extra of these cards. Some of them, as in the real game, advanced players toward winning, but additionally, my cards included silly things on them – stand on one foot and hop around the table – or surprise prizes, like getting a bonus star for the star chart or five M&Ms. This not only lent excitement to the game, it also allowed a certain amount of general movement, which cut down on inappropriate restlessness.

One afternoon, I was playing Jesse's version of the game

with him and Billy and another little boy named James, who came in occasionally for reading help.

Jesse had had a bad day in general. His tics tended to wax and wane both in frequency and in strength, and in the previous week or so, some of the noisier, more intrusive ones were definitely on the increase. We were also having to give him more time to do things, like answer questions, because his tendency to get caught obsessively repeating words slowed everything down. Billy was relatively patient with this, but James found it annoying.

"Come on, kid, take your turn," he kept saying, which only increased the time necessary for Jesse to answer.

I reached across and touched his arm. "That isn't helpful, James."

"He takes forever. We could have played this game about six times, if he'd just hurry up," James replied.

"He's doing the best he can," I replied.

"He's got tics," Billy offered. "That's how come he's taking so long."

"Don't talk about me like I'm not here," Jesse muttered.

"Yes, you're right," I said. "I'm sorry. Can you take your turn now?"

Jesse's shoulders twitched. He held out his card and studied it carefully. I could tell by the expression on his face, he was mentally repeating something. There was this huge sense of expectation. He was *just* on the edge of speaking, but –

"*Geez,*" James finally said. "This is taking *forever.*"

That was it. Jesse exploded. He leaped up abruptly from the table, knocking the playing board off with one swift movement. The cards fluttered everywhere. Within the space of a breath, Jesse was over the table and had hold of James.

"Hey, hey, hey!" I said and pried them apart. "Jesse. Over there. At your table. Get your folder out and start your work. James, here. Sit over here. Billy, to your table, please."

"Geez! Do something to him, would you?" James squawked. "He's not getting away with hitting me."

"You let me take care of this," I replied. "You sit here. You've only got ten minutes left anyway."

Jesse couldn't sit down. He tore around the classroom in a way that I knew would end in mayhem if I didn't physically reorient him. I looked over to Julie, who was working with Gwennie. "Could you get him? Help him sit down and get on with his work?"

"I could help him," Billy offered cheerfully.

"Thanks, Billy, that's kind of you, but I think it would be more helpful if you just sat down at your own table and started your folder. When you're done, you can check to see if Zane needs help with his work."

"I don't!" Zane replied testily.

"Yes, well, whatever," I replied. "You do your work and Billy can do his. And you, James, on with yours."

Julie managed to catch Jesse and get him seated, although this meant leaving Gwennie, who was trying to work on a report on peanuts for her other class. This was proving a real trial for her. Gwennie clearly had no idea what the whole point behind doing a "report" was. Even as basic as the requirements for a third-grade report were, they were too abstract for her. The previous time she'd had to do such a report, she'd simply reproduced what she'd read verbatim, so Julie and I had been trying to get the concept of summarizing across to her. Not easy. And Gwennie found it stressful. She resorted to numerous distraction techniques and persistently endeavored to get the conversation around to her favorite topic: foreign countries. And the more stressed Gwennie felt, the more likely she was to engage in autistic-like behaviors, such as spinning her pencil or echoing back words and phrases said to her.

Julie got Jesse to sit down and open his folder, at which point one of the twins needed attention and she went there. I stayed with James, as his time in the room was almost over. Peace reigned for three or four minutes, which was about as long as I'd expect peace to reign with this group.

"Fuck you!" Jesse cried out. I could tell by the way he said it, it was a tic and not actual swearing. This wasn't a common tic for Jesse, but it did happen occasionally.

I ignored it and bent back over the work with James.

"Fuck you!" Jesse cried out again.

"Aren't you going to stop him?" James asked in amazement.

"He can't help it," Billy said. "Just like you can't help being a nosy bastard."

I put a finger to my lips and looked over at Billy. "But *you* can. So get back to your work."

"Fucker!" Jesse cried again.

And then suddenly, "Fucker!"

We all looked up. It was Gwennie. She had her head down and continued concentrating on her work. But just as Jesse barked out his swear word, Gwennie echoed it.

A surreal moment followed. Back and forth they went. Over and over. Jesse was aware of what was happening, but the stress and the attention made him unable to control his tic. Gwennie was blithely oblivious.

"Fuck you!"

"Fuck you."

"Shithead!"

"Shithead."

Billy started to laugh. "Listen to you guys!"

"Man, you're crazy in here," muttered James, who had clearly had enough of us for that day. He collected his stuff together and prepared to go.

"Poophead!" Zane shouted, not wanting to miss out on this fun.

"Yeah, Poopyhead!" said Shane.

It deteriorated from there. All the boys were laughing uproariously by that point. Even Jesse, who was still barking out swear words, joined in. Gwennie started to laugh too. They all laughed. Raucous laughter. Lots of swear words. More laughter. More swearing. Everyone was holding their sides with hilarity.

I laughed too. And let them play noisily with the various words until everyone fell panting into their seats.

The only person who didn't find this merry was Julie. She stood apart and smiled tolerantly and waited for all the hoots to subside before she said very tactfully, "It probably isn't very kind to laugh at Jesse's and Gwennie's challenges."

Billy turned to look at her. "It felt good. That was fun."

"How would you feel if someone laughed about something you couldn't help doing?" Julie asked.

"Well, sometimes you shouldn't. But sometimes, I think it is okay. Because just now we weren't laughing at them. We were laughing because it was funny," Billy replied.

There was a moment's pause.

Billy continued, "If we stopped laughing when Jesse said something funny because he's got something wrong with him and we don't want him to feel bad, then what we're *really* thinking about is that Jesse's got something wrong with him. But that's not what we *were* thinking then. All we were thinking was that he said something funny. Which means we forgot he wasn't just like everybody else. So, I think that's okay. Sometimes you got to laugh. Sometimes stuff is just funny."

The other person not included in the laughter of the classroom was Venus. This was because she wasn't there. Again. Her attendance had never been spectacular. Even during the first months at school, Venus tended to be absent quite a lot, but since she had returned from homebound education, she often missed a day or more every week. I had chased this matter up on a number of occasions only to be met by the same two excuses: she was sick or Wanda had forgotten to bring her.

When she was there, despite the tentative first beginnings of a relationship between the two of us during the time we spent alone together, she remained almost catatonic in class. Each morning Wanda brought her up to the classroom, she took her seat, and she remained there, silent and immobile, unless one of us went over and physically reoriented her. Sadly, because she was so silent and motionless, it was all too easy to ignore Venus entirely. To include her fully in our activities would have required a full-time aide to make sure that she changed from activity to activity physically and to ensure that she picked up a pencil or other item when appropriate and made the necessary motions to use it. We didn't have such resources. Left to her own devices, she just sat. Her folder, once passed out, remained unopened in front of her on the table. Her pencil lay untouched. Venus sat throughout, enigmatic as an Easter Island stone head.

I was uncertain what to do with her during these times when I really needed to tend to the other students. I tried to ensure that at a minimum of once an hour during the school day, I sat down with her, talked directly to her, orienting her face, if necessary, to look at me, and endeavored to get her to try something. If she categorically refused all effort at participation, I kept it up for about five minutes and then moved on to the other children. I couldn't do more, as I had a lot of students during the time the resource children were coming and going and had to keep to a fairly strict schedule to give everyone their appropriate amount of time. And, of course, with Billy, Jesse, Zane, and Shane, who could be very demanding, even when the resource students weren't there, I was usually fully occupied.

Julie's attitude was that it was more than okay to leave her, that it was actually the right approach, that Venus needed time to feel comfortable with us, and when she finally did feel secure enough, she would start to respond. I wasn't willing to go that far. Given that Venus had already spent half a year with us and was not yet showing any signs of "feeling more comfortable," and indeed, she had already spent the two previous school years "not comfortable," I didn't feel leaving her alone was an "approach." It was a make-do measure, because to do more would have been to do miracles. But because Venus was starting to act with some spontaneity during the time we spent alone, I was able to live with her inertia, at least for the time being.

Chapter Nineteen

During our twenty minutes alone each day, Venus and I were cautiously starting to explore a relationship. After the dancing episode – or episodes, because we danced for three or four days – I managed an even bigger step.

The other children had thundered out into the hallway with Julie to go to recess that particular afternoon, and Venus had hung back. I expect that if I'd given her the opportunity that day, she would have again extended her foot forward onto mine, her code to dance, but I wanted to see if we could advance things just a little more. So I crossed the room to the reading corner, leaving Venus over by the door.

"Come on," I said. I'd not done this before. Previously I'd always guided her from where she stood to the reading corner.

Venus regarded me.

"Shall we read?"

She hung back.

"Or do you want to dance? We can dance, if you want. Come on over here."

Was she going to come? Or was I expecting too much in wanting her to cross the distance of the classroom to me of her own volition?

I waited.

Venus hung back.

I acted as if it didn't matter. "Perhaps you would like to choose something different to read today. There are so many books here. Maybe you want something different. Or we could read Frances. Or Frog and Toad."

Minutes dragged by. I kept up the friendly chatter. Venus stood by the door. There wasn't the usual vacant look in her eyes. She was fully engaged in watching me, in listening to me. I could tell by the way she leaned forward and watched that she *was* weighing up the possibility of crossing the room to me, but finding it very hard to do. Such a seemingly little thing for a seven-year-old to do – walk fifteen feet across a room – and yet the challenge of it was clear in her face.

As I talked, I was picking out books that had become jumbled in the shelves and laying them on top of the low bookshelf. I sorted the books out and put them back, one by one.

Very, very slowly, Venus stretched out one foot. It hovered a moment before she lay it on the floor in front of her.

Then her other foot. She moved like a child playing one of those old-fashioned games: "How many steps may I take, Mother?" "Five baby steps." "May I, Mother?" "Yes, you may." Step, step, step, step, step. Pause. "How many steps may I take, Mother?"

I kept talking nonchalantly, lifting up books I was sorting, pretending not to notice her approach. Or rather, pretending like it was normal. We had only five minutes left before the others returned. It had taken Venus a full fifteen minutes to cross the room.

But she made it. Finally, she stood beside me.

"We haven't much time to read," I said. "But there's still a little, little bit. What shall it be? Frog and Toad?" I held up *Frog and Toad Together*, which I perceived to be her favorite book.

Venus lowered her eyes and looked across the bookshelf. There was a pause. Then in contrast to all the hesitation involved in coming across the room, she reached down quite straightforwardly and picked up the She-Ra comic book from a pile on one shelf. She looked back at me.

I had actually thrown the comic away once. I hadn't realized it had been put back on the shelf. It hadn't been cared for. The cover was now ripped off and the first page bent over.

"You want to read that?"

Very faintly, Venus nodded.

I knelt down beside her. "Come here." I pulled her in close with my arms around her and opened the comic. "We're almost out of time today, so we'll just look really quickly through it now, okay? Because everyone will be returning soon. And then tomorrow, I'll read it to you."

I turned the pages of the comic, pointing out the highlights of what was happening. "See, there's Adora. She's really She-Ra. That's her secret identity. No one else knows this. And look, there's Spirit, her horse. What's happening here? What's happening on this page?" I pointed to the picture. "Something's happened. Adora needs to use her magic powers to change into She-Ra. See? She holds up her magic sword and she says 'For the honor of Grayskull! I am She-Ra!' "

I looked at Venus. "That'd be good, wouldn't it? To have magic powers like that. Can you do that?"

Venus stared back at me.

I rose to my feet. "See, she spins around like this and holds her sword up." I grabbed a nearby yardstick and pointed it up in the air. "Then she says, 'For the honor of Grayskull!' – I turned around dramatically – 'I am She-Ra!' "

"Whatever you say."

I jerked my head sharply and dropped the yardstick. There was Julie standing in the doorway. She laughed. I laughed. Venus went blank.

The next afternoon, I repeated the procedure. I left Venus alone by the door once the others had left and crossed to the book corner. I picked up the comic.

"I saved this out," I said and held it aloft. "Do you want to read it today?"

Very faintly, Venus nodded.

I sat down, cross-legged, on the rug in the reading corner. "Okay." I patted the floor beside me.

Venus remained by the door.

I opened the comic. Bending over it, I feigned great interest. " 'Oh dearie my! Here I am trying to brew up a fresh batch of magic potion,' " I read. I ran my finger over the picture. "That's Madame Razz. She's a witch. Funny looking, isn't she? Because she wears her hat way down over her eyes. Look at her."

I held the book up, as if expecting Venus to be able to see from her place by the door. Then I went back to reading.

My hope was that by reading, by not demanding that she cross the room first to sit down with me, I would encourage her to do this spontaneously. Or at least more or less spontaneously. Come on, come on, come on, I was thinking as I read, trying to will her across the room telepathically.

Six or seven minutes of reading She-Ra aloud to myself in the reading corner and no sign of movement out of Venus. What should I do now? Stop? Give up? Go back to what I'd done the day before in concentrating solely on getting her across the room? Things had seemed so positive when she had crossed and then chosen the comic. Had I jumped ahead too fast?

I kept reading. And kept thinking. What was making all this such hard work for her? Her IQ? Was she just too delayed to be able to go more than one excruciatingly slow step at a time? Was I expecting too much?

And thus the entire recess period passed with Venus remaining by the door and my reading She-Ra aloud to myself across the room.

The following day, Venus was not in school.

The previous week, I'd complained to Bob about this system of having Wanda bring Venus to school each day, as it just was not working. He'd contacted Teri. He'd reassured me it had been sorted out. Now this week, the same thing. Wanda forgot. I complained again. Bob tried again. He reassured again. I had no doubt that the next week, it'd be the same thing again.

On this occasion I went so far as to suggest we call Social Services in on this case, because the truth of the matter was, this kid was not getting much of an education. Bob told me that Social Services had already been called as a result of my complaints on two or three occasions. He said that the last time he had contacted Social Services, they had reminded him that the family had nine kids, and they were dealing with problems on every single one of them, so school absences had to be taken in stride. Social Services were doing as much as humanly possible.

As far as illness went, Venus did seem to be unwell a lot. She had a permanently snotty nose. She had cold sores. She had impetigo. Indeed, her skin was always crusted over with scratches and scabs of one sort or another. I kept my eye out for signs of abuse, but it was hard to know because she always wore long-sleeved tops and pants and often several layers. The sores were more the marks of a poor immune system and questionable cleanliness. In other years and with other children I had taken a more active role, providing soap and water and a place to wash, helping with hair, finding new clothes in the donation box, but there were increasing restrictions on doing these sorts of things due to litigation and child abuse worries. Moreover, with Venus I would have hesitated anyway. It is easy to overstep this mark and be invasive. In a child who as yet still did not feel comfortable coming across the room on request, it seemed inappropriate to initiate something so personal.

But the absences bothered me, if for no other reason than it made my job harder. Two or three days of achingly slow progress and then she'd be gone, then there'd be a weekend and by the time we started again, we were back nearly to where we'd started. Trying to question Wanda regarding Venus's whereabouts was an exercise in frustration, if ever there was one. So, in the end, I decided to have another visit with Teri.

Again, this was not straightforward.

On a Friday afternoon in February, I went over to their trailer after school. As things worked out, Venus was not in school that day, so this seemed a particularly appropriate time to visit.

We'd had snow the previous week. In the interim it had become very cold – well below zero – and the snow had gone hard and squeaky. Teri greeted me at the door when I arrived and invited me in. The first thing I noticed was that it was unpleasantly cold inside the trailer. I doubt it was up to sixty degrees. Several of the children were sitting around watching television. Two had gloves on and another two had a ratty blue blanket pulled up over them.

"The heater don't work so good," Teri said. "I'm sorry about that. It's kind of cold. I hope you don't mind."

She looked tired. At some point in her life, she must have been a very attractive woman, and the ghost of beauty still lingered in her high cheekbones and her well-proportioned features. But a heavy-lidded tiredness lay over everything, giving her the look of those women in charity ads for Third World countries. Seeing her – really looking at her – the question momentarily flickered through my mind of why it was often more acceptable to help the poor and outcast of other nations and not our own.

I explained why I was there, that I was concerned about Venus's frequent absences.

Teri shook her head wearily. "I told Wanda."

"I know Wanda is supposed to be bringing her, but this doesn't seem to be working out very well. Wanda doesn't seem to remember often enough."

"Well, I got to be at work. I work the night shift at the supermarket. You know. Downtown. I do shelf stuff. Stacking. Inventory. I can't be here to make sure Venus gets out. I don't get off until eight, and so, I'm not getting home in time."

"Who is here then?" I asked.

"Danny. Usually."

"So he's here at night?"

"Sometimes. Sometimes he pulls the night shift too. He's a porter at the hospital. But Wanda's here then. And the other kids. Cheryl. LaTisha. They're old enough to be caring for Venus."

"Except they need to get her to school," I said. "It's very important that Venus come to school *every* day. Venus is delayed in a lot of ways. To help her, I need to be able to work with her every single school day."

Teri leaned forward, putting her arms on the table and pushing her hands against her face. "All of my kids been delayed in some way or another. Not just Venus. She's no special case. People keep coming around here talking about Venus, but all my kids need attention."

I nodded. "Yes, I can understand how you feel. But Venus is the one I have. And I like Venus very much. She's a sweet little girl. But to help her, I need her to attend school more regularly."

Just then, the door to the trailer opened and Danny appeared. He looked at me very suspiciously when he saw me, crossing to stand over me. "I didn't know someone was coming," he said to Teri.

"This here's Venus's teacher from school."

"I don't care who it is. You never told me no one was coming here." He looked at me. "What you here for?"

"I've come to discuss Venus's absences from school."

"She's going to school," Danny said flatly.

"Not often enough," I said in as calm and unprovocative a manner as I could.

He pulled off his coat. He wasn't a big man. He was shorter and lighter-boned than I. His mousy hair was combed back in a greasy ducktail, and his skin was very bad, even though he must have been fifteen years past the hormones of adolescence. "You never told me no one was coming," he said abruptly to Teri.

I could read from the undercurrent that this was not good, that he was angry with her for letting me in the door, that he did not like things happening in his home that he did not ordain. Indeed, I got a very nasty sensation off him, so I hastened to make it clear that I, not Teri, had instigated the meeting.

He was not easily deflected. "You done this because you knew I was going to be out this afternoon. You done this behind my back on purpose."

Teri shook her head. "I didn't. She just called ... Nothing I done."

"Listen," I said, "*I* arranged the meeting. I insisted on coming. It's about Venus not coming to school. She *must* attend more regularly. The truant officer is going to impose fines if we can't work something out, and I know that isn't what any of us wants."

"Well, you the fuck try and send a truant officer around here," Danny said to me.

"I just came about Venus," I said.

"Well, fuck Venus. I don't care. And you don't do it when I'm not here," Danny replied. "Is that clear? So, get out."

I sat. I didn't *feel* like sitting. Admittedly, I felt very much like getting out. But I sat.

"May I see Venus?" I asked.

Danny's eyes narrowed. Teri lowered her head and supported it with one hand.

"She wasn't in school today. May I see her?"

"She's sick," Danny replied.

"With what?" I asked.

"Got a cold."

"May I see her?"

"She's sick."

"I know. I'm okay with that. May I see her anyway?"

Danny rolled his eyes. "*JE-sus. No,* you can not see her. You go. Get out. I already said that. You got no right to be here."

I sat. I was wishing very much that I'd brought Julie with me on this home visit, because I wasn't feeling nearly as brave as I was trying to give the impression of being. However, a nebulous concern was rising inside me. The more he refused to let me see Venus, the more intense my concern for her became.

"She's sick," he said a third time.

I sat.

"Go on," he said. He came over to the table where I was sitting with Teri and pushed my shoulder. It wasn't a hard push. It wasn't particularly aggressive, but the meaning was clear enough.

Finally Teri rose. "I'll go get her," she said in her weary voice.

"Sit down!" Danny demanded.

"I'll just get her," Teri offered meekly.

"Sit down." Then he looked at me in a really angry way. "I'll fucking well get her myself."

He disappeared down the corridor of the trailer. There was the sound of his angry voice, muffled noises, and then there he was, pushing Venus ahead of him down the hall.

She was barefoot and dressed in a red plaid flannel boy's bathrobe. When she saw me, her eyes went wide with undisguised surprise.

"There, you satisfied?" He brought Venus over until she stood about six feet away from me.

What I noticed was that she appeared to be wearing nothing other than the bathrobe. This caught my attention because it was four in the afternoon and so an odd time to be taking a bath or the like. And because it was so cold in the trailer. Perhaps she had a short nightie on under the bathrobe, which I couldn't see, but my sense was of nothing. Just the bathrobe.

"Hello, Venus. I was worried because you weren't in school today."

She stared at me. It wasn't in the blank way she often stared at school, but it wasn't in a particularly aware way either. She stared at me like I was someone she didn't know, like I was an amazing, unreal sight and she didn't know whether to be happy to see me or frightened of me.

"I hope you will be coming tomorrow," I said. "I missed you."

"Okay. Happy?" Danny asked.

I nodded slightly.

"Go off now," he said to Venus and pushed her aside.

She didn't move. She just stood, staring at me.

"Go!"

She didn't move.

"*Go*!" He pushed her shoulder.

Venus turned and disappeared back down the corridor of the trailer.

Chapter Twenty

The next day, Wanda came struggling up the stairs to the classroom, Venus trailing behind.

"Her come to school," Wanda said as I met them at the door to the room. "Beautiful child come to school today."

"Yes, that's right. Thank you for bringing her, Wanda."

"Beautiful child go to school."

"Yes, thank you, Wanda. You brought Venus to school today, didn't you?"

She twisted her hands and gave a shrug. "Beautiful child go to school."

"Yes."

Shabbily dressed in a tentlike garment and heavy tweed man's overcoat, Wanda stared at me in an almost beseeching manner. I noticed she had no gloves on, despite the cold weather, and no hat or muffler. She twisted her hands again.

It occurred to me that perhaps she was saying in her own way that she, too, wanted to come to school. What was being done for Wanda? I wondered. Anything? Did she wander aimlessly, her days empty? Except perhaps for Danny. At that unsavory thought, I made a mental note to talk to Bob about her. In the meantime, I took notice of her hands, still twisting.

"Your hands would feel warmer with gloves or mittens on, Wanda," I said. "Do you have a pair?"

"Beautiful child go to school."

"Yes, that's right. But do you have a pair of gloves at home, Wanda? This is the weather to put them on."

Wanda stared at me.

"I can try to find you some in the donation box, if you want. Shall we do that? Before you walk home? Shall we go down and see if there are any gloves for you?"

Only Jesse had arrived, and he was busy putting a puzzle together. I guided Venus over to her desk and then took Wanda downstairs to the office.

"Who's at home now, Wanda?" I asked. "Is Danny there?"

"Wanda go home," she replied.

"You're going home? After bringing Venus to school?" I was uncertain what she meant. "Is Danny there?"

"Don't like Danny," she muttered.

"Why is that?"

We were in the back office. I'd taken down the box of donated clothing that was kept on top of the cupboard and began to sort through it for gloves of a size that would fit Wanda. I couldn't find a matching pair.

"Don't like Danny. Danny says 'Sleep in the bathroom.'"

"Sleep in the bathroom?" I asked, looking up. "Who does he say that to? You? Do you sleep in the bathroom?"

"Beautiful child."

"Venus?"

"Cold. Cold hands." She put her hands up against her ears. "Makes cold. Don't like Danny. Don't want to go home."

"I see." I didn't see. I wasn't sure what Wanda was talking about except that it wasn't good, that someone – she or Venus or maybe both of them – was being mistreated. "I'll see what I can do. Okay? Perhaps you can stay here for a little while."

Wanda's eyes grew wide. "No. No go to school."

"No, I know you don't go to school here. But if you want to stay here a little while instead of going home, I'm sure it would be all right."

"No!" She seemed quite alarmed at this and backed off. "No go to school."

"Okay, okay. Here." I helped her pull the gloves on her hands. One was black. One was brown. They were all I could find that fit. I looked her in the face. "Those will keep your hands warm."

"Go now. No go to school."

"All right." I started for the door with her, but then paused. "Wait. Wanda? Would you like a doughnut?" I pointed to the box of doughnuts kept on the counter beside the coffeemaker. "Have a doughnut, Wanda."

She took two, and her face broke into a broad smile.

I wanted to stop then and there to talk to Bob about all this. Wanda's conversation had given me a very bad feeling. But it was spot on nine o'clock, so I needed to get back up to the classroom.

I watched Venus through the morning. She was very much her usual self, totally clocked out most of the time. There was no way to get her to do any kind of academic work other than one-to-one, and even then, it was I who was doing the work, moving her hands, opening the folder, making the connection between this item and that. It was February and in all this time Venus had made absolutely no progress academically. I had no idea what the homebound teacher had done with her, but I couldn't imagine it was much. Venus did absolutely nothing in the classroom still. She sat. This student literally did nothing but sit.

I suddenly felt disheartened. "Progress" for Venus had thus far consisted of getting her to walk across the room by herself. Not even spontaneously. Just walk across the room. After much urging and coaxing. What kind of progress was that? And now this horrible suspicion something very bad was happening at home. I didn't get down moments often, but I had a very big one just then. Everything about Venus seemed suddenly hopeless.

During morning recess I went in search of Bob. I found him in the teachers' lounge.

"Can I talk to you a minute?" I asked. "Privately?"

He got up from his chair. We stepped outside into the hallway.

"I stopped by to talk to Venus's mother last night about her poor attendance. I asked to see her. This Danny character was there. I asked to see Venus. This is because I've been over there on two or three occasions now and I never see this kid around when I'm there. So I asked to see her. She was supposed to be ill. That's why she didn't come to school. Anyway, he did go get her, but she was poorly dressed. Looked like just a bathrobe and nothing else. Maybe it was nothing. Maybe she was changing clothes. Maybe she had a short nightgown on underneath. I don't know. But then Wanda comes in this morning saying something about Venus sleeping in the bathroom. Or at least this seemed to be what she was saying. You know Wanda. But …"

Bob nodded slowly.

"I dunno. I realize none of this really constitutes 'evidence of abuse,' but it's giving me very bad feelings."

"I'm not sure what we can do about it," Bob said.

"Can we just raise it with Social Services? Let them know I'm concerned. In case they're concerned as well and it is just a matter of corroboration?"

"I think they already *are* concerned. I know the whole family is considered 'at risk' regarding abuse. There's been abuse with previous boyfriends, so Social Services is keeping an eye on them. They know there's stuff going on there. You and I know that. I think everybody does. It's just a matter of *proof.* It still is a free country, Torey. Not a police state. We can't interfere in people's lives based on suspicion. And awful as that feels in instances like this, it's still the way we've got to be to have a free society."

"I thought this Danny was being brought up on drug charges," I said.

"Apparently it's been dropped."

I sighed. "I was hoping we had some excuse to get him out of the home. He gives me the creeps."

Bob's shoulders sagged. "They *are* concerned, Torey. Social Services are up to their necks with this family. I'm not saying they're doing nothing."

I studied his face.

Finally he nodded. "But yeah, okay. I'll phone them again."

At recess that afternoon, I didn't push the issue of getting Venus to cross the room. Instead, I stayed with her at the door until the other children were out and then put a hand gently on her back and guided her to the reading corner.

"What shall we read?" I asked. I had left the Frog and Toad books, the Frances books, and the She-Ra comic all lying in plain view on top of the bookshelf.

Venus paused.

I waited.

Then without further hesitation, she lifted her right hand and gestured faintly toward the comic. She looked up at me.

"She-Ra? Okay. Let's find out what happens to She-Ra."

I took the comic and sat down on the rug. Then I reached up for her and pulled her down onto my lap. Venus still did not sit naturally in laps. A stiffness always remained that kept her from molding against my body.

I started reading.

It was a surprisingly complex story for a kid's comic and had a broad cast of characters. I had forgotten how many creatures peopled the imaginary worlds of He-Man and She-Ra – witches, elves, sorcerers, storm troopers, robots, magic cats and horses – a strange mix of very ancient and very modern, where rocket ships appeared alongside magic cauldrons. Certainly this was not the world of Frog and Toad, who concerned themselves with nothing more complex than what time to get up or how to find a lost button.

Was Venus listening? Was she comprehending? There was no way to know. She sat in the same still, stiff fashion throughout.

I pointed out the various characters. I commented on their strange clothes, their unusual mannerisms, their relationships to one another. It all flowed back with a wave of nostalgia, returning me to long-ago moments when He-Man was such an important part of classroom life. Small moments with other classes, other children peeped in around the corners of my thoughts as I read to Venus.

Then, finally, came the dramatic moment in the story, where ordinary, everyday Adora drew her magic sword, held it aloft, and turned herself into the superheroine She-Ra.

"Look. See how she's doing that?" I said, running my finger over the picture. "Wouldn't that be good? Would you like to be able to do that? Pull out a magic sword and turn into a superhero? Have super strength? Be able to whack away the bad guys with your sword?"

Venus leaned forward slightly to look at the picture better. She studied it intently.

"Shall we play that?" I asked. "Practice it? Shall we see if it works for us?"

I lifted her off my lap and went over to the chalkboard where the yardstick was. I brought it back to the reading corner.

"Do you think if I spin around and say 'For the honor of Grayskull,' I'll turn into She-Ra?"

Venus had gone wide-eyed.

"Shall I try?" I asked. I laughed and held aloft the yardstick. "Shall I try to turn into She-Ra?"

And she nodded. Only very, very faintly, but it was a nod.

I kept the yardstick in the air and spun around. "For the honor of Grayskull! I am She-Ra!"

I looked down at Venus. "Did it work? Did I turn into She-Ra?"

A very slight shake of the head. And a smile. She got the joke of it.

"What about you?" I asked. "What if you try?"

Venus's eyes went wide again with surprise.

"I bet it might work for you. I bet it will. I bet you might turn into She-Ra. What do you think?"

Very, very faintly she shook her head.

"You don't? You don't think you will?" I replied in exaggerated surprise. "Well, let's see. Prove it to me. Prove to me you're not She-Ra. Because I'm thinking Venus is probably really She-Ra's secret identity. *Really* her secret identity."

Venus shook her head quite openly then.

"No? Aw, you're kidding me. Prove it to me. Spin around with the sword here and show me."

She shook her head again. "Not," she said very, very softly.

"You're not? Awww. I don't believe you." I held out the yardstick. "Here. Prove it to me."

There was a long, long moment between us. I began to doubt she was going to respond. Then, in a slow, cautious movement she held her hand out.

I gave her the yardstick. I grinned.

Venus took the yardstick and held it up. Not high. Only a small part of it was higher than her head, but she clutched it tightly and started to turn. She closed her eyes and turned all the way around. Her movements were slow and stilted, but she did make it, her small face screwed up tight in concentration, her black hair bouncing slightly against her shoulders.

She stopped. She opened her eyes and looked at me.

I opened my hands wide in a gesture of amazement. "Hey, Princess of Power, it's you!"

And Venus laughed out loud.

Chapter Twenty-one

February – the 3 a.m. of the year.

At last I had what I wanted: a reasonably cohesive, unified group. The strict behavior modification program had had its desired result in terms of focusing the children's attention on specific behaviors and decreasing all the negative acting-out stuff. I still operated the class largely by use of the traffic lights, and although I was not, by nature, someone inclined to such a rigid approach, I realized that the familiarity of the system itself had become reassuring to the boys. They knew precisely what was expected when and what the consequences would be, if they chose to disobey. For the types of problems most of them were coping with – poor attention span, hyperactivity, impulsiveness – this highly structured routine gave them the security they needed to stay calm enough to work.

What kept this rather strict program from becoming austere was the singing. I hesitate to call it music. While Jesse and Billy clearly had musical abilities, none of the rest of us could be relied on to stay on tune or remember all the words to whatever song was struck up. Perhaps for this reason, we very often made up our own words and, on occasion, our own melody as well! And every once in a while, we'd get downright operatic, singing back and forth to one another things like "I don't think you're going to get your work done!" "Oh yes, I am." "I don't think so; recess is coming." "Oh yes I am, I am, I am." The pleasure singing gave us – the silly, off-the-wall spontaneity of it – kept everyone smiling.

The boys, while still volatile and prone to the most awful fights, had also begun to think of one another in small, but significant ways. Billy, in particular, had started taking a brotherly interest in Shane and Zane. He referred to them as "the little guys" and often said things to me such as, "Don't worry, I'll look out for the little guys," when they were going down to recess. Or coming in from lunch one day, he told me, "They ran out of Jell-O, but that's okay, because I went and grabbed two extra when I saw there weren't many left, so the little guys would have some." The "little guys" didn't always reciprocate this thoughtfulness especially well. Neither Zane nor Shane was making a lot of progress in terms of controlling their impulsive, often aggressive behavior. Each gain was slow and hard won for them, but Billy, and even Jesse, seemed to be reaching a point where they could accept that the "little guys" had some problems, and sometimes, as Billy put it, "you had to not take things personal."

Billy and Jesse were also forming a friendship, but they had a harder time with each other. In part, it seemed just to be a difference in personality. Billy had a big, noisy, expansive personality. He was enthusiastic with a capital *E*. Jesse, on the other hand, was one of life's natural Eeyores. He wasn't a particularly shy or quiet boy. He spoke up often; he joined in. But the world always seemed a little gloomy through his eyes. As a consequence, he found it hard not only to feel Billy's eagerness for everything, but also to put up with Billy for experiencing it. He was forever telling Billy to calm down, shut up, or stop goofing off.

There was also a certain amount of rivalry between the two of them. Shane and Zane were the "little guys" in the classroom, so this automatically cast Billy and Jesse as the "big guys." Although Jesse had very poor academic skills – more in line with Shane's and Zane's than Billy's – he saw himself in competition with Billy. He wanted to be included in anything Billy got to do. He tried very hard to keep up and keep his self-esteem intact by besting Billy – not easy in the circumstances. But the one place he shone was musically. Because of our crazy habit of singing, Jesse was thus allowed to reign in one area. He could remember words to songs best of any of the children. He could remember tunes. Indeed, he could easily play out tunes on the tinny little xylophone, our only real classroom instrument. And when singing or playing music, Jesse's tics seemed to fade away. So I got used to Jesse's requests to have a song whenever he felt threatened by Billy in the classroom.

The end of the first week in February marked Gwennie's last day with us, as her family was moving across the country to Washington, D.C. I was genuinely sorry to see Gwennie go. She was a lively little character whose quirky comments about population and land mass of foreign countries had often injected a much-needed distraction into the grim realities of keeping the boys under control. However, I did also feel a sense of relief at her going. She needed a different placement than our class. We hadn't met Gwennie's needs particularly well. She was ahead of all the children academically, but needed careful one-on-one work to develop her very deficient social skills, and we simply didn't have the setup to give her this. None of the boys was patient with her, and she had never proved the companion and workmate for Venus I'd hoped. Moreover, her intolerance of Jesse's sudden, noisy tics had often made life in the classroom extremely challenging. So I bade her good-bye on that Friday and wished her well in her new school.

Venus remained an almost invisible member of the class. None of the boys interacted with her at all. Indeed, most of the time, everyone behaved as if she were not there. Even so, she had improved. She was more controlled now. Since she'd returned to our class from homebound, there had not been a single outburst in class like we'd had in the fall. Even on the playground she seemed to be better. We still operated our "security system" of aides to watch her, but as the weeks drew out, Venus behaved herself.

To mark this newfound stability, we had two "celebrations" in February. One was the Shoe Party, which we held on February 8. This was a Friday, and we were due to have our "party" in celebration of so many people managing to keep their traffic lights on green that week. These parties were never much. Given this group's intolerance for unstructured situations, it seemed pointless to have a genuine party, which would degenerate into chaos all too easily. Instead, we did cooking. The "party," consequently, consisted simply of making something nice to eat and then eating it. That, and putting on the local pop radio station while we did it. For some reason, the boys perceived this as a particularly sinful treat. "Like getting to watch cartoons at school," as Billy put it. So our "party" wouldn't have been very partyish by most people's standards, but it was enough fun to be enjoyable.

On the preceding Monday, however, I told them we were doing something *special*. Instead of a Friday party, we were going to have a ceremony! After all these months I said that I finally felt we had reached the point where everyone could finally keep their shoes on *in class*. This was dependent, of course, on everyone's managing to keep their traffic lights on green so we could have the party. And dependent on not having one single knock-down-drag-out *all week*.

The boys took this news very seriously indeed. So seriously that Jesse, who was inclined to be the class policeman anyway, annoyed everyone else by reminding them constantly to be on their best behavior. And it was no doubt helped by the fact Billy was home sick with a cold during the middle three days of the week.

To give a celebratory feel to the day, I ordered a sheet cake from the bakery. I had them make it a very special cake with a big chipmunk design on it and the words "Happy Shoe Day" and each of the children's names underneath the chipmunk. It arrived at lunchtime full of lots of icing flowers and fancy bits, and from then on, there was talk of nothing else.

Mindful of the chaos at Christmastime, I did everything I could think of to keep order throughout the afternoon until it was time for the party in the last half hour. Both Julie and I patrolled constantly among the tables, our hands full of yellow and red traffic disks, just as a reminder. And we made it to party time without giving out a single one.

While Julie had kept everyone occupied after recess, I'd discreetly wrapped a bit of ribbon around each pair of shoes and attached a little blue ribbon medallion that said "First Prize." Not exactly appropriate, but it was all I could find at the teacher supply store the evening before. And it would do. I knew they'd all like getting a first prize, even if there hadn't been a contest.

To start the ceremony, I had everyone sit in their chairs

and then I took down the box of shoes from the top of the cupboard where I usually put them. The first pair of shoes I drew out were Zane's. I held them up, showing off the ribbon and the medallion. "Zane, may I have the honor of presenting you with your shoes?" I said as regally as I could. "And present you with this Medal of Good Conduct?"

Zane broke into a grin that spread from ear to ear.

"Go up there," Jesse said in a stage whisper.

Billy wasn't so discreet. "Hey, Zane, get off your butt."

He got out of his chair and came up. I pinned the First Prize ribbon on his shirt and then gave him his shoes. I had to help him. He still couldn't tie them himself. But once he had them on, he held his feet up, one after the other, as if no one had ever seen shoes before. Everyone clapped uproariously.

Next came Jesse's shoes. I went through the same ceremony.

The third pair out were Venus's. I held them up, showing off the shoes and the ribbon, just as I had with the two boys. "Venus, may I have the honor of presenting you with your shoes?" I asked.

The boys all turned to look at her.

She was watching me. I could tell she wasn't clocked off. Indeed, when I'd first held the shoes up, I saw her start forward in a way that made me think she was actually going to rise from her seat. But then the boys looked at her.

"Just give 'em to her," Billy said. "She won't come up and get 'em. And I haven't got my shoes yet."

I came down the aisle between the tables to where Venus sat. "Shall I help you put them on?" I asked.

She lifted her feet off the floor. It was only a small movement, but she did it without urging. She lifted them enough so that I could slip her shoes on.

"And what about your Medal of Good Conduct?" I had risen back to my feet and was standing beside her table. I held the blue ribbon out.

Unexpectedly, she stood. Venus simply pushed back her chair like any other kid and stood up.

"Wow!" Billy cried, as if she had accomplished a most amazing feat.

I pinned the ribbon on her chest. "Shall we give her a round of applause for her good conduct in getting her shoes back?" I asked.

Everyone clapped wildly.

Venus stood a moment longer, then sat down again. I think there might have even been the shadow of a smile on her lips.

Our other February event was building Lincoln's cabin.

Because this group had been so contentious and difficult, we had done virtually nothing all year outside the strict structure of the behavior modification program and each child's individualized education plan or IEP, which was the "academic prescription" I was required by law to write up for each child, laying out his or her academic program. In other years I'd had field trips, activity days, and special classroom projects. This year there had been nothing. But in honor of our newfound stability, I decided it was time to try something fun.

Since it was February, I landed on the idea of doing a unit on Abraham Lincoln, in commemoration of his birthday on February 22. I read the children the story of how he had been born in poverty in a log cabin near Springfield, Illinois, and how he had worked so hard to get an education, including doing his schoolwork by the light of the fire. I went on to explain how he had grown up to be president of the United States and about the Civil War and his part in emancipating the slaves.

We did several related activities. Billy wrote a report about Lincoln's assassination. Jesse found a picture of the Lincoln Memorial in Washington, D.C. Zane and Shane counted Lincoln pennies. But our "fun" project was Lincoln's cabin.

Initially, I intended to replicate a project Pam, in the classroom next door, had tried one year. She had had her students make little Lincoln cabins out of graham crackers and icing with construction paper roofs. She'd taken pictures of them and showed them to me, so I thought that's what we would do. But further thinking made me realize that Shane and Zane probably did not have the patience, much less the dexterity, required to assemble these and would become frustrated. Then we'd have lots of fighting and throwing of graham crackers. Next, I found a version in a teaching magazine. This one was made with pretzels and glue. It made a cabin that looked more realistic than Pam's version, but I realized this would take too much concentration for my group. Plus, they'd spend the whole time pigging on grungy gluey pretzels. I considered alternatives – construction paper strips glued onto paper, drawing, painting. But nothing seemed quite right for what I had in mind.

Then, when I was up in my attic looking for old teaching materials, I saw the perfect – and obvious – solution: Lincoln Logs. Similar to children's building blocks, these were notched wooden sticks that were designed to slot together to build rustic log cabin-type structures, and indeed, had taken their name from Lincoln's cabin. They had been a very popular toy in the 1940s and 1950s but had gone out of fashion in the following decades, as Lego and other more sophisticated building toys arrived on the scene. I had inherited a huge set of these many years earlier from a friend when she and her family had moved away. Because they were bulky, she hadn't wanted to take them along on the move, and so she'd thought I might like them for my classroom. I'd never taken them in because too many of the notched sticks were small – just the right size to lose or pocket or slip on or throw. But now …

I pulled open the lid on the container. Of all the classes I'd had through the years, this one was not a good candidate for a barrel full of small brown sticks and the accompanying green roof slats, which were about the size of a skinny ruler. It was not hard to imagine what I was letting myself in for. Indeed, because this group was so feisty, I'd long before removed all the small, potentially missilelike toys, such as Lego.

Yet …

I struggled down from the attic with the cumbersome barrel-shaped container holding the Lincoln Logs. I had to decant them into two apple boxes to fit them into my car.

The next day after morning recess, I said, "We're going to do something special today. But we're going to have to start by rearranging the room. I want to make a big space in the middle of the room, because guess what we're going to do? We're going to build cabins like Abraham Lincoln lived in. Each person is going to get to make his own. But – and an important 'but' here, everybody – "

I caught myself saying that and paused, waiting for Billy to leap in with one of his wiseacre literal comments about butts, but he didn't. He was leaning against the radiator, listening.

"But," I said, "there are lots of little pieces, lots of things that can be stepped on or slipped on. So I want everyone to be a very careful Chipmunk. If we're going to do this, we've got to be careful."

We moved the tables back so that there were three along one side of the room and two along the other. I had Jesse and Billy carry the two apple boxes to the center of the room and then carefully empty them into two piles, one on either side of the free area. I showed them how the Lincoln Logs fitted together.

"Hey, cool!" Billy shouted enthusiastically. "You mean we get to build with these things?"

"Each person can make a Lincoln cabin," I said.

"Wow. We'll have a town then," Jesse said.

"Yeah, Springfield, Illinois!" Billy interjected. "That's where Bart Simpson lives!"

"I don't think so, Billy," I replied. "There are lots of towns named Springfield."

"Well, it might be. You don't know."

"Bart Simpson's famouser than Abraham Lincoln, I bet," Jesse said.

"I'm gonna make Bart Simpson's house," Billy said. "Then it *will* be that Springfield." He grinned, knowing he was pushing his luck.

"I'm gonna make a grocery store," Zane chipped in.

"Yeah, me too," said Shane.

Sitting down cross-legged on the floor, I pulled Venus onto my lap. "Here, I'll help you."

There was a certain amount of silliness. Straightaway, Billy had to see how high a structure he could build. "This is gonna be a watchtower. Probably they had a watchtower, huh? 'Cause that was back in the days when they were fighting with Indians. So, this is gonna be a watchtower."

"Yeah, like one a million feet high," Jesse replied. "Like they'd have one that big. It's not going to fit in with anything else."

"So?" Billy replied, like this was an answer.

Then Zane discovered that you could pull back the end

of the rather springy green roof slats and it made a satisfying smacking sound when it hit something, and, indeed, delivered a satisfying smack. He tried it out on Shane's behind. Shane let out a yelp and leaped up, fists flying.

"Hey, hey, hey," I said in a warning voice.

Jesse was quicker. "Guys, don't, okay? We're having fun. And we won't get to keep doing it if you guys start fighting."

To my surprise, Shane did stop himself. He bared his teeth at his brother, then knelt back down over his cabin, shifting it away from Zane and over closer to Jesse.

I'd intended the activity to last only half an hour, which was pretty much the limit of this group's attention span, but when the half an hour was up, all four boys were still deeply engrossed in creating their log cabin town on the floor. They were planning together, discussing the layout, helping one another find the right-sized logs to build with. There was even the odd comment about Abraham Lincoln in the conversation. So I let it continue uninterrupted.

I concentrated on getting Venus to add logs to the small building I was constructing. It took about twenty minutes but she finally joined in, cautiously adding the wooden sticks, if I handed them to her.

"Can we leave this up when we're done?" Jesse asked.

"Yeah, and can we leave the room this way?" Billy added.

I nodded. "If you want. As long as everyone is careful not to trip."

"We could make more and more," Shane said.

"Yeah!" Billy cried. "We could make, like, a log cabin *city*. All around the room. Can we? Please, please?"

"I don't think there are enough logs to make that many buildings," I said.

"But we can leave it up?" Zane asked. "Can we keep adding to it?"

I nodded.

"*And* leave the room this way?" Jesse added. "Leave our tables side by side like that?"

"Okay." I was tempted to put provisos on it, as in "Yes, if you can keep from fighting," but I thought that didn't sound like I had much faith, so I kept my mouth shut.

The boys went back to building.

"You know what?" Billy said suddenly. "If this was Abraham Lincoln's time, Jesse and Venus would be slaves. They probably wouldn't even get to come to school."

Jesse bristled slightly. "Well, you wouldn't even be in this country. You'd still be in Mexico. Probably they'd be shooting at you."

"No, they wouldn't," Billy said indignantly.

"Boys," I said gently, "let's see if we can keep from arguing."

"Yeah, but he said – " Jesse replied.

"I *said* if this was Abraham Lincoln's time, you and Venus would be slaves. I didn't say I *wanted* you to be slaves," Billy retorted. "So don't get so hot and bothered."

"Yeah, well, I didn't say I *wanted* you to get shot at either."

There was a long pause. Jesse reached over to sort through the pile of logs for the size he wanted. Billy watched him. Then he went back to building.

A long, busy silence followed.

Billy paused again. He looked at Jesse and then around at the others.

"Know what?" he said to no one in particular. "I didn't used to like black kids. Before I came in this class. That's 'cause there's these black kids over at my brother's school and they're always beating people up. They beat me up once. And my brother says that's 'cause they're black."

"Yeah, well, it's stupid to think like that," Jesse replied. "What color you are doesn't mean you're gonna beat people up."

Billy nodded. "Yeah. I know. I figured that out. I'm just saying what it was before."

There was a pause.

Billy watched Jesse as he worked. "You and me are friends, huh?"

Jesse shrugged.

"That's what I told my brother. The other night I was saying that to him. I said I know a black kid at school and he's my friend. So don't go saying anything bad about black kids or I'll pop you," Billy said. " 'Cause that's what I do, if someone insults my friends."

Jesse nodded slightly. "Yeah, you're my friend too. I told my grandma that."

A pause.

"She said, 'You don't got no friends,'" Jesse continued. "She said, 'That's 'cause you got Tourette's and that's what makes you the way you are. So it makes it so you can't get friends.'"

"That ain't true," Billy said. "That's the same as being prejudiced, huh, Teacher? Like saying you got no friends 'cause you're a black kid. That's what I was talking about. That's what I meant. Before, *before* I knew Jesse, I didn't think I could be friends with him, 'cause he was black. But now when I look at Jesse, I don't *think* about him being black. And it's the same about Tourette's. 'Cause when I didn't know you, Jesse, I thought all your jerking and stuff was weird. But now I don't see it. You don't see how people are different, if you know 'em. You just see how you're alike. Huh, Teacher?"

"That's what I said to my grandma," Jesse replied. "I said, in my class, I got friends."

A moment passed in silence as the boys worked on their buildings.

"You know what?" Billy said. "I think we're lucky to be in this class. I told my brother that. I said this here was the best class I ever been in. I'm glad I don't go to any other school."

"Me too," Shane said.

"Yeah, me too," Zane said.

Jesse nodded. "Yeah, me three."

"That should be 'me four,'" Billy interjected. "Me," he pointed to himself. "Me too," he said, and pointed to Shane.

"Me three." He pointed to Zane. "And me four." He pointed to Jesse.

Jesse laughed. "Yeah, me four too, then."

Chapter Twenty-two

Over the following weekend I went out to garage sales early Saturday morning with a girlfriend, Beckie. This was an activity I did purely in the spirit of friendship, as I have transformed through the years into one of nature's natural disposers. I could see the point of *having* garage sales – how wonderful to palm off all your old junk on someone else – but the point of *going* to one to acquire what other people were trying to get rid of was lost on me. I went along, mainly because the outings always ended with a leisurely Saturday morning breakfast at one of my favorite restaurants.

Beckie was the sort who could browse through garage sale offerings for hours, particularly for clothes. She bought half her wardrobe from garage sales and was always after me to do the same, showing me all the great stuff she'd acquired over the years, much of it for only a few dollars an item. Clothes – new or used – didn't have quite the same appeal for me, so I usually trawled through the bric-a-brac. On this particular Saturday, we hit one garage sale with racks and racks of clothes, much to Beckie's delight. I went off and checked out the kitchenware, then the boxes of books, then the secondhand toys, then the tools, then the hodgepodge stuff like old florists' vases and empty Avon bottles. When I'd seen every conceivable thing, I went back to find Beckie *still* looking. I wandered off again.

To while away the time, I struck up a conversation with a young girl who was obviously the owner of the toys being sold. She looked about ten. We talked about outgrowing Barbie dolls and how you might still like the dolls themselves, but you didn't need that pink plastic camper anymore, and so, what did you do with it? She then told me she was trying to make ten dollars selling her stuff so that she could buy a jewelery-making kit. I told her I regretted not being able to buy anything, as I was looking mainly for boys' toys.

She was a natural little entrepreneur, this kid. When she found out that I hadn't seen anything I liked, she wanted to know if I'd like to see some stuff they had kept back to put out the following day. It was just in through the back. Come on, she said. Maybe there was something I'd like.

In among the things waiting to be put out was a cardboard box full of children's videos. I leaned down and sorted through them. That's when I saw it: *She-Ra, Princess of Power*. I picked the video up.

"How much for this?" I asked her.

"Fifty cents."

So it was a done deal.

When I finished my lunch on Monday, there was still almost half an hour left before the bell rang for the start of the afternoon session. So I packed away my things and went down to the playground to find Venus.

She was over by her wall. She wasn't up on top of it. She wasn't allowed up there during school hours, but she leaned against it. She spent most outdoor periods like that, leaning against the wall.

I knew better than to try and call her over, so I crossed the playground to where she was. I knelt down in front of her. "Do you want to come inside? I have something special for you."

She regarded me.

I smiled.

No response.

"Guess what it is? A She-Ra cartoon. It's on video. I thought, if you wanted, we could go up to the classroom now and watch it on the VCR there."

No response.

"Would you like to do that?"

No response.

It was unrealistic to expect an answer here in the noisy,

exposed playground, so I simply rose back up to my feet and held out my hand. "Come on. Let's go watch it."

She remained immobile.

I reached down and took her hand. "Come in with me."

She came willingly enough.

We walked into the dim corridor and up, up, up the long staircase. I opened the door to the classroom, but since we were going to watch the video, I didn't turn on the lights. Crossing the room to my desk, I took out the video. Removing the tape from the cover, I handed the cover to Venus.

"See? Here it is. Have you seen any She-Ra cartoons before?"

No response.

I pulled out the stand that held the TV monitor and the VCR. "Let's pull it over here so that we can sit on the cushions in the reading corner." I shoved the stand ahead of me.

Venus remained by the door, the video case in her hands. She looked at the picture on the front.

"Come on," I said. I returned to where she was standing and led her over to the reading corner. Turning on the VCR and monitor, I then sat down. I pulled Venus onto my lap and wrapped my arms around her.

It was a rather thin plotline about a pirate who would work for anyone who paid him until he met Adora, who worked for the resistance movement on the planet Etheria. That's when he realized he really wanted to be a good pirate and work to free Etheria from the evil Horde too. The crowning moment came when Adora transformed herself into She-Ra accompanied by a very catchy tune and a cascade of glittery light. I could feel Venus's little body tensing as she watched the transformation. Her fingers gripped the cloth of my jeans and she sat forward, enthralled.

There was a second cartoon on the tape, but we didn't have time to watch it. Only about seven minutes remained before the afternoon session began, so I rose up and turned the VCR off.

"That was good, wasn't it? Did you like that?" I asked.

Very cautiously, Venus nodded.

"Here," I said and handed her the yardstick. "Shall we practice turning into She-Ra? You turn around and do the sword thing. I'll sing that good tune, okay? I'll sing the 'She-Ra! She-Ra!' part."

Without any real hesitation, Venus held the yardstick aloft and started to turn around. I did the musical accompaniment.

"Yes, that's good. But you forgot something. You forgot to say, 'For the honor of Grayskull!' It wouldn't work without that, I think. Here, try it again. I'll do the 'She-Ra! She-Ra!' "

Venus held the yardstick aloft again and turned slowly around. I saw her open her mouth but I couldn't hear anything.

"Here, try again. I think it needs to be louder. Like this: 'For the honor of Grayskull!' " I shouted.

Venus's eyes went wide.

"Can you say that really loud?" I asked. "Let's hear you try."

"For the honor of Grayskull," she mouthed.

"Hey, yeah! Almost got it. Can you try it just a little bit louder?"

"For the honor of Grayskull," she whispered.

"Almost there. Louder?"

"For the honor of Grayskull," she said, again in a whisper.

"Louder."

"For the honor of Grayskull," she said and it was almost a normal voice.

"Just about there. A little louder."

"For the honor of Grayskull," she said and it was at a normal level.

"Great! You are so good! You can do it, can't you? Now, let's get all the action too. Here. Hold up the sword. Spin around. And don't forget the words. Let's see you transform into the Princess of Power!"

Venus held up the yardstick and turned around. I sang, "She-Ra! She-Ra!"

Venus ventured the yardstick a little higher. There was a pause … the pause started to draw out … it threatened to become a silence. Then suddenly, "For the power of Grayskull!" she said in a clear voice.

"Wow! Wowie!" I clapped my hands to my cheeks. "And there you are! The Princess of Power! Right in front of me!" I reached down and grabbed her to me, hugging her in against my body.

Venus giggled happily.

The two of us spent the next few days watching the video during the lunch hour. Once Venus knew what we were going to do, she came willingly. She still would not risk declaring her allegiance openly by crossing the playground to me, but instead, she started lingering by the door, waiting for me. On the third day I saw a smile touch her lips when she glimpsed me through the glass of the door.

I looked forward to our lunchtime meetings almost as much as she did, I think. Sensing we were on the cusp of a breakthrough, I filled much of my spare time with thoughts of how to get the next response. How much could I ask of her? How much would she do?

I also spent much time pondering what was behind all her extremely unresponsive behavior, because even now, even after all these months of being up close with it, I found it unusual. She was so persistently unresponsive, even when it was apparent that she could, indeed, talk.

I still had never heard spontaneous speech out of her. Venus would now very occasionally talk, after a fashion, when we were alone together. Or rather, she would either grunt out "yes" or "no" or she would repeat something I told her to say. This was not enough speech to clarify in my mind the degree to which she could speak normally. There was still the specter of retardation haunting our activities. Venus was so unresponsive it had been impossible to administer any kind of assessment test, such as the WISC IQ test. Consequently, we didn't know. It was possible she did not speak because she simply did not have enough intelligence to do so. Or maybe she had brain damage or aphasia or the countless other things that might lead me to a dead end.

Bob rather sardonically pointed this out to me one lunch hour, as I was finishing up my sandwich in preparation to go down and watch the video with Venus.

"You really are a most amazing person, you know that, don't you?" he remarked as I packed up my things.

I looked up questioningly.

"The way you get by on so little reward." He tipped his head, as if gesturing about someone in the room. "I mean with Venus."

"She's rewarding," I answered, perhaps a little defensively.

He raised his eyebrows. "Come on, Tor," he said in disbelief.

I looked over at him.

"You don't have to lie to me. I came up through all the liberal idealism too. We've both got the swinging sixties in our blood. Love, not war. All that crap. I've served my time worshipping at that altar. But we're also both old enough now to know when the odds aren't in our favor. And they sure aren't with this one."

This remark irritated me. "So what are you saying? That I shouldn't be doing this?"

"No. I'm just saying you're putting a lot of effort into what is likely to be very little return."

"I don't think that's a value judgment I should be making, Bob."

"Perhaps there's another way to put it. One's got to pick one's battles, Torey," he said. "When I was saying that about the swinging sixties, I was meaning we were both idealistic back then. When you and I started working together, we thought we could save the world. But the truth is, we can't. And you know that. I know you do. I know you're not half so idealistic as you come across."

"I'm realistic," I said, "more than idealistic."

"Which is what I'm saying. Realistically, you'll never accomplish much in this case. And I see you spreading yourself thin. I know you're taking personal time to work with her."

"Then get me another aide. Get me enough help in my classroom so that I can adequately attend to all the children I have, because I can't do it now. I can't work with this girl during class time, not the way she needs to be worked with, because what would I do with the others?"

"No, what I'm *saying*," said Bob with a note of exasperation in his voice, "is that – "

"This one isn't worth saving," I said.

"No. Let me finish. What I'm saying is that I don't want to see you overextend yourself. I *can't* get you another aide. I know as well as you do that you should have one, but tell that to John Q. Public at the next mill levy, because the money just isn't there. In the meantime, this is all we can do. And yes, sadly, it means we've got to pick our battles."

"I don't work that way," I said and picked up my stuff and left.

The conversation with Bob left me disgruntled. I was experienced enough and realistic enough to know that, yes, sadly, one *does* have to make difficult choices. I had no delusions about being able to "save" every kid I encountered. There were not the resources. There wasn't the time. And in some instances, I simply wasn't the right person. But I resented very much the implication that Venus should be considered expendable on the basis of an IQ people were only guessing at or her potential for "return" on time invested, which to me was as discriminatory as excluding her based on socioeconomic level or race. I simply did not think this was a judgment I should be making. If Venus was responding, then that was sufficient reason to keep working with her.

And she *was* responding. In the privacy of the unlit classroom, in the shadows of a cartoon princess, we slowly began to build up a relationship.

"Here. Do you want to put the video in?" I asked one afternoon.

Venus stood, her eyes growing wide.

"You don't know how? Come here. I'll show you."

Hesitantly, she came up to the machine.

"Here. Take the tape. Then you push it in here. There. Like that." I demonstrated. Then I popped the videotape back out. "Now, here. You try it." I put the tape in her hand.

Venus looked down at the videotape with an amazed expression, as if it were a most unusual thing.

"Lift it up here."

She looked up.

"Lift it up. Here." I put a hand under her elbow to make her raise her arm. "Now, put it into the slot."

She didn't move.

I put my hand over hers and moved it toward the machine. "There. Push it in." I guided her hand with the tape until the tape went into the slot. "Good! That's right. Now, you try it." I popped the videotape out again. I gave it back to her.

Venus hesitated a very, very long moment. Then slowly she raised her hand and gently put the tape against the VCR slot.

"Okay, good. Now push it in."

She wasn't using enough pressure, so the little flap on the slot wouldn't open.

"Push a bit harder. You won't break it."

Venus pressed it a little more against the flap, but it still wouldn't open.

"Harder. Keep trying. You're almost there."

Venus kept the tape pressed against the flap. There came another one of these long, long moments, so long, in fact, that I thought we weren't going to manage this. But I just waited. And smiled.

She hesitated. Then, at last, she gave it a little push and in it went. The machine purred to life and the cartoon flickered up onto the monitor as the tape started to move.

"Wow! You did it! You did that all by yourself, didn't you!" I cried and I grabbed her up in a big hug. "Wow! Princess of Power!"

Venus smiled. Indeed, she did more than smile. Her face broke into a wide grin, showing two missing top teeth.

We both laughed.

Chapter Twenty-three

Despite my visit to Venus's home and the talk with her mother and Danny, Venus still did not attend school regularly. I found this frustrating in the extreme. We would have two or three good days together and then Venus would be gone. It didn't matter how well we had been doing when she left, inevitably there would be a small slip back, even if she was gone only a day. If I had her crossing the room, but she was out the next day, then the first day back was lost trying to get her to cross the room again. If I had her putting the tape in the VCR, but she was out the next day, then the first day back was lost trying to get her to put the tape in the VCR again. It never failed.

"Something has *got* to be done about this," I said to Bob.

"I know," Bob replied, running a hand down across his face in a gesture of frustration.

And Bob did know that. Indeed, Bob did try. He sent the district truant officer to the home to talk to the parents about their responsibility in getting Venus to school. He notified Social Services for the umpteenth millionth time. He even brought in the police at one point and a female officer was dispatched to the home. Despite all this effort, however, there continually seemed to be crossed lines of communication. The police officer went *out* to the home. We were informed of that. What we weren't informed of was that she did not see Venus. The truant officer went *out* to the home. We were informed of that. What we weren't informed of was the fact that he found no one there when he arrived. Social Services went *out* to the home. We were informed of that. What we weren't informed of was the fact that this was this particular social worker's last day and she didn't fill out all the appropriate reports before leaving her job and moving to another part of the country. And on and on. So, while the right moves were being made, it was never communicated that they weren't being fully executed. Bureaucracy tripped over itself. And in the end I was none the wiser for why we could not keep Venus in school.

She-Ra cartoons had long since stopped being shown on television, but I was determined to find more videos; so I spent several Saturday mornings with Beckie "garage-saling," as she liked to call it. Doing this, I managed to acquire half a dozen more She-Ra videos. In addition, I found two or three She-Ra picture books and about ten comics.

Venus and I made a routine of watching the cartoons together during the lunch hour. Venus would now wait by the door onto the playground for me to finish my lunch and come get her. Then she'd follow me upstairs without being directed, help me push the monitor across the room, put the tape into the VCR of her own accord before finally joining me on the pillows in the reading corner. She liked sitting on my lap and often wrapped my arms tight around herself, if I didn't do it quickly enough myself.

During the afternoon recess, we started role-playing. Venus was always She-Ra, of course. Using the yardstick, she transformed herself into the Princess of Power half a dozen times during the twenty minutes. We then acted out small sections of whatever cartoon we had watched at lunchtime or perhaps a scene from one of the comics. These were usually very, very simple scenes. Her favorite was for me to pretend to be the evil character Catra and sneak up on her from the other side of the low bookshelf.

"Here I come! I'm going to destroy that She-Ra. Meeee-ow. Then Etheria will belong to meeeee," I'd say, pretending to creep along in a very evil way.

Venus found this delicious fun. She would swing the yardstick and laugh and squeal. After the first few times, she managed to work up the courage to come after me. She wasn't able to let her guard down enough to actually run, but she managed to speed around the classroom at a fast walk, trying to tap me with the yardstick.

It was low-level stuff, the sort of games you might play with a three- or four-year-old, and it evoked the same giddy laughter from her. I didn't try to do more. I didn't push for speech. I didn't endeavor to make it more age appropriate. I didn't try to make it educational. All I wanted was to engage Venus, to help her realize this was a good place to be, a fun place, a safe place.

Unfortunately, almost none of this freer behavior was carrying over into the classroom. Venus remained very much her usual closed-in, inhibited self around Julie and the other children. I could occasionally get her to move of her own volition, if the group was working near to her. She would come willingly to stand by me or sit on my lap so that I no longer had to go get her and move her physically. And very, very occasionally she would nod or faintly smile. But these were all still very much exceptions to the rule. Most of the time, she just sat, catatonic as ever.

Because of this, I thought maybe I could make the transition by moving She-Ra into the classroom.

I'd been reading an old favorite of mine – *Treasure Island* – to the children after lunch. I always did this every year because I loved the book and because I found that whatever age the children were, there was an innate fascination with pirates that lent itself to many other activities. In this case, we decided to make pirate chests as an art project. I'd brought in a big container full of colorful clear plastic chips from a nearby factory to use as jewels, plus an assortment of colored foil and cellophane and other shiny items to be turned into appropriately gaudy treasure chest contents. Then we used cereal boxes to create the chest itself. The boys all took to this enthusiastically, of course. And Venus just sat, of course.

Once it was clear that the boys were well occupied, I took out a large piece of cardboard I'd cut from the side of an apple carton and brought it over to Venus's table.

"You know what I'm thinking?" I said as I pulled out a chair and sat down. "I'm thinking that instead of making a treasure chest, what you *really* need is a proper Sword of Power. Don't you? I mean, we've been pretending with the yardstick and that's been okay, but I think we should have a *real* one. Don't you? One just for you? That is your own?"

Venus's eyes went wide.

"I was thinking we could use this cardboard. I'll help you draw a sword shape and we can cut it out. Then you can stick fancy jewels on the handle. What do you think?"

Venus's face lit up. Very, very slightly she nodded.

I drew a freehand sword and cut it from the cardboard. Taking silver foil, I showed Venus how to fold it over the blade and glue it to make it shiny silver. She wouldn't try it at first. I sat with her, taking her hand and moving it over the foil to smooth it onto the cardboard while Julie walked among the boys, helping them.

As the afternoon passed, Venus slowly became involved.

She chose some colorful wrapping paper for the hilt, which I helped her stick on. Then working on her own, she carefully picked out "jewels" from the assortment of plastic chips I'd laid on her desk and glued them onto the sword.

I rose and moved among the boys to see what they were doing. Venus continued to work. She was very self-contained, sitting hunched over her table, her movements tight and constricted. She gave the impression of intense concentration, as if she were crafting the most delicate masterpiece, and, indeed, it turned out she was, as she added the plastic chips, the sequins, the glitter in a delicate pattern on the hilt of the sword and then eventually up along the blade of the sword too. As she worked, she never looked up or around to see what any of the others of us were doing. Instead, she kept her head down, her shoulders forward, and added decoration after decoration to her Sword of Power.

My fly in the ointment was Julie.

After school had finished that afternoon and we were wiping glue off tables and picking bits of paper off the floor, she said, "I'm not sure I'm comfortable with this."

"Not comfortable with what?" I asked, having no idea what she was referring to.

"Your using this cartoon thing with Venus. Does Bob know? Have you talked it over with him?"

No, I had not talked it over with Bob. I didn't generally clear my lesson plans with my principal, so it had not even occurred to me to talk it over with Bob. I was irritated, not only for her rather casual implication that I didn't know what I was doing, but also simply because I was the teacher here and she was the aide, so it wasn't her responsibility to continually question my actions.

"What bothers you about it?" I asked.

"It's not a very good standard of material. Do you think? I mean, that whole series was just designed to sell toys. Just consumerism gone mad. There's no depth to these characters. No literary value to them. Wouldn't it be better to choose something ... well, more *educational* to stimulate the children? And something more nonviolent. And ..."

"Yes?"

"Well, in Venus's case, something more culturally appropriate. Venus is African–American. Have we got the right to shove some blonde, white bimbo with pneumatic boobs at her?"

Admittedly, I hadn't even considered that. My sole goal had been to engage Venus. When she chose the comic as one of her first acts of self will with me, I just took it and ran.

"Julie, I'm about as color-blind as a person can get. I can't remember the last time I even noticed the color of Venus's skin."

"But that isn't color-blind, Torey. That is just blind. We get so used to thinking from the point of view of white, Anglo-Saxons that we aren't even aware we *are* prejudiced.

You don't question if it's appropriate to be giving this girl these kinds of role models because you're assuming our culture is right *without* questioning it. But if you were truly color-blind, you would be embracing heroines and role models of all colors. Equally."

"This doesn't make a lot of sense to me," I said, "this idea that I have to be conscious of someone's race in order to be not conscious of it. Venus's skin color is immaterial, just as the length of her hair is or the material of her shirt. I chose what I chose because that's what she showed an interest in. My goal is simply to wake this kid up again, because when she came into the classroom, she was the walking dead. So, if she'd taken an interest in Spam cans, I probably would have gone with that. I just went with what was there. 'Culturally appropriate' never even crossed my mind."

"Yes, I know. That's why I'm saying this."

There was a pause.

"This isn't me putting you down, Torey," she said. "I know we always end up like this, always on opposite sides, and I don't mean that. I really admire the way you work. You're the most spontaneous teacher I've ever known. You can make a lesson out of anything. On the spot. Without any preparation. I could never do that. I have to have everything planned down to the last word in the plan book. So, I really admire this about you, because it would be so hard for me to do it. But sometimes, because things *are* so spontaneous, I think maybe you're not aware of all the sides to it. I mean, couldn't you just try to choose an African-American heroine for this girl? Someone she could be proud to identify with? Say, like, Rosa Parks?"

"Rosa Parks instead of She-Ra?" I asked, hoping that if I said it aloud, the absurdity would strike her.

It didn't. She nodded approvingly.

"They're not really in the same category, Julie. I think Rosa Parks is a fantastic person and a wonderful role model, but she just doesn't represent the same sort of thing that She-Ra does. It isn't even She-Ra, per se. It's someone powerful and strong."

"And you think Rosa Parks isn't powerful and strong?" Julie replied.

I sighed in exasperation. "Yes, of course she is. But in a different way. She isn't a comic book superhero. And just at the moment we *need* a comic book superhero."

"But *why*? Why some unrealistic comic book Barbie doll that Venus will never be like in a million years? Why not someone she can genuinely model herself on?"

"Because I think she *can* be like She-Ra. These are *qualities*, Julie. They have nothing to do with culture or race or gender or any of that crap. Everybody is capable of them. These are human qualities. And they are easier to see in a cartoon character, in a superhero, simply because they *are* exaggerated. It's easier to know exactly what they are and how you behave to get them. That's all I want right now."

"I can't agree with you there."

Picking up the scraps of paper I'd collected, I crossed

the room and threw them into the trash can. "No, I can see," I said because I could. We were on two different planets in this conversation. I didn't know how to change that.

The conversation bothered me. Long after the school day had ended and Julie and I'd gone our separate ways, I was still thinking about it. *Was* I being inadvertently racist because I had exposed Venus to white superheroes? Was I somehow disenfranchising her by denying her real-life role models of color? In She-Ra's world of Etheria where people transmogrified into pink cats, did color matter? Truth was, I felt it was Julie who was being racist by putting limits on what Venus could enjoy, by saying, "The only appropriate role models for you are those who look like you, even in your imagination." But the truth was, I didn't know the answer to this one.

Julie's conversation ruined things a little for me. The next day I did not come quite so innocently to our lunchtime cartoon viewing. I now paid attention to who was what color, and the truth was, in Etheria, many of the characters were not even human. There were robots and purple-faced witches, rainbow-colored owl-like things that flew by flapping their ears, and a sorceress who was faceless altogether. But the good guys – Adora, She-Ra, her boyfriend Bow, her friends, Glimmer, Bright Moon, and Flutterina – were all white.

Still, imperfect as it was, She-Ra's world remained my common ground with Venus. She watched the cartoon enthusiastically, her small body tensing with the action. She pulled my arms up tight around her and smiled at me when I hugged her close. After the cartoon, we went to find her Sword of Power where I'd put it to dry on the back counter after art the previous afternoon.

Venus moved ahead of me to get it. There was no hesitation in her actions. She could have been any little girl then, going to get a favorite item. Reaching for the sword, she lifted it up.

"Wow! Look at that! Magic or what?" I said. "Let's see you turn into She-Ra."

Holding the sword pointing upward, Venus closed her eyes and twirled around. "For the honor of Grayskull!" she called out.

"Wow! That works perfectly!" I said.

Venus gave the sword a test swing.

"Come here," I said. I pulled her over toward the full-length mirror in the dressing-up corner. "Look, do you see? See how great that magic sword looks?"

I had her standing in front of me, a little girl with scraggly hair and dirty skin. Her clothes were worn and ill-fitting. Her nose was crusty. She had sores along the sides of her mouth.

"Aren't you beautiful?" I said and smiled at her reflection. "Look. That sword's made you every bit as super as She-Ra, huh? Don't you think so?"

Her eyes sparkled. A slow smile spread across her lips. She nodded.

"I'm looking in that mirror and I'm seeing someone who *really* is a Princess of Power. Someone who *really* knows how to use a Sword of Power." I knelt down and wrapped my arms around her.

Venus kept her eyes on her reflection in the mirror. She nodded.

"You know what I'm thinking?" I asked in a chummy sort of way.

Venus raised her eyebrows in question.

"I'm thinking, what if you stay changed into She-Ra this afternoon?" I asked. "When the other kids come?" I was hoping that this was the magic she needed to be brave enough to talk and interact in the classroom. Perhaps with the Sword of Power at her side, she would risk it.

The expression in her eyes changed slightly. Concern clouded the joy.

"You could keep the Sword of Power with you, if you want. At your table. What about it? What about between now and recess? You could be Princess of Power for that time."

A long pause followed.

Venus kept her eyes on her reflection in the dressing-up mirror, and as I watched her, she transformed. Without a movement, without a word, the joy drained out of her.

"You don't want to do that?" I said. It was more of a statement than a question, but I wanted her to know it was all right to make that choice. That she could. "That's okay."

She shook her head. "No," she said, which surprised me, because I hadn't expected her to say anything.

"No, what? What's the matter?"

We were still in front of the mirror. I still had my arms around her in a sort of backward hug. We were talking to each other through our reflections.

"I don't want to," Venus said very softly.

"That's okay. It was just a suggestion. If you don't want to, you don't have to. In here you decide."

She regarded my reflection. The fun was gone from her dark eyes.

"Does it make you feel afraid?" I asked.

She nodded.

"Of what?"

She didn't answer.

"The boys?"

She didn't respond.

"Do the boys frighten you? I know the boys are noisy. And pretty rowdy. But they don't want to hurt you. You're safe in here. I wouldn't let anything happen."

She shook her head. I wasn't altogether sure what she was meaning by that.

A small silence came.

"I'm not really She-Ra," she said finally. "It's just a game."

"I see." Then I nodded. "Yes, you're right."

"That makes me scared."

"Oh?"

She didn't reply.

"I'm not sure I understand," I said. "Can you explain it more?"

A long silence.

"I'm not really She-Ra. Not for real."

"Well, no. Because she's just pretend, isn't she? She's just a cartoon. But the things about her – being strong and able to do things that are good – those things are real. And you do have those things inside you. For real. You do. I know. In here." I tapped her chest. "When we pretend with the sword, we're just letting them out. But they're already real. Inside you, you're strong and able to do things that are good, just like She-Ra."

Venus shook her head.

"Yes, you are," I said. "You've got lots of good things inside you, Venus."

Venus shook her head more vehemently. "No," she said.

"Well, I think differently, because I can see those things in you. And I'm not the only one. Wanda can too, can't she? That's why she calls you 'beautiful child.'"

"No. She just says that 'cause that's something retards say."

I looked at her. "Who told you that? That isn't true."

She dropped the Sword of Power on the floor and left it there. Her eyes shrouded. The vacant expression returned.

I looked down at the cardboard sword. Something had happened. I'd inadvertently ruined something. But I wasn't sure what.

Chapter Twenty-four

That was my first real conversation with Venus. Up until that moment, I had never had a multisyllabic exchange with her, much less an actual conversation. It wasn't until it was over that I even fully comprehended what had happened.

On the one hand, I was astonished. It answered so many questions. For instance, obviously she was capable of genuine speech. Her grammar and vocabulary were acceptable. The concepts she was expressing were reasonably sophisticated. While not erasing entirely the concern that she might be developmentally delayed, the conversation was well within normal limits for a seven-year-old. So, even if she were delayed, it was nothing near the level of Wanda's difficulties. This was positive, valuable information.

On the other hand, I was saddened. The conversation gave evidence of a repressed, unhappy little girl.

And then, of course, the next day she wasn't there.

Of all the students, the one who was making the most heartening progress was Billy. At the beginning of the year he had been "everywhere" – buoyant, wildly enthusiastic, noisy, explosive, unable to focus himself on anything for long. His academic work had been appalling because he'd never stayed seated long enough to finish any. His uncontrolled enthusiasm was more annoying than charming, because he burst in on everything, hogged the limelight, and ignored everyone else. He spoke loudly and often aggressively. And his off-the-wall sense of humor, usually expressed by taking any figure of speech literally and catching the unwary speaker out, wore thin long before Billy would give up the joke.

Billy's had been one of the few cases where I'd found the district's insistence on interminable student assessments to prove valuable. Discovering that Billy was a gifted child when previously he had only been identified as a troublemaker had given me something concrete to work with. Reframing him as an underchallenged, poorly directed child of considerable ability, I'd set about to find something for him to sink his teeth into. This had been difficult initially, because Billy's academic skills were nowhere near where they should have been for a boy of his apparent ability, so, when necessary, I'd had to come up with a way to jump-start some of these skills. For example, to allow him to work on projects that would engage him more, Julie and I recorded huge chunks of resource materials, such as encyclopedias, onto cassette tapes. Or I armed *him* with the cassette recorder to interview people instead of writing it down. And I looked for interest areas, knowing that if he were genuinely gifted, they must be there somewhere. But these proved hard to find. His flighty approach to everything meant he pursued everything with equal enthusiasm but stuck to nothing.

The real turning point for Billy, however, was our traffic light system. He was such an impulsive, scatterbrained personality that the tight structure of the behavioral modification program seemed, for the first time, to give Billy the necessary framework for inner discipline. He thrived in the new, rather rigid setup. Even so, self-discipline was still a hard-won virtue. Although he participated enthusiastically and was very motivated to earn the treats and the stars, he had been the last of all the children to actually manage it. Even the twins learned how to keep their traffic lights on green before Billy did. But he made it in the end, and was he ever proud of himself!

What I discovered with Billy that I hadn't previously appreciated was that once something was learned, it stuck. Once he mastered breaking the time before recess down into chunks that involved sitting and working, interspersed with chunks specifically meant for getting up and moving around, he was quickly able to generalize it to the period after recess. And then to the afternoon as a whole. And eventually to the rest of his week. Once he figured the system out, his behavior became much more reliable.

I found it interesting the way his mind worked on issues like this. There was always a conscious "click" for Billy. But he had to not only understand it but also experience it logically. Not just consciously, but logically – this part connects to that part which then connects to this part, and all of them together result in this outcome. My telling him to sit down and work, because once he had worked for twenty minutes he could get up and have free time, did not penetrate. Seeing the schedule written down on the board with the traffic lights and experiencing the clockwork regularity of twenty minutes of work time, ten minutes of free time, which meant the traffic light stayed on green, did not penetrate straightaway either. He kept saying, "Why?" "How's it go?" But finally, when he experienced it, talked about it, wrote it down, considered it from all sides, and told it back to me half a dozen times, it suddenly "clicked" for him. Suddenly he understood the point of what he was supposed to be doing and how each individual behavior contributed to it, and from then on, he was reasonably successful.

With this newfound ability to keep himself in his seat for twenty-minute blocks, Billy started to make startling progress on his academic work, particularly in reading, which had been much further behind than his math. And this, of course, brought its own rewards. There *were* things he was interested in. But Billy, being Billy, didn't have your ordinary nine-year-old-boy interests.

The first thing he took to was flowers.

One day he showed up with a beautiful coffee table book about tulips. I had no idea where it came from, as I knew Billy's family did not live well and there would have been no money for such an extravagant book, but I didn't query it. And Billy loved this book. It had numerous exquisitely drawn pictures of tulips, including dissections of the bulb and the flower. These fascinated him. Noting this, I brought in other books. I had been a biology major in college, so I brought in one of my botany textbooks. I explained to Billy how, as part of our college course work, we had had to dissect flowers and draw the parts, and when we did, we kept a notebook and drew pictures and diagrams of what we'd seen. This intrigued him. He wanted to try that too. As it was February when I told him this, we did not have a lot of flowers growing outdoors for such an activity, so Julie brought him in a lily left over from a display at her church. With care and remarkable concentration, Billy spent the late morning "dissecting" the flower and making detailed drawings of everything he found, working meticulously to identify stamens, pollen, etc.

As a consequence of all this growth, I felt Billy would be ready to return to the regular classroom after this year in our class was over, as long as we could guarantee placement in a relatively structured program. To prepare him for this, Bob and I decided to try mainstreaming him into a regular class in the building for part of the day. This instantly hit problems. Where to put Billy? He was nine, going on ten, so he should have gone into the fourth grade. His overall academics made him more suitable for third grade however. So should he go into third grade, despite being older and intellectually gifted? This seemed like asking for trouble to me. Yes, he was only at that level academically, but he was improving steadily. It seemed inevitable that he would soon be unchallenged, if put in with younger children, and I genuinely felt that this lack of challenge had fed significantly into his behavior problems in the past. So I stuck my neck out. There was an advanced placement or AP class for gifted children in a neighboring school. They catered to children across a greater age range, so I suggested Billy go there. Not for all day. Not even for every day. I knew the teacher of the class slightly. I knew she had the children doing special projects of their own interest two afternoons a week. What if Billy went over and joined them for those two afternoons?

Bob did some serious eyebrow raising at this suggestion. Send a behaviorally disordered child with poor academics to an AP class? Send a child who could hardly read and write when the other nine-year-olds there probably read at tenth-grade level? He shook his head in amazement at the sheer chutzpah of the idea. Nonetheless, it appealed to him. He contacted the teacher. We had a meeting. She came again and visited with Billy, who, as with everything else, was joyfully enthusiastic. She was smitten.

Yes, she said, she'd be happy for him to come two afternoons a week.

Every once in a while – on those rare, rare occasions – things really work out. Offbeat as they sound, they work. And this did. Armed with his tulip book and his notebook, Billy left that first afternoon bravely. No hesitation. No worries about where to find the rest room or if the bus driver would remember to come to pick him up from this different school. "I'm going to my special class," he told Jesse at lunchtime.

"You're already in a special class," Jesse remarked.

"This is a different one," Billy replied.

"Why? Is something else wrong with you?"

Billy shrugged. "No. It's where I might go next year. Who knows."

"How come you got to go to a different special class, though? How come you don't just stay here?"

"This other one's a special class where kids do special stuff they want. That's what the teacher says. Mrs. Sprang. That's her name. And she says I can do tulips all afternoon if I want, and the other kids'll be doing just what *they* want all afternoon."

"What kind of class is that?" Jesse asked. "Is it school? It doesn't sound like school to me. What grade is it?"

"It doesn't got grades," Billy replied. "Like in here. Like we don't got grades in here."

"Have they got kids who are eight, like me?" Jesse asked. He looked over at me. "Is this for real? Is he telling the truth?"

I nodded.

"You mean that he gets to do what he wants? That there's a special class just for that?"

"Well, not exactly," I said. "They do schoolwork too. Just like every other class. It's just Billy isn't going over there then. He's going over during project time."

"Wow, lucky," Jesse muttered.

"Yeah, that's me," Billy replied with a smile.

And that was it, smooth as could be. Billy went into the AP class two afternoons a week and did beautifully. Yes, he was a little wild, a little over-the-top in the way only Billy could be, but he didn't punch anybody. He didn't swear uncontrollably. He didn't have any aggressive outbursts. Nothing gave away the fact that he spent the rest of his time in a class for behavioral disorders. Carol Sprang, the teacher, handled him confidently. Although the children were given a lot of latitude in terms of choosing the projects they would pursue, she was a structured teacher by nature and so put emphasis on order and commitment, and this suited Billy's needs well. He came back after each visit that little bit happier and more confident. I felt as if I were seeing him mature right before my eyes.

As a consequence, Billy very soon started to think of the AP class as "his" class too. There was no favoritism in his attitude. He enjoyed his time in with us and was generous in his pleasure with our system and our Friday parties and the company of the other boys, but he also liked his "other" class and the friends he made there. Thus, when March rolled around and his other school announced a school carnival, this was *all* Billy could talk about.

"Know what? My class is going to have a stall at the carnival," he said to us. "It's going to be an eggshell game. You pay a quarter and then you got to guess what egg is whole. See, most of them are broken-in-half shells. There's the big tray with sand in it and they are all pushed in halfway. So it looks like every one of them is whole. But only one is. So, you pay your money and you get to choose. And if you don't pick the right one, you still get a prize. You get one of those little fun-size candy bars. But if you do pick the whole egg, then you get a big prize."

"Like what?" Jesse asked.

Billy shrugged. "Dunno. They haven't told us that. But probably something good. And guess what, *I* get to work on it. Mrs. Sprang said."

"How come we don't get a carnival at this school?" Jesse asked, a bit miffed.

Shane ran up at just this point. He was having a silly afternoon. He had put an old knit bobble hat from the dressing-up box on his head and pulled it way down to his eyebrows. All afternoon he had insisted on wearing it like that.

"Yeah, I know what our stall could be for this class," Billy chirped. "Guess the twin! Guess who was who. Zane or Shane." He laughed.

Jesse laughed too and reached over to pull Shane's hat

down over his eyes. "Not much problem if you still got the stupid hat on, Shane."

Shane lashed out at him but Jesse took it in a playful fashion, wrestled him a moment, and then let go.

"Will you guys come?" Billy asked. "It's on next Friday night. Will you come to my stall? I'd let you have a turn for free."

This pleased Jesse. "Hey, man, you bet. I'll get my grandma to take me. You just tell me where this school is and I'll be there. And probably I'll win your big prize. I might even win it twice. I'm good at guessing games."

After school I asked Julie if she wanted to go with me on the following Friday to visit Billy's school's carnival. She hesitated, then nodded slowly. A slight smile crept across her features. "Yeah, okay," she said. She sounded surprised that I'd invited her.

When I arrived on the Friday evening to pick Julie up, she came out of the house carrying a small child in one arm and a car seat in the other. She opened my rear door and set the car seat inside.

"This is my son, Jon-Paul," she said and fastened the little boy into the seat.

This shocked me. Six months together and I had had no idea Julie was a mother. I had assumed she was not married because she wore no wedding ring, but beyond noticing that, I'd had no idea if she was in a relationship. She'd never mentioned a husband or a boyfriend, so I'd assumed she didn't have one. But then she'd never mentioned Jon-Paul either. This lack of knowledge astonished me. How was it we knew so little about each other? When had we stopped talking? Because obviously we had and obviously we had quite some time ago.

The school carnival was in full flow by the time we arrived. I always enjoyed this sort of thing and regretted the years I worked in schools that did not have one, because I liked the planning involved in carnival stalls and the happy, relaxed atmosphere that such events evoked.

The stalls were set up in the corridors of the school. It was a relatively modern school, built in a U shape, all on one level. This necessitated going down one arm of the U and then doubling back and going down the other.

Jon-Paul loved all this excitement. He was three, a lively, chatty little boy with an angular face and dark, doelike brown eyes, who delighted in taking both our hands and trying to swing between us. He was too little for most of the stalls, except for the fishing one, which was run by the fifth grade. That involved casting a fishing line over a sheet whereby some fifth-grader on the other side tied on a small gift to be reeled in. Jon-Paul wanted to do this game about fifty times.

It took us a while to find the AP class's stall. When we did, we found Jesse there too. Billy had him helping set the eggshells back into the sand. Jesse's tics were rather bad. He grimaced and jerked, but he was clearly enjoying being included in the running of the stall. There were four other children from the AP class helping too, plus Carol Sprang.

She greeted us cheerfully.

"I see you've acquired another of mine," I said and tipped my head in Jesse's direction.

Carol nodded. "Billy says, 'You can't leave out my friend,' and, well, when Billy says something, we tend to pay attention. Don't we, Bill?" She rumpled his hair.

"Yup," Billy confirmed in a pleased tone. He reached over and grabbed my arm. "Here, take a chance. Me and Jesse set this one up. Take a chance. You can do it for free. I gave Mrs. Sprang a dollar so that all my friends could have a go."

"That's wonderfully generous of you, Billy," I said, "but I'm happy to pay." I held out a quarter.

"No, I *want* you to do it for free." He smiled up at me. "'Cause this is my class here too. And I want you to have a good time visiting. On me."

"Well, thank you." I reached over and chose one of the eggs in the sand.

Billy pulled it up to reveal it as just an eggshell. "Whoops, you lose. But you don't really lose, 'cause here's a candy bar. What kind do you like best? I'll give you a choice."

I chose a minature Mars bar.

We stayed a few minutes longer, buying two more tries for Jon-Paul, who left gleefully clutching a mini candy bar in each hand.

As we were leaving, I said to Julie, "You want to go get a drink somewhere?"

"I can't really take him in any place," she said, nodding toward Jon-Paul.

"No, I wasn't thinking alcoholic. Just coffee or something."

We ended up at a nearby McDonald's that had a play area for Jon-Paul. He was a very lively little character. Despite it's being almost 9 p.m., he was still full of energy and ran off at full speed toward the play equipment.

"My sister thinks he's hyperactive," Julie said, watching after him. "She says I ought to get him on Ritalin. Her son Luke is on Ritalin. He's six. She says it's helped a lot."

"What do you think?" I asked.

Julie was silent a long moment. Finally she gave a little shrug. "I dunno. I hate the idea of drugs. But he is a handful. I come home so tired some nights and he's just bursting with energy and I think, 'Oh God, please. . . .' But that'd be so totally the wrong reason to medicate him."

Jon-Paul came running back to the table. He clambered up over me and into the seat on my other side.

"Jon-Paul, what do we say when we do that?" Julie asked. "Excuse me. When we want to get by someone, we say 'Excuse me.' "

"Excuse me," Jon-Paul said to no one in particular. He reached over for his drink. Grabbing it by the rim, he tugged at it. The cup tipped over and Coke ran everywhere.

"Oops," Julie said in her usual calm voice. "Spilled drink. Let's wipe it up."

"I want that one," Jon-Paul cried. "Gimme that one."

He reached for Julie's. She handed it to him before getting up to get napkins to mop up his drink.

While Julie was up, Jon-Paul attempted to climb over me to get back out.

"Why don't you leave the drink here?" I suggested and lifted it up before he could grab it.

"No," he replied curtly. "Gimme!"

"See the sign there. It says 'No food. No drinks.' If you want to play, you need to leave your drink here," I said.

"No!" he said emphatically and made an angry noise.

Julie was back. She mopped up the Coke and handed him the wet napkins. "Here, go throw these away. All right? Please?"

This distracted him and he ran off with the napkins.

Julie flopped down into her seat and took what was left of her drink. "He does go like this all the time. Probably my sister's right. Probably I should get him checked."

I was thinking that perhaps clearer limits, less Coke and candy, and a scheduled bedtime might help, but I didn't say that. Instead, I asked, "What does his father think? Does he give you much input?"

Julie shook her head. "His father doesn't see him."

A pause followed, one of those kind usually referred to as "pregnant." Julie was watching Jon-Paul as he rushed around the play area.

"Truth is," she said in a soft voice, "I don't even know who his father is."

I looked over.

"When college was over, I left for a year of hiking around Europe. It was something I'd always wanted to do, and so I'd had all these summer jobs and stuff and saved money. I only got as far as France. I liked it there. I hung out a lot in Paris. Then I was in Lyon for a while with some friends. And then in Normandy. Then back in Paris. And then I was pregnant." She shrugged slightly. "Everyone else came home with pictures. I came home with Jon-Paul."

"Wow," I said. And it did amaze me. With her long hair in its demure, childlike style, her youthful looks, her quiet manner, Julie seemed the quintessential small-town girl.

"So that's how I ended up working at the school. I needed work, but it had to be part-time because my mom could watch Jon-Paul in the mornings, but not in the afternoons, and that was the only job I could find. It's better this year. He's at the day care center. So that's why I could work full-time."

"I see. Were you planning to go into teaching before this?" I asked.

"No. I certainly didn't plan any of this. Got my degree in history. But what good does a history degree do anybody?" Julie replied and smiled ruefully.

I looked up then, looked across the table at her. She met my eyes briefly and looked down.

"I guess I like it. I like the schedule anyway. But I never planned it." A pause. "I *planned* big things with my life. I planned on being a lawyer. Maybe politics. The state senate. My mom was a state representative years ago. Did you know that? Margaret Nicholson? Ever hear of her? I thought, 'Maybe I'll do that.' Only maybe the senate instead. That seemed classier. Be a lawyer and do some politics. I like politics a lot. I like issues. You know, fighting for them. But then I went to France. Went off to see the world and came back with my future." She nodded toward Jon-Paul, who was tearing around the play area. "And so that was the end of any plans I made."

I gave a slight shrug. "I never planned this either. I got my degree in biology. I was going to be a wildlife biologist. Study bears in Yellowstone Park. I love Yellowstone. I've spent some part of every year of my life there, and that's just what I wanted to keep doing."

Her eyes widened. "So how did you end up doing this?"

"I was poor. I took a job to see myself through college and it just happened to be in a program for special ed. kids. I walked through the door and that was it. I never left."

"How come?" Julie asked.

"The first day I arrived, the director said, 'There's this kid you can work with,' and he pointed out this little four-year-old girl who was hiding under the piano. And I said, 'What am I supposed to do?' And he said, 'You'll think of something.' And I was scared shitless. I mean, what did *I* – some eighteen-year-old biology major – know about doing this? And I said that. I said, 'Whatever am I supposed to do? What if I make a mistake?' And he said, 'At least try. Your mistakes will still be better than her life is right now, over under that piano. And nothing can change until someone tries.' And so that's what I did. And by the end of it, I was thinking, there is nothing – *nothing* – that I could enjoy doing more than this."

"You're lucky," Julie said. "Most of us don't live such a charmed life."

Chapter Twenty-five

The following Monday, Venus again did not turn up for school. This angered me. When I hung out the attendance slip, I underlined Venus's name and wrote "AGAIN!" in big red letters, hoping it would spur someone in the office into checking on what was going on. However, with the other children there, at that point I was unable to look into the matter myself.

After morning recess I was settling the boys with their folders to do math. It was about 10:40 and I was with Zane, doing counting, when there was a heavy knock at my door. I rose and went over.

Wanda stood in the hallway. She was totally inappropriately dressed. Even though we had reached mid-March, the temperature remained below freezing and there was still snow on the ground. Wanda, however, wore what looked like an old-fashioned housedress – the sort made of printed cotton that snapped up the front – and a cardigan. No coat, no hat, no gloves. And on her feet she was wearing pink fluffy slippers. This, however, was nothing compared to how Venus was dressed. Venus did have a coat on. However, underneath it she wore a red polyester football shirt about three sizes too big and what looked to be the flannel bottoms of a pair of boys pajamas. That was all. She wore overshoes on her feet.

"Her come to school," Wanda said. "Beautiful child come today."

"Yes, you've brought her. Thank you, Wanda. But it's late this morning."

Wanda looked at me blankly.

"Did you oversleep?"

"Beautiful child come to school," Wanda replied.

"Where are your proper clothes, Wanda?"

A baffled expression crossed her face. She looked down at herself.

"Where are your gloves?"

Wanda looked at her hands. "No gloves."

"No, I see no gloves. Remember I gave you gloves last time you were here? Where are they?"

"No gloves."

Giving up, I sighed. "Okay, thank you for bringing Venus. Good-bye now." I closed the door gently on Wanda, who was still standing in the hallway. Putting a hand on Venus's back, I guided her over to the little area beyond my desk where the hooks were for outer clothes.

"Here, let's take your coat off."

Venus stood, unresponsive.

"Can you help me? Hold out your arm, please."

She did nothing.

I was cursing to myself as I lifted her arm to remove her coat. This is what always happened. I'd make a little progress with her, then she'd be absent and lose it all. This was a hopeless situation.

I knelt down. "Let's take off your overshoes."

Because Venus was in her totally unresponsive mode, this meant I had to lift her leg myself and pull off the boot, but when I did, it came off easily. That's because there was no shoe inside. There wasn't even a sock. She was barefoot inside the plastic overshoes.

"Oh dear, look at this," I said. "You left the house without your shoes on."

I looked up at her, shabbily dressed in the oversize shirt and flimsy flannel bottoms, and now, no shoes.

"What happened? Did Wanda put out your clothes?"

It occurred to me to wonder for the first time how she got ready for school in the morning. I had yet to discern if she was as unresponsive at home as she was at school. There seemed no reason to think otherwise. If so, she'd have to be dressed because she wouldn't do it for herself. Most days she came with reasonably appropriate clothing, so either she *was* doing it herself or someone was laying the clothes out for Wanda. Or maybe Teri dressed her. Whatever, the system had failed this morning.

"I think you're going to have to leave your boots on," I said. "It's too cold to go barefoot in the classroom."

Venus watched me as I spoke. Her eyes weren't vacant. It had actually been quite a while since she'd given me the absolutely vacant stare. Now, even when she was totally unresponsive, she still gave the impression of someone being home in there behind her eyes. At home. Just not answering the door.

Lunch was a familiar round of conversations with Bob after I told him about how Venus had arrived an hour and a half late and dressed inappropriately. What was the status with Social Services? Was the truant officer following up on these absences? What was happening with Venus's older brothers and sisters? Were they absent as much as she was? What could be done for Wanda, who seemed to be simply wandering around miserably?

I was full of angry frustration. I told him that here it was March, almost April, and not only had we made very slow progress with Venus, I had not even managed to determine what her problem was. Despite having visited the home, despite having talked to Teri, I didn't even know yet if Venus was as consistently unresponsive at home as at school. *After all this time.* No reliable test data had been acquired. Teri's answers had always been vague and disorganized, never giving useful information. I had no idea of her academic abilities, no understanding of the source of her problems, *nothing*, really. How was it I could see this child day in and day out and still know so little? How was it we could have a child registered in the school and targeted by Social Services and goodness knows how many other government bodies and we still never accomplished anything? Something *had* to be done for this girl.

Bob was as frustrated as I was. He said this was an instance of bureaucracy tying itself in knots. He told me how he'd been onto Social Services again about Venus. The social worker told him she'd been out to their place about something else. She hadn't seen Venus but she had talked to Teri and she brought up Venus and her irregular schooling. That was about as close as we were probably going to get with Social Services, Bob muttered.

Bob said at the end of the day, this was a "poverty problem." He said he knew this was difficult for us to deal with, but sadly about as much was being done as could be done in the circumstances. Which was probably true. Other than the bothersome truancy problem, there was no concrete evidence of law breaking. Just careless or inept parenting. And a lot of stuff that "shouldn't" happen. But in the real world it did because society had yet to come up with effective, civilized ways of dealing with people who were overstretched by too many children and too little money, of dealing with the subculture surrounding many of them, which was so misunderstood by the middle classes, of dealing with the complex machinations of the modern family, which often contained related and unrelated combinations, including adults who sometimes had little interest in providing a stable home for children who were not theirs. When Bob said it, I knew his term "poverty problem" was not derisive, either of Venus and her family or of the local Social Services. It was just a statement of the facts. Our town, largely built on the steel industry of the nineteenth century, had been in decline for decades as steel prices fell and contracts had gone elsewhere. Unemployment ran almost three times the national average. The downtown area was full of vacant buildings. Across the railroad tracks were empty, crumbling factories. Venus and her family were not exceptions in our community and certainly not in our school, which drew largely from the poorer part of town. These were things one just couldn't think about too closely; otherwise it was a temptation to give up before one ever got started.

When I came downstairs after my lunch, there was Venus, waiting for me by the door. I opened it and let her in. She came willingly, clomping along in her shoeless galoshes. With the black humor one tends to develop in circumstances like these, I thought, At least I don't need to worry about her attacking anyone today. If she tried, the boots would trip her up and she'd fall flat on her face.

Upstairs, I took one of the She-Ra tapes out of the file drawer and held it out to her.

Venus had stopped just inside the door. She looked at me and at the tape in my hand.

"Do you want to put it in the VCR?" I asked.

She didn't move.

"Come here."

She didn't move.

I crossed over to her. Kneeling down, I put my hand on her arm. "What's the matter?"

She regarded me.

I reached up to touch her face. There was a faint movement from her, a very slight pulling back, but she did let me touch her. "My feeling is that something is wrong. Can you tell me what's the matter?"

Unexpectedly, tears welled up in her eyes and they were down over her cheeks before I even realized what was happening.

"Come here, lovey. What's wrong?" I pulled her against me.

With that, she let out an enormous, noisy sob.

"Hey, hey, hey, poor you," I said. I sat down on the floor right there by the door. Pulling her onto my lap, I wrapped my arms around her.

Venus cried in loud, inelegant sobs.

This was the first time I had seen her cry thus. Previously she'd only cried angrily in response to being thwarted in the middle of one of her explosions.

"What's wrong, sweetheart?" I put my hand on her forehead. "Are you not feeling well?"

She wouldn't answer me. She just sobbed.

Then the bell rang. We were still on the floor by the door. The sound of children pounding up the stairs began to fill the hallways. Venus tensed. She pulled away from my arms. Although I had the box of tissues down with us, she rubbed her forearm across her face, quickly mopping up her eyes and nose. And she closed back up. It was quite amazing to see, because it was an actual phenomenon, like a time-elapse film of a flower closing. The tears vanished. Her eyes shaded. By the time the boys burst through the door, she looked as if nothing had happened.

After school Bob stopped by my room. I was on my own, as Julie had had to rearrange her schedule that week to accommodate a day care problem with Jon-Paul and had thus left right after the bell.

I assumed he was coming in to talk to me about Venus. One of the plans we'd come up with over the lunch hour had been to try and pull together some kind of coordinating conference with Social Services, the police, and everyone else who was involved with the family to see if we could get some agreement not only about how to proceed, but also about how to communicate better with one another.

Sitting at the middle table, I was grading work and preparing the children's folders for the next day, so I shoved out the chair across from me with my foot and invited him to sit down.

"About Venus ... ," he started.

I looked up.

"Well, not about Venus. This isn't a continuation of what we were talking about at lunch," he said and sat down.

"There's another matter with Venus." He paused. "I've had word about there being a … well, sort of … a racial concern."

My eyes went wide.

"I hate to bring this up with you, Torey, but I'm afraid I need to. I need to be clear on this. What's the scoop about your using racially inappropriate material with Venus? Is this the cartoons? Those videos?"

"Julie?" I asked back.

Bob paused. Then slowly he nodded.

"She's been bearing tales to you?"

"Not 'bearing tales.' "

"No, it *is* bearing tales. And quite frankly, Bob, that's what I consider inappropriate."

"She says she has talked to you about it, so she wasn't coming to me without having spoken to you first."

"Well, yes. She did speak to me but I thought we were over it. She's reading into things what isn't there," I said. "It's more a difference in style than anything else."

"Fine line here, Torey. Because while I don't dispute that you're a good teacher, I must say, your 'style' is very much your own. And I've been aware of this. It isn't simply a matter of Julie bearing tales. I've been aware of it on my own."

I regarded him. "Such as?"

"Let's take your classroom singing, for example. Now, I think what you've done is really cool in a way. I mean, it is like one of those stories out of *Reader's Digest* or something. A bunch of tough little boys who have been tamed by music. A behaviorally disordered class that works like an operetta. I mean, that's cool. It *sounds* cool. But out in the real world, how much of it is going to transfer? Are they actually learning to *control* their behavior? Do I need to give all my other teachers singing lessons? Or more to the point, inhibition lessons, so that they can happily burst into song anytime they need to interact with one of your students? Because that's the ultimate goal here – to get these children out of your class and into theirs. You've hit on a very creative way of gaining control in your classroom, but is it a way that will allow these children to rejoin regular education?"

If I was honest, such questions had never even crossed my mind once. I was surprised and, indeed, a little hurt that Bob should consider this innocent activity unsuitable. It had never occurred to me that our singing would be thought of as anything other than positive.

"And now I'm hearing that you are using some toy-company cartoon character as practically your whole way of interacting with Venus. She's spending her time at school – a sizable chunk of her time at school – indulging in a fantasy world that is both educationally and culturally questionable."

"Oh geez," I said angrily. "This is *Julie*, saying this. Doing this."

"No, no, don't go off. Yes, it is Julie saying this, but it's me too, Torey. I'm the one in charge here. I'm the one who has to meet the parents and the school administrators and the people raising the mill levies. I'm the one who has to justify what's happening in my school building. And so *I've* been watching you too. I know about the cartoon videos and all that."

"Because I haven't tried to hide them. Of course, you know. Because I don't think I'm doing anything wrong."

"But is it appropriate?" Bob asked.

"It is, if it helps her talk. It is, if it brings her out of her shell. Bob, you know how this works. *Geez*, you taught me how to be this way. *You* taught me to think laterally to help a child. So how can you question it now? This is just a means to an end. Venus showed an initial interest in this cartoon, so I just picked up on it. I needed a hook. And this one seemed as good as anything. I didn't think, 'Let's find the whitest, flimsiest charactered creation Hollywood has ever come up with and use it to subvert this child's mind.' I just took what was there and worked with it for my own purposes."

"This is a fine line, Torey."

"It's a means to an end."

"And that still makes it a fine line. I'm not sure I *am* comfortable with you reading comics and watching cartoons with this girl, because you *are* a teacher and this *is* a school and there are hundreds of rounded, well-portrayed, characters full of vigor and integrity in the books in your classroom. Somewhere, somehow, we have to draw the line on what makes appropriate role models for children, and as educators, we have the responsibility to elevate that when we can.

"I'm even more concerned to hear the term 'culturally inappropriate' rear its head in regards to role models. This is a serious issue, Torey. We are in a racially mixed school here and I've worked many long years to meet the needs of my students equally, whatever their background. I don't want anyone leveling accusations at us on this account."

"Race has nothing to do with this," I said. "It doesn't now. It never did. The whole thing was just a hook. Honest. Venus showed an interest in a She-Ra comic I'd brought into the classroom, so I leapt on it. Period. It went no deeper than that. For the first few months this girl was here, *nothing* got a reaction out of her. So I simply thought here's something that interests her. Let's build on that. Let's use the positive characteristics shown and help her see them in herself. It never even crossed my mind that because her skin color was different from She-Ra's, I might be being racist. And it still doesn't make sense to me. I'm working with the *kid*. Not her skin."

"No, I know," Bob replied. "And I know you didn't have that intention. But this is why I'm bringing it up. It is a complex issue and we're often blind to how these things can be perceived. And as I've said already, this is a fine line."

"But it shouldn't be," I said. "We shouldn't come to the place where we are so sensitive to the possibility of offending each other that we therefore fail to help each other. It's gone too far when that happens. Venus is important to me. Her well-being is important to me. She *matters*. And finally ... *finally* I've got something that allows me to start relating to this kid. And now you want to hog-tie me with political correctness?"

"No, I just want to raise your awareness. I'm not saying stop, Torey. For the time being, carry on. I'm just saying, be *aware* of what you're doing. Start thinking of alternatives. If you can, switch. We're better people for being aware."

I lowered my head.

Silence then.

I looked over. "You do know what the real problem is here, don't you?"

"What's that?"

"Julie."

Bob nodded.

"I don't know why," I said. "I don't know what went wrong. But we're just on different planets. Everything between us just seems … slightly out of kilter. We're just not a match made in heaven."

"No, I've sussed that," he replied.

Silence again.

"She can't be enjoying it any more than I am," I said.

He nodded.

There was a pause.

"Any chance of her transferring?" I ventured. "Of giving her a different placement?"

"It's gotten that bad?" Bob asked.

Until that moment, I hadn't appreciated that it had. Throughout the year, I'd tried very hard not to think about

Julie and me, about why we didn't work together. There wasn't really anything wrong with Julie. She wasn't a terrible person. She didn't have a horrible personality. And while her methods were different from mine, they were not glaringly bad. Inept and inappropriate sometimes, but not bad. And no doubt she thought the same of some of my methods.

I didn't like admitting that I was not able to adapt to her in the classroom. I liked to think of myself as a flexible, easy-going person; I liked to believe I had enough charisma that sooner or later I could win anyone around to liking me, to liking my way of doing things. To acknowledge that Julie and I were not working out was also to acknowledge that these things weren't really true.

"Has she said anything to you?" I asked, because it would have been easier if Julie were also uncomfortable enough with the situation to have spoken to Bob about it. Then I wouldn't feel like it was just me, unable to cope.

"Well, not specifically on that. But she's mentioned all these little disagreements often enough to me that I'd gathered things weren't going well for you."

I looked over. "So, any chance … ?"

"Of a different placement? I don't know. I'd have to look around. And we'd have to coordinate it with Casey Muldrow, because she's still working with him in the mornings, of course. Plus, it's whether she wants to do it or not. I couldn't make her, because quite frankly, Torey, she hasn't done anything wrong. And do remember this too – even if she would want to move, there's also the question of whether there'd be another aide to come in and take her place. The alternative might be just you alone for the rest of the year."

"I see. So, basically, no choices except bad choices," I said.

"Or, as my psychology professor used to call these things," Bob replied, "only inelegant solutions."

Chapter Twenty-six

The next morning Venus wasn't there. I didn't wait this time to discuss it with Bob or anyone else. When lunchtime arrived, I piled into my car and drove over to her home.

When I arrived, there were two kids lounging on the wooden steps that served as a small porch at the door of the trailer. One was Venus's sixteen-year-old sister and the other I didn't recognize. They were leaning back against the wall of the trailer and smoking cigarettes.

"Hi, I'm Venus's teacher. Is your mom here?"

"Uh-uh," the sister replied. She took a long, slow drag on the cigarette and all the while looked me up and down in a lazy sort of fashion.

"Where is she?" I asked.

"Out, I guess. I dunno. But she ain't here."

"Can I see Venus?"

"You got to talk to my mom's boyfriend," she replied. "He's baby-sitting."

"Okay. So, where's he?" I asked.

"*Danny*!" she shouted with such sudden loudness that I stepped back in surprise.

A few moments later Danny appeared in the doorway, but he didn't open the screen door. His eyes were heavy-lidded, as if he'd been asleep. Or maybe he was just hung over. It was hard to tell.

"Yeah?" he said, as if he'd never laid eyes on me before.

"I've come about Venus. I'm her teacher. She isn't in school today. She's supposed to be in school."

"We been told she's going on homebound again. We been told not to send her to school," he replied.

Startled, I peered at him through the screen door. "No one's told me anything about that."

"That's what Social Services said. Said she's going on homebound."

"Social Services wouldn't arrange something like that," I replied. "Not without consulting us. And I've heard nothing about this. Why would they put her on homebound anyway? We're not having any problems with her behavior."

"Said it cost too much."

"Homebound costs more than sending her to school does," I replied.

He shrugged. "Don't ask me. This is just what they said. Said all them aides there to watch her special cost too much money."

I couldn't believe this. Surely Social Services wouldn't arrange such a thing. Surely they couldn't without Bob's input. And surely Bob wouldn't do it without talking to me.

"Anyway, so we're not supposed to send her to school. A teacher's coming out," Danny said.

"This can't be right."

He shrugged. "Well, you'll just have to talk to them. But we're just doing what we're supposed to." And he backed away from the screen and shut the inner door in my face.

I was dumbstruck. All the way back to my car, all the way back to school, I was too overcome with surprise to be able to puzzle anything out. Why wouldn't Bob have told me, if this was a consideration? Indeed, it *couldn't* be a consideration, because he'd been just as annoyed about her late arrival the previous day as I had been. But maybe the reason she'd arrived so late and so disheveled was due to the fact that Wanda had mistakenly thought she should be at school and had gotten her ready herself. That might explain that. Perhaps this even explained Venus's unexpected tears, because she knew herself she wasn't coming back.

All the pieces were coming together, but I was still baffled. Could Social Services do this? For the most part, we had a pretty good relationship with the people from Social Services. A lot of the children in our school were on their rolls, and both Bob and I had had many dealings with them. A couple of the social workers were a little dim and all of them were horribly overworked and horribly weighed down by the usual red tape of government bureaucracy, but for the most part, they were reasonable. Why would they have done this out of the blue without telling us? Had communications broken down that much between us?

Unfortunately, by the time I got back to school, the bell was almost ready to ring, so I couldn't go talk to Bob. Instead, I went on up to the classroom. Julie was in there, straightening up the materials left out from the morning. It was the first time I'd seen her since Bob had come in for his little chat, and I found myself uncomfortable. Indeed, between her going to tell Bob about the things she disapproved of my doing and Danny's telling me that Venus was supposed to go on homebound, I felt a little paranoid. Maybe Bob *was* in on something to take Venus away. Maybe this was all some grand scheme everyone else knew about except me.

The afternoon was awful. I felt uneasy with Julie in the room. I felt concerned Bob knew things he hadn't told me. I felt worried about Venus and her whole situation.

Billy burst spontaneously into song as we were standing around, waiting for the recess bell to ring, and I felt too self-conscious to join in.

"What's the matter?" Billy said.

"Nothing," I said.

"You're not acting nice today," he said.

"I am acting nice. I'm acting just like I always do. You pay more attention to how you're acting."

"How come you're mad at me? I didn't do anything?" he asked.

"I'm not mad."

"You are mad. You've been mad all afternoon and no one's done *nothing*! You'd make *me* go sit in the quiet chair if I was in a bad mood all afternoon."

"Billy, everything is fine. You're reading things that aren't there," I said and hated myself for lying. And hated him for being Billy and having to comment on everything. The recess bell didn't ring a moment too soon.

After school, I went down to Bob's office. I told him what Danny had said about Venus going back on homebound.

Bob's eyes widened. "Homebound? No. Not that I know of."

"He said Social Services arranged it."

"They wouldn't do that. Not without talking to us, certainly. No, I don't know where he's gotten his information, but it's wrong."

"Social Services *couldn't* arrange something like that, could they?" I asked. "Without our input?"

"I can't imagine they'd want to. Did he tell you why?"

I shook my head.

"Something funny's going on," Bob said.

"He was very straightforward telling me. Seemed to know what he was talking about, because he referred to those extra aides that have been hired."

"Yes, but it isn't true."

"You're sure?" I asked.

"It can't be true, Torey. We'd have to know. Homebound is an education issue. Even if Social Services did want to do it, even if it was some kind of emergency, they'd talk to us before or at least at the same time as the parents."

"You're *sure*?" I asked again. "Because *he* certainly sounded sure. And the way the right hand never knows what the left hand's doing with us and Social Services and the police and ... you're absolutely certain?"

"Yeah, I am," Bob said. "And I don't like this guy. He's got more tales than Paul Bunyon."

Back in the room, I put my books and papers together. It had been an uncomfortable day and I didn't feel like staying at school to do my plans so, I decided to pack up and go home. It was only about four-fifteen.

As I was going to the parking lot, I saw Wanda at the far end of the playground. She was picking dandelions from the long grass that grew against the playground wall. She clutched them in a tight fist, like a five-year-old would.

I crossed over the grassy playing field to her.

"Hi, Wanda," I said.

She looked up.

"Where's Venus today?"

"Her come to school," Wanda replied cheerfully.

"No, actually, she didn't. Did you forget to bring her?"

"Her no come to school."

"That's right. She stayed home today," I said.

"Beautiful child."

"Yes, beautiful child. Beautiful child didn't come to school. Do you know why?" I asked.

"Beautiful child."

"Yes, that's right. She didn't come to school. Why, Wanda? Why didn't Venus come to school today?"

"Her come to school."

"No, she *didn't* come to school," I said, a little frustrated.

Wanda lifted up the fistful of flowers.

"Tomorrow, Wanda, *tomorrow* can you bring Venus to school? Will you try to remember that?" I asked.

"Tomorrow?" she asked quizzically.

"Yes. Tomorrow. When it is day again. Will you bring Venus to school?"

"Her come to school."

"That's right. She must come to school. Will you try to remember that? Please? For me? Will you try to bring her to school tomorrow?"

"Beautiful child," Wanda replied to no one in particular.

"Yes. Beautiful child."

Bringing the dandelions right up against her nose, she sniffed them deeply. They made her nose yellow.

"Please? Can you remember?"

But she didn't answer. She just turned and wandered off.

The next morning Venus arrived at school all by herself. Indeed, she was already at the school when I arrived. I saw her over by her wall, just leaning against it in the cool morning sun, and it occurred to me for the first time that she no longer sat on top of the wall. I hadn't seen her up there in several months.

I crossed over to where she was standing.

"Good morning. You're very early. Would you like to come into the classroom with me?"

She regarded me with dark, soulful eyes but did not speak.

"Here," I held out my hand to her.

No response.

I didn't take her hand. There were still thirty minutes before school started, so if she didn't want to come inside, she had that choice. I waited a moment longer and then I turned and headed for the building.

She followed me. Staying about ten paces behind, she came with me to the door.

I paused there and held it open. Without speaking, we went inside and up the stairs to the classroom.

"How are you this morning?" I asked as I took out the keys to unlock the classroom door. "I missed you yesterday."

She watched my face.

Inside the classroom, I put my things away. Venus took off her coat and hung it up. She was more appropriately dressed, although her clothes were wrinkled and shabby. This was not particularly unusual. She'd never come well dressed.

"Did you know I went to your house yesterday?" I asked. "I was looking for you."

She regarded me.

"Did you know that?"

She shook her head.

"Danny said you were going to be taught at home again. He told me that. He said you weren't coming to school again." I pulled out the chair of my desk and sat down.

Venus was watching me very, very closely as I spoke, and as I did, I saw tears welling in her eyes.

"Is something going wrong?" I asked.

She didn't respond.

"I'm beginning to have that feeling," I said. "I'm beginning to think something isn't right for you at home."

Her face dragged down into a grimace of tears and she began to cry.

"Here. Come here, sweetie." I reached out and pulled her up onto my lap.

Venus wept with the same heavy sobs as she had on the previous occasion.

"Can you tell me what's wrong? What's happening to you?"

She didn't answer.

I was starting to have a very bad feeling. If Danny had made all that up, *why?* What was going on here?

"It's important you talk to me, Venus," I said gently. "Remember the other day when we talked? That was good. That was helpful. It's important for you to tell me things because then I can help you."

No response.

"Can you tell me what's wrong?" I asked. "I can see you are unhappy. What's the matter?"

She just cried.

How could I get her to open up? I had to be very careful what kinds of questions I asked if she did not volunteer information, because if there was anything illegal going on I could prejudice the outcome by asking the wrong questions. Indeed, I knew personally of two instances where abusers had gone free because their victims had been asked leading questions by psychologists or the police.

"Sometimes things go wrong at home," I said quietly. "When that happens, it's very important to tell grown-ups you can trust. Sometimes there are very big problems and they are too much for you to fix by yourself. Sometimes the problems are with moms or dads. Or stepdads. Or mother's boyfriends. Sometimes there are problems with brothers or sisters. When that happens, the right thing to do is tell another grown-up. A safe grown-up. Like me. Or Mr. Christianson. So that we can help you solve it. So we can make it better again."

Venus wiped away her tears with the cuff of her shirt.

"It's okay to tell. Sometimes people say that you shouldn't tell, because something is a secret. They say you should keep secrets. But that's not true. The only kind of secrets that are right to keep are fun secrets. Surprise secrets. Like what you are giving someone for their birthday. But bad secrets shouldn't be kept. If someone tells you to keep something secret that's bad, you don't have to keep it."

Laying her head against my chest, Venus sat quietly.

"And sometimes people say you shouldn't tell, because if you do, they'll do something bad to you. They'll hurt you. Or they'll hurt someone you love. Or they'll take something away from you. Sometimes people even say they'll kill you, if you tell. But none of this is true. They are only saying that to scare you. *They* have done something bad and they are afraid someone will find out and punish them, so they try to scare you into keeping their secret. But this is wrong. You shouldn't have to do that. If someone says those things to you, you should always tell a safe grown-up who can help you."

Venus never said a word.

For what felt like the umpteen millionth time in the last few days, I went down to Bob's office.

"I see Venus is back," he said.

"I'm getting really uncomfortable about all this. Why would this guy tell us that about homebound, if it wasn't true?" I asked. "My gut instinct is that he's trying to cover something up."

"Probably. The question is: what?" Bob replied. "He's a sleazy character. I wouldn't trust him as far as I could throw him. So he's probably capable of being up to all sorts of things."

"No. I'm thinking specifically to do with Venus. I mean,

the law says, if there's the suspicion of child abuse, we need to report it. I think it's time to go official," I said.

"Venus has told you something?"

"Well, no ..." I explained her uncharacteristic tearful behavior. "That, in conjunction with her absences and her inappropriate clothing the other day and that Danny's strange excuses yesterday. I'm thinking something's happening to her that's making it so she *can't* come to school these days."

Bob was thoughtful. Finally he shook his head slowly. "I don't think that's enough to actually file a report, Torey. A hunch isn't enough. We need bruises or her saying something or ... something more concrete. About all I can do is alert Social Services to your suspicions. Again. Because I think they're probably waiting to nail this guy too."

"What about you?" I asked. "What's your take on this?"

Again, Bob was thoughtful. Moments drew out as he considered. "That you're probably right," he said quietly. He looked over. "That I wish I could save the world in the way you and I thought we were going to be able to back in the seventies. I wish it had turned out as easy to do as we'd believed it would be."

Chapter Twenty-seven

In the middle of all this drama over Venus, I was starting to make the usual end-of-year plans for the children. Billy, I was certain, was ready to be mainstreamed back into the regular classroom. We didn't think he was capable of handling the AP class on a full-time basis. While he was an intellectually gifted boy and identifying this exceptionality had gone a long ways toward helping him straighten himself out, Billy remained in need of considerable learning support. He still lagged behind his age mates in both reading and math, although he was starting to approach grade-level work in reading. And his behavior was still a little too ebullient for the average classroom, so it was important that he be in a program that maintained a fairly strict structure. We did want to keep him in the AP class part-time, as we felt this had made a real difference for

Billy. Unfortunately, all the regular classes at the school where the AP class was operated under an open-plan, learning-center system, which meant a fairly noisy, chaotic learning environment. Both Bob and I felt this was asking for trouble with Billy, who needed no help getting excited. So in the end we opted to keep Billy at our school, planning to place him in the regular fifth-grade class there and have him come into my room for resource work. In addition, he would continue to attend the AP class two afternoons a week with the hope that eventually it might be an appropriate full-time placement for him.

Jesse had also made very good progress during the year, and his aggressive behavior had improved dramatically. He was still inclined to "fly off the handle," as Billy always called it, but he was gaining an increasing ability to pace himself, to understand what sorts of things triggered his outbursts, and to know how to withdraw gracefully from a situation until he was back in control. Indeed, Jesse had begun taking pride in his newfound self-control and often pointed out to the rest of us when he had managed something difficult.

The tics caused by his Tourette's syndrome still gave Jesse a big challenge in terms of returning to a regular classroom. They varied in intensity, and sometimes he went through spells where they were not a big disruption. However, they tended to frequently worsen dramatically, especially when he was feeling stressed or unwell. His barking in particular could become almost nonstop on these occasions.

Through no fault of his own, this made him a noisy, distracting student. I was concerned that he might be bullied or, worse, be goaded back into his old acting-out behavior if he returned to regular education. His worst problem, however, remained his academics. He had made steady progress in both reading and math but still lagged more than a grade level behind his peers in both. I felt that he would do better in a more protected environment for another year, so in the end we decided to keep him at our school as well. He was to go into the regular fourth grade for half of each morning and afternoon and spend the rest of the time in the resource room with me. We hoped eventually to get him back full-time into the regular classroom, but this seemed the safest route for the time being.

This left me with the twins. For them, there would not be a less restrictive alternative. Both boys continued to be highly challenging children in an educational setting. Neither could sit still any length of time; neither could concentrate for more than a few minutes; neither seemed to retain much of what they were taught from day to day. They had mastered the tightly structured traffic light system, but it had to be applied with unerring consistency to keep them at it. The slightest deviation, such as a party where I forgot to monitor behavior with the traffic lights, and they would both lose the plot. We'd have to start all over with learning the rules of it the next day, as if it were something completely new to them.

I liked Shane and Zane. Indeed, they had moments of

being truly charming little boys, as they were both affectionate and eager to please. There was nothing particularly malicious in their misbehavior. They just could not keep their focus from minute to minute, so they required constant monitoring to keep them on-task and achieving.

Consequently, it was deemed unrealistic to try any kind of mainstreaming with either twin. Their parents were pleased with their current progress in the resource room, as were we. So we decided to keep them right where they were.

And Venus?

Bob and I didn't even discuss her future. We were having too much trouble as it was with her present.

Then the weather turned. Down out of the north came a massive cold front. The temperatures, which had been on their seasonal climb upward into the fifties and sixties, suddenly plummeted toward zero Fahrenheit. Snow began to fall, weighing down the newly opened daffodils. And it fell and it fell until the daffodils disappeared altogether. We were paralyzed under almost two feet of the stuff. Everything came to a standstill.

The storm occurred on a Thursday. School was canceled for Friday because no one could move. I spent a relaxing day home by the fire, watching an old movie on TV, my enjoyment dampened only by the fact that Friday was normally my shopping day and I had almost no food in the house. So I had to make do with a supper of casseroled butter beans and an endive salad.

Saturday was spent digging out. Sunday, the weather turned nasty again. We still had almost all the snow, although the temperature had risen to near freezing, so it had gone soft. On Sunday came a second storm, only this time it didn't go so cold. Instead of snow, the precipitation came as freezing rain and quickly turned to ice. Within hours, everything was glazed.

I'd never seen anything like it. The snowdrifts outside my door were like crème brûlée – if you tapped the hard surface, it cracked into shards to reveal the soft snow underneath. But I was unable to explore any farther than the door, because ice covered everything. It had glazed the shoveled sidewalks and plowed streets quite thickly, making it almost impossible to keep one's footing. Driving too was treacherous. The town went eerily silent as everything came to a standstill for the second time in three days.

And then the gunfirelike banging started. The weight of ice clinging to the power lines started to bring them down all over town, and the noise came from arcing transformers. Before nightfall I'd lost my electricity, as had many other neighborhoods.

So school was canceled again for Monday. And even though a thaw had set in by Monday afternoon, it was canceled on Tuesday. Electricity still had not been restored to many parts of town, and driving remained a dangerous prospect on the slippery roads.

Not until Wednesday did we venture in again, and even then, there were many absences. Julie didn't make it to school that day. And neither did Venus, although this came as no particular surprise. Almost without exception, she missed the first day back from any kind of break, planned or unplanned.

Billy was his usual enthusiastic self, bouncy as Tigger. "Guess what we did, Teacher! Guess! We went sledding, only we made our *own* sleds. 'Cause we didn't have enough. Not enough for my brothers and me and the kids next door. So we made 'em. Out of cardboard. You just cut up cardboard into squares and you know what? Works good as a store-bought sled. It does. I'm telling you that for real."

"Billy, it's not gonna be as good as a store-bought sled," Jesse muttered. "How could it be as good as a store-bought sled? Otherwise why would people go pay money for something they could get just as good for free?"

The twins seemed to have suffered from their confinement. They were everywhere. Jumping up over the chairs and playing tag across the tables. I tried to snag them and get them to settle down.

"Well, it is as good," Billy remarked. "Because I had just as good a time. If we'd had just our sled, we would have had to tooken turns and that would mean, like, about ten kids and one sled. But we made each our own with the cardboard, so that way we could all sled all the time. And it was *fun*."

"Shut up," Jesse said and hunched forward in his chair.

"Yeah, well, I'm right."

"You dickhead," Jesse snarled. "You're just boasting.

You're just a big boaster all the time. You think you know everything."

"Jesse," I said.

"Well, tell *him*. He's the one who's always spouting off."

"Billy, take your chair," I said.

Billy couldn't resist this slip on my part. He grabbed his chair and spun it up over his head. "Take it? Take it where?" he chirped.

I grabbed the traffic disks and waved them menacingly. This was too late for Jesse, however. He lunged out of his chair and punched Billy. Not hard, probably not so much because he hadn't meant it to be hard but because he came at an angle and it glanced off Billy's shoulder. This was enough, however, to cause Billy to lose his balance and fall over and for the chair to come crashing down on top of him. And enough, for some reason, for Shane to feel he should join the fray. He bolted over the adjacent table and kicked Billy in the leg.

"*Hey!*" I cried. "Hey, hey, *hey*! What's gotten into you today?" I jerked Shane off and plopped him firmly into the nearest quiet chair. "What's all this fighting? We haven't had fighting like this in ages. Jesse, get over in that quiet chair."

Billy was howling, although I couldn't tell if it was from pain, surprise, or hurt pride. I put my arms around him and gave him a tight hug.

"That was kind of silly, wasn't it, spinning that chair like that."

"It wasn't my fault," he sobbed rather too dramatically. "*He* hit me. I wouldn't have dropped it, if he hadn't hit me. It's *his* fault. He could have killed me. He could have made that chair fall right on my head and killed me."

"Well, thank goodness that horrible scenario didn't happen, huh? Are you okay?"

"Noooo. I hurt my elbow."

"Oh, poor you," I said and rubbed Billy's elbow. It was the wrong one. He held the other up and I rubbed that. "Now, sit down in your chair. And stay there. You've got work to do."

I looked over at the others.

Zane was sitting in his chair. "I'm being *good*," he said cheerfully.

"Well, thank goodness someone is. Have you got your folder? Can you get started?" I asked.

I looked over at the other two in their quiet chairs. "Okay, guys. If you can keep yourselves together, come back to your tables and get started."

Shane, who was still a little flighty, bounded back to his seat. Jesse shuffled to his table and took out his chair.

I came over and knelt down beside him. "You seem to be having a hard day. Did something happen before you came to school?"

"No."

"You seem like you aren't in a good mood."

His tics confirmed his stress. His head twitched and twitched.

"This is like the old days with you and Billy and everyone fighting all the time. But that hasn't happened in a long time. Everyone's pretty good about staying in control now. So, when I see you so angry, it makes me think there must be a reason."

"No."

I waited quietly beside his chair.

"I had to stay in the *whole* time," he muttered.

"You mean while the storms were on?" I asked.

He nodded. "My grandma wouldn't let me go out. She said it was too dangerous."

"That must have been upsetting. Especially if you saw other children having fun," I said.

Jesse nodded. "I couldn't go out at *all*. She said, 'Maybe you'll get a tic and fall down on the ice,' and I said, 'I won't,' but she said, 'This boy in Illinois slipped on the ice and hit his head and he died.' She said it happened when he was walking to his grandmother's. Like *that* made a difference. Like, just because I've got a grandmother and he got a grandmother, the same thing is going to happen to me. But I couldn't make her see that. I had to stay in *the whole time*."

"You must have felt very fed up," I said.

"I *was*."

"And you must have felt angry when you heard what a good time Billy had. Is that maybe what happened this morning?" I asked.

Jesse shrugged.

"Gosh, I'm sorry when you tell us that," Billy said.

"Gosh, that sucks. The *whole* time? Gosh, that sucks big time, Jesse. No wonder you were so mad. I'd be mad too. Probably I'd punch a hole in the wall, I was so mad."

"God, Billy, there you go bragging again. Everything you say is a brag, you know that?" Jesse retorted.

Standing up, I put a hand on his shoulder. "I don't think he's bragging, Jesse. He's being sympathetic. That means he's trying to share your feelings."

"Yeah. 'Cause I'm your friend. *Trying* to be your friend, if you don't keep punching me," Billy said.

"Well, you could have come over and got me. If you were really my friend, you would have done."

"I couldn't. We couldn't drive our car," Billy said.

"You could have talked to me on the telephone."

"You could have talked to *me* on the telephone. You could have told me what was happening and maybe my mom could have talked to your grandmother or something. It isn't just my fault."

There was a little pause.

"Anyway, I'm sorry when you tell us you got shut in," Billy said. "I was thinking of you, Jesse. Really I was. I wanted you to come over. We would have had fun."

After school I was sitting at one of the tables and doing my lesson plans for the next day when Bob stuck his head in through the door. When he saw I was there, he came on in and shut the door behind him. He crossed to the table, pulled out a chair, and sat down.

"Well, I've got some good news for you," he said, but there was a rather resigned note to his voice, as if it were good news with reservations.

"Yes?"

"You're getting a new aide."

My eyes went wide.

"I had a long conversation with Julie," Bob said. "It started out on Wednesday evening. We ran out of time that night and were going to continue it on Thursday, but then the storm came. But the gist of it was that she felt her place in the room had become untenable. She said she'd become very uncomfortable, that you were cold and distant all the time, that the two of you had lost whatever rapport you'd managed before this."

"I wasn't 'cold and distant,'" I replied.

"Well, it felt that way to her."

The awful thing was, I knew I hadn't been all that great on Wednesday. I was feeling self-conscious. She was probably right about the rapport being lost. But I felt defensive about being called "cold." Which probably meant it was true.

"Anyway, she's feeling more and more uncomfortable about the situation. So, she called me over the weekend. And I've been making some calls around to see if I could resolve the problem. And here's what I've come up with. Julie is going to transfer over to Washington Elementary for the rest of this year and take up a place in the preschool program for developmentally delayed. And you're going to get their aide. Rosa Gutierrez. I don't know a thing about her, other than she's worked for the district a long time, so she must be decent. She'll do Casey Muldrow in the mornings and be in here in the afternoons, same as Julie did."

I nodded.

A pause came between us.

"Look, I'm really sorry for this," I said, and I was. "I'm embarrassed we couldn't work this out between us. And I'm sorry for all the trouble this has caused you."

Bob nodded. "Well, it happens."

I nodded. I felt guilty, as if I'd somehow cheated my way out of a bad spot. And I did feel embarrassed, because it left me with the sense of being somehow socially inadequate. But I also felt very, very relieved.

Chapter Twenty-eight

I felt quite tired that evening when I came home from work. Due to the disruption to our routine that the storm had caused, the children had been rather unsettled and overexcited all day. It was also harder work without Julie there at all, because most of my resource students came in the afternoon. I'd needed to give up my break to lay out materials, so that I would have enough time with the children. As a consequence, I came home, kicked off my shoes, and opened a bottle of wine.

Stretched out in the recliner, I was about halfway through my second glass of wine while watching a rerun of *Star Trek: The Next Generation* when the phone rang. The first thing I did was look at the clock on the VCR underneath the TV. 6:43. Then I got up and answered it.

Bob. "I'm just ringing you to warn you that the police are going to be calling you," he said. His voice was tight.

"What's happened?" I asked in alarm. "What's wrong?"

"I can't say too much. I'm not supposed to, because they want to interview you. But it's over Venus. I just wanted you to know it's coming."

"What's happened?"

"They'll talk to you."

"Can't you even clue me in a little?"

"No. Just be prepared. It's nasty." And he hung up.

I looked at the half-drunk glass of wine still in my other hand. Normally I never drank other than with meals, so why I had done so that evening I didn't know. It had just sounded good to me. Now I regretted it mightily. I wasn't tipsy, but I'd taken it on an empty stomach, so I could feel it. Whatever they wanted out of me, I hoped it didn't involve driving. I put the wine down and went into the kitchen to find something to eat to ameliorate the effect.

I never seemed to have in the refrigerator the food I needed for the moment. I liked to blame this on my rather meager teacher's salary, but the truth was, I never shopped in a very organized fashion. Consequently, the only "quick" food I could find was a package of sliced pepperoni sausage and a can of pork and beans. I threw these together in a dish and popped it in the microwave just as the phone rang.

It was a police sergeant named Jorgensen. He said they were investigating allegations of child abuse involving

Venus Fox and would like to interview me. They were sending two officers to the house.

I ate my odd little supper and washed it down with the rest of the glass of wine, which didn't really go with sausage and beans, but what the heck. A rather shocky nervousness had come over me, the same sort one gets when coming unexpectedly across a traffic accident. I knew that if no one was telling me anything, it was done to avoid prejudicing my testimony. And this meant, I knew, that it was serious.

Two officers arrived shortly after seven-thirty in the evening. One was a tall, blond man named Millwall, who was about my age. The other was a female detective who looked to be in her late thirties. She was one of these slim, athletic-looking women, the type who run marathons for fun. Her name was Patterson, but she said I could call her Sam. "Short for Samantha," she said in a friendly sort of way, which seemed out of character with their otherwise official demeanor.

I suggested we sit down in the living room, but Sam said she needed to record this interview and it would probably work better if they could put the cassette recorder on a table. Consequently, we ended up sitting around the kitchen table, still cluttered with the work I'd brought home, dirty dishes, and the open wine bottle. Embarrassed, I shunted everything off onto the counter.

"We have Venus Fox in the hospital at the moment," Sam said. "She was taken in early this morning. Now, my understanding is that you had spoken to your principal only last week saying you suspected child abuse. Can you give me more details about what you said?"

"First," I interjected, "can you tell me? Is she okay?"

"She came in unconscious."

There is a real sensation behind that phrase "my blood turned to ice." Mine did just then. A horrible cold, sinking feeling went right through me. "What happened? Can you tell me that?"

"It appears to be hypothermia, but the hospital is still giving us the details."

Hypothermia? I was baffled.

"Anyway, Miss Hayden, I'd appreciate it if you could tell us more."

"Torey. Call me Torey," I said, because suddenly that seemed important to say to her. All sorts of ridiculously small things seemed important to me just then. I noticed the open bottle of wine I'd put over on the counter, for instance, and wondered if I should tell them I didn't normally drink. Because I didn't. But they wouldn't know that.

Sam nodded in a sympathetic manner. "It's difficult, isn't it? I know dealing with things like this are shocking. But if you could …"

I thought a long moment. Bracing my head with my hands, I tried to bring back to mind all the details of the last weeks that had made me say that to Bob. I was dismayed how, in the circumstances, my mind went blank. All the things that had seemed so important, so suspicious, so oddly out of character for Venus now evaporated. All I could think of were the minor discrepancies. Or maybe they were all "minor discrepancies" that had just accumulated.

"It was more just a feeling than anything else," I said. "I didn't see any bruises or anything like that. No evidence of physical abuse. She isn't very well cared for. And she tends to wear these long-sleeved shirt things and pants all the time, so it would have been hard to see. And Venus doesn't talk much. This is one of the reasons she's in my class. As I'm sure you're aware, I teach children with behavioral disorders. In Venus's case, she is in the class because she's very unresponsive and virtually mute. It's difficult to know what's going on with her because she's extremely withdrawn."

Sam nodded. "Yes, I've been on this case for some time now. We've been liaising with Social Services over this family and we're aware of the behavioral problems with Venus. And the lack of speech. Indeed, all this very difficult behavior. It's made it almost impossible to monitor anything that is going on with her."

"But she has been starting to respond," I said. "Since about February. The major problem for me has been her poor attendance. She misses two or three days a week routinely."

"And this has been all along?"

"Yes," I said. "She was out of my class for about eight weeks in the autumn, when she was placed on homebound – where the teacher goes to the child's home instead of the child coming to school, and that was a different teacher – but otherwise, yes, she's had this attendance problem all along. We've reported it to Social Services. We've had the district truant officer on the case. In fact, I think someone has even reported this to you."

Sam flipped back through the pages of her notebook. "We probably wouldn't be notified about something like school attendance," she replied.

"But I think you were," I said. "I know we reported it."

"Yes, but it would have stopped with your district truant officer, wouldn't it?" Sam asked.

"But my principal reported it beyond the district. I know he talked to Social Services about it because it was so bad, and I know they said they talked to you. They said an officer went out."

Sam was reading through notes taken earlier in her notebook. "Well, an officer's been sent out to that home a good number of times. Over all sorts of things. But I don't see anything noted in connection with the girl's absences."

"It *should* have been. We reported it."

"Yes, well, anyway. So, you were saying about this suspicion that you mentioned to your principal?"

I tried to explain what had made me go to Bob on that last occasion. I told Sam and Officer Millwall how Venus had cried, and this had been unusual for her. I mentioned her peculiar clothing on the one occasion. I tried to explain how, even though she was not communicative, there was something about her behavior that led me to think she was in distress, that something *was* wrong, but I had to admit it was largely based on just a sense I had rather than concrete evidence.

Sam really hooked into this idea that it was a "sense." She kept trying to pin me down on it. *What* specifically made me have this feeling this time? This sense that something was amiss with Venus?

"I don't know," I said. "Beyond what I've told you, beyond those two times when she cried and just acted funny, I don't know. Just a gut feeling."

"Intuition?" Officer Millwall interjected.

"Yes, I suppose you could call it intuition."

"We've got to be as precise as possible. As I'm sure you can appreciate," Sam replied, "intuition isn't going to get the perpetrator caught."

I nodded.

"I do know what you mean. I'm not trying to demean what you're saying, but this is a tricky one," Sam said. "We've got a kid who doesn't talk, who has serious behavior problems, who now can't tell us if she wanted to because she came in unconscious. So I'm not questioning whether you've got good intuition or not. I'm just saying if someone is responsible, I want to find out who and I want to make sure they never get the chance to do it again. So, as much precision as possible is very important."

We didn't talk much longer. There wasn't a lot more I could say at that point. I kept anecdotal records on the students for my own use, but these were in a notebook at school. I wasn't sure there was anything in there that would be helpful to the police, although I'd made quite a few notes on Venus and her behavior through the year. And Bob, of course, had all the evidence for her absences.

Sam and Officer Millwall rose, thanked me for my time and cooperation, and said that no doubt they'd be back in touch. I showed them to the door. We shook hands and they left.

I came away from that meeting shaken by the news of Venus's hospitalization and vaguely disgruntled. Her absences *had* been reported to the police. At least that's what I'd been led to believe. If not, who had been deceptive? Bob? Social Services? Or was it less deception than a depressingly common bureaucratic cock-up, where each party involved had passed the buck to the next party and no one ever bothered to check back and find out if things have been carried through? If the absences had been reported, then why did the person in charge of the case not know that?

Unable to get the events out of my mind, I phoned Bob.

We discussed the matter. He told me that from what he'd managed to piece together, Venus had been found unconscious at home and her mother had taken the girl to the hospital emergency room. Bob didn't seem to know any more than I did what was wrong with her. He too had been told it was hypothermia, but he said he didn't think hypothermia could keep you unconscious for a long period of time, not if you were warmed up again, which obviously you would be if you were in the hospital. I said I didn't know. I wasn't very well informed about the specifics of hypothermia beyond knowing that it happened when the body temperature dropped too low. We talked about hypothermia in general then, and Bob mentioned it was an odd sort of diagnosis for child abuse. I asked if there was any chance of going to see Venus in the hospital the next day. He didn't know.

That night I couldn't sleep.

I couldn't get Venus out of my mind. Abused. When had it started? How long had it been going on? I played back incident after incident with her in class, probing all the corners of the events to see if I could apply new meaning to them, now that I had hindsight. All I could come up with was the knowledge we'd failed her. That much was clear. Me, as much as anyone. Could I have seen this coming? I lay awake in the darkness, seeking the answer to that.

News travels fast. In the teachers' lounge the next day, all the talk was about Venus. Between her violent behavior on the playground and the fact that almost all the teachers at the school had had her siblings at one time or another, everyone felt the situation personally. The rumor machine geared up. One person heard they'd arrested Danny and Teri both and all the children had been taken into care. Another said, no, Wanda was still wandering around. Someone else said she'd heard Venus had stopped breathing and they'd had to resuscitate her and she was on a ventilator. Several people speculated about physical injuries. The fifth-grade teacher said he'd heard on the radio that there were twenty-two healed fractures. I said I didn't think this could be Venus's case. I was pretty sure there were reporting restrictions. The fifth-grade teacher said there wouldn't be two cases happening at the same time. We weren't in that violent a town.

The truth was, no one really knew. And none of us could find out. As the tension built up, the atmosphere in the teachers' lounge was sparky to a point of irritability.

I desperately wanted to keep all this from the children. At some point or another they would need to know something had happened to Venus, but until *we* knew, there seemed little value in sharing it with them. Moreover, this was distressing news, so it would be important to handle it appropriately. I didn't want them overhearing frightening gossip among the teachers or out on the playground, if at all possible.

In the end, it wasn't possible. Little Mr. Big Ears came in the form of Billy. Who else?

We had just come in from afternoon recess when he stopped by my desk, where I was putting away the whistle I used when we were playing games.

"What are people talking about?" he asked.

"What do you mean?"

"I'm hearing people talk. Like you guys. Like all the teachers. Like some of the big kids. What's happened?"

Jesse had wandered up. "What's happening about what?" he asked.

"What have you heard, Billy?" I asked him, because I thought this would give me a better handle on what to tell him.

Billy's forehead wrinkled. "Did somebody get killed?"

"No," I said.

"Was it Venus?" he asked, as if he had not heard my answer.

"No."

"Somebody said Venus got killed. They said she got run over by a car and both her legs got cut off."

"*No*," I said. "You're hearing gossip. That isn't true at all."

"That's what Devon said," he replied. "You know Devon? That kid who's in Mr. Jamieson's fifth grade? He's a friend of Venus's brother, Frenchie, and I thought that's what he said. I thought that's what I heard him say to this other kid when they were talking about it."

"No, that's not true at all."

"Is Venus dead?" Jesse asked, his voice softening with awe.

"No, Jesse. Come here. Let's sit down. We'll talk about it."

The conversation went right over the twins' head. Very quickly it became apparent that they did not have the comprehension to understand what Jesse, Billy, and I were talking about. They were curious when I said something had happened to Venus and she was in the hospital, but within moments of my telling them that, their attention was distracted onto something else and they grew restless. So I gave them puzzles to work on while Billy, Jesse, and I explored the matter more deeply.

I explained to the boys that I didn't know very much myself and that probably none of us did, including Venus's brother's friend, Devon.

"How come?" Jesse asked.

"Because no one has told us more," I said gently.

"How come?" he asked.

"Because … they haven't, that's all. Because none of us knows Venus's family personally and none of us works at the hospital and those are the usual ways of finding these things out."

"Yeah, but Devon knows Frenchie and so he knows them personally," Billy said.

"But what he's said is wrong."

"How do you know?"

"Because Mr. Christianson and I have talked with the police and they told us she is in the hospital. So I know what Devon says is not true. But beyond that, I don't know either," I said. "We have to wait until the hospital can give out information, and at the moment they can't."

"How come?" Jesse asked.

"Because at the moment it's private."

"Why?" Jesse asked.

I smiled at him. "Because at the moment they don't know what caused Venus's injuries and so they're looking into it and until they know more, they don't want to say more."

"Who's 'they'?" Billy asked. "Is it the police? Because Devon said Venus's brother said the police came to their house."

"Yes, the police went to their house."

"Why?" Jesse asked. "Did somebody break into her house?" His expression grew worried. "Did she get hurt by a burglar?"

"No, it wasn't a burglar to my knowledge," I said. "I don't think they're quite certain how Venus was hurt. And when someone gets hurt and people don't know quite how it happened, the police usually come to help find out."

"Somebody bad came to our house once," Jesse said, and I could hear the fear in his voice. "They hit my grandma on the head and stole her money and she had to go to the hospital. Now my grandma has got bars on her windows downstairs, because that's how they got in."

"We got a gun," Billy replied. "That's how we keep safe. If a burglar came to our house, we'd shoot him dead. Your grandma ought to get a gun."

"She says guns aren't good for people to have unless they're policemen or something. She says if we had a gun, more than likely we'd shoot one of us. That's what happens mostly to people who got guns."

"I don't think that's true," Billy said.

"My grandma says."

Billy shrugged.

There was a pause.

Billy turned his head and looked over toward the window.

A moment or two passed with his attention absorbed there. Jesse was twitching badly. His shoulders jerked up around his ears and his head twisted.

"I wonder what it would be like if someone in our class died," Billy said, still not turning from the window. "It'd feel weird."

"I don't want to think about it," Jesse replied.

"Kids aren't supposed to die," Billy said.

A pause.

"I didn't like her very well. She was stupid. First, she used to attack me all the time. Like, she just went psycho if you looked at her wrong," Billy said. "Then she was just weird. She never talked. She just sat there and stared at me. But not liking someone isn't the same as wanting them dead."

"Kids get dead for all sorts of reasons," Jesse added. "Lots of kids *do* die, you know. They get run over by cars. I knew this kid once who got hit by a car and he died. He was getting off the school bus. His brother was in my class when I was in kindergarten."

"Wow," Billy said, impressed.

Jesse gave a self-deprecating little shrug. "Well, I didn't actually *know* him. But I knew his brother."

"Wow. Weird."

"And some kids get shot by guns. Like my grandma says," Jesse said.

"And you can get drownded," Billy added. "I heard about kids getting drownded."

"Or you could get sick. Like cancer or something," Jesse said.

"Or electrocuted. I heard once on the TV where some kid got electrocuted on the railroad line. 'Cause he was playing where he shouldn't."

"There's lots of ways you can get dead," Jesse said.

"Wow. Weird."

Both boys were thoughtful for a long moment, and then Billy looked over at me. "What happens to you when you die?"

I smiled gently. "I wish I knew, Billy, but I don't."

"You should. You're a teacher," he replied. There wasn't the note of teasing in his voice I'd expected. He looked at me earnestly.

"Sadly, just because I'm a teacher doesn't mean I have the answers to everything. I don't. No one does," I replied.

"But you could look it up … ," he said, his tone rising toward the end of the phrase hopefully. "Isn't there someplace special where teachers can look stuff up?"

I smiled again. "No. Just the same places you use."

"There should be. Should be, like, this giant answer book. That's got all the answers in the world in it." He grinned.

"We go to heaven," Jesse said. "If you take Jesus for your savior."

"But you got to be good too."

"Yeah, that too," Jesse agreed.

"But I don't know about this heaven business," Billy said. "When my gerbil died, our priest said he wasn't going to go to heaven because he doesn't have a soul. Only things with souls get to go to heaven."

Jesse wrinkled his nose. "Oh, I don't think that's right. My dog got run over and *he's* gone to heaven. My grandma said."

"Maybe he's got a soul," Billy offered. "Dogs probably do."

"Gerbils probably do too," Jesse said. "I think everything's got a soul. Like, even rocks and stuff. It's just we don't know it. And because we don't know it, we don't think it's true."

"Yeah, you're probably right. A lot of stuff's that way," Billy said.

A pause.

Billy turned to me. "But you know what I think about? It's not being dead. I don't think I'd mind being dead, because probably it's just like being alive, only different. But what I wonder is what it's like to *die*. I wonder what it *feels* like. Do you think it's really scary? Because I always think it must be scary."

"Yeah, I'm scared to die," Jesse said.

"Yeah, me too," Billy agreed.

"Me too," I said. "But I think that's just nature's way of making sure we concentrate on staying alive. Because otherwise we might forget to take good care of ourselves. But I don't think dying probably feels scary. If it is something we all do, it must be a natural thing, like growing up is. So, I think that when the time comes to do it, we probably feel ready for it and so it isn't scary. For instance, when you are very little and you look at a bigger kid going to school, you think, 'That looks so scary. I'll have to leave Mom and go away from home all day. I'll never be able to do that.' But when you are old enough to go to school, you think, 'This is pretty interesting. I can't wait to go.' And you get to school and you see the big kids reading out of their schoolbooks and you think, 'That looks so hard. I'm scared I'll never be able to do that.' But when you get into fourth or fifth grade, you have the same books and you look at them and you think, 'This is pretty interesting.' That's because by the time you get there, you've grown up enough, and what seemed scary before, when you weren't ready, now seems just right. So, I think it must be just the same with dying. When it comes time to do it, I think we probably feel ready. I don't think it's so scary then."

A pleased smile crossed Billy's face. "Hey, I get that! Yeah, you're probably right."

Jesse was not so easily placated. "But what about little kids? What about when little kids die? They can't be ready yet."

A pause then.

I looked at him. "I'm not sure, Jesse."

"A lot of this stuff doesn't have answers really, does it?" Billy said.

"No," I replied.

Jesse shook his head in a weary sort of way. "It shouldn't happen to little kids," Jesse said. "Little kids shouldn't have to die."

"Yeah," Billy said. He sighed. "A lot of stuff shouldn't happen to little kids. A lot of stuff shouldn't happen, period."

Chapter Twenty-nine

The weekend came, and those two days had an odd time-warpish feel to them, as if we were trapped in some form of suspended animation. We all desperately wanted information about Venus, about how she was, about what had happened, and it was almost impossible to get anything reliable. The police had placed restrictions on discussing the case, which meant Social Services went mum. They wouldn't talk to Bob or me. Close as we were to the case, we remained outsiders.

I contemplated just turning up at the hospital and seeing if they would let me in, but, despite having a fairly strong personality, I didn't have all that bold of one. I was scared of being caught out, of not knowing what to say, of being chased off for being in the wrong place at the wrong time. I was put off by the thought that someone might perceive my interest as nosiness and my presence as interference. So while I wanted to, I didn't. I stayed home and waited by the phone, like everyone else.

The suspended animation feeling came from the fact that it was hard to get on with other things without being constantly drawn back to thinking about Venus, and this was a dead end. I had brought home the IEPs and other end-of-year materials I needed to work on in preparation for getting the children ready for their new program the next year, but I kept being drawn to Venus's. What should I do with hers?

I looked over her IEP – individual educational plan – which was the "prescription sheet" I needed to do for each child, laying out the next steps of learning necessary to reach various educational goals. The idea was that it gave some sort of accountability to the education process. Here was what the child needed to learn. Here was what I was going to teach. Here was how long we had to do it in. Looking over Venus's current IEP, it was wildly optimistic. "Venus can identify sounds associated with consonants." I hadn't even managed to get Venus to speak reliably. I didn't even know which sounds she could make, much less which ones she could identify. I was almost positive she hadn't a clue what consonants were.

Where was I with this kid? I don't think I'd ever had such an enigmatic child. The better part of a whole school year together, and I knew very little more about her than I had when she'd arrived. I clearly remembered that first day when I'd come down the long sidewalk from the parking lot and seen her on her wall, leaning back, her face into the sun. I remembered that sense of languorous mystery about her. I'd thought of old-time screen goddesses, because of the manner in which she was turned away from all of us beneath her on the ground, the way she was relaxed back and oblivious to the comings and goings below the wall, as if they were of no concern to her, as if they were not part of her real world. And I don't think they were. But what Venus's real world consisted of, I still didn't know.

Despite this wide gap, I didn't feel a sense of failure with Venus. I didn't feel frustration. While those feelings happened with some children – I knew I was getting nowhere or I was off base – with Venus I'd felt all right. Subtle as it was, I'd always had the sense that she and I were connecting. But ... it was not the stuff that could be written down on an IEP. What would I say? The goals I was setting: "Get her to walk across the room without urging," "Get her to take a videotape and put it into the VCR by herself" were increments that were too small for the IEP. And they weren't IEP stuff anyway. IEPs were for *education*. Reading, writing, and arithmetic. Many school districts had them computer generated and not personally written out at all, because despite the "individualized" label, the goals were not really individual at all. I stared at hers with all its formalities so carefully filled in. What was going to happen now?

To add to the general chaos of that period, I got a new girl in the class. Her name was Alice and she was eight, although she looked much younger because she was tiny as a kindergartener. She had long blonde hair pushed back with a headband à la Alice in Wonderland, whom she would have made a pretty good stand-in for, except that her hair ended in a tangle of loose curls that lent her a wild edge, and she had huge, dancing brown eyes. This gave an impishness to her that was heightened by her quick, lithe movements.

She had arrived in our town about two months before with her family. They had previously lived back east, and Alice had attended a private Montessori school, where education was dependent on reaching "developmental" stages and children progressed very much at their own pace. As a consequence, her academic skills lagged well behind what would be expected for her age. She'd been placed in a regular third-grade class in a school across town near where her family lived and given resource help, but it soon became apparent Alice had more than academic problems.

Truth was, Alice was very, very strange. There was no other way to put it. For one thing, she talked to her right hand. Stretching it out in front of her, she would focus intently on it and start talking to it, as if no one else were in the room. Her hand even had a name – Mimi – and she spoke to it rather the way younger children do with imaginary companions.

Alice also had the tendency to say the oddest things.

These were just off-the-wall utterances that seemed to have nothing to do with anything, but they were often almost poetic in their form. When she met me, for instance, her first words were, "No one cries. With tears. No one eats. With gulps. No one asks. With pleas."

I said, "You can sit here, Alice." And I put her at the table where Gwennie had been before.

Alice replied, "Any child when abandoned withdraws and waits."

"Do you want to hang your sweater in here?" I showed her the little side entrance where we kept our outerwear.

"They honed their buckles sharp as blades," she responded.

And yet Alice could talk normally at other times. She greeted the boys appropriately when they came in. She asked Billy where he bought his Adidas jacket. And she could do academic work. Indeed, while she might not have been up to the expected level of your average eight-year-old, she was considerably more able than Jesse and quickly did the worksheets I'd hastily reproduced from his book and put into a folder for her. Indeed, she could rival Billy in reading.

The morning went appallingly. Not in any big way, but rather in the all-too-familiar way of everyday schoolrooms. First Billy and Shane got into a knockdown drag-out fight while I was trying to get Alice started on some work. I don't know what it was over. Something to do with a pencil, but I never found out whose or why. I separated them and pushed them into quiet chairs.

Jesse's barking was particularly intrusive. I don't know whether he was stressed by Alice's arrival or whether he was just having a bad day, but he kept yelping.

"Why's that boy do that?" Alice asked.

"Jesse has Tourette's syndrome," I said and explained briefly that as a result sometimes he made sudden noises or body movements.

"He sounds like a dingo," she replied.

"She's calling names," Billy hollered.

"No, I'm not. He sounds like a dingo. That's not a name. It's an animal. And he *does* sound like a dingo."

"What's a dingo?" Zane asked.

"It's a dog. A wild dog in Australia," Alice explained. "And it sounds just like that kid. Ark! Ark! Just like that."

"Okay, I think that's enough discussion," I said.

"She's making fun of him," Billy said irritably. "Why are you letting her get away with it?"

"I'm not 'letting her get away with it,' Billy. Alice is new. She's learning the rules. And I'm just about as annoyed with you when you say 'him.' Jesse is right here. If you talk about people when they are present, use their names. Otherwise, it's rude. It makes you feel less than human to have someone talk about you in front of you that way."

"Well, shit, don't come over all bitchy with me," Billy said. "I didn't know that, did I?"

I pointed to the quiet chair. "That isn't the kind of language we use in here and it isn't the way you talk to your teacher."

"No," he said defiantly.

"*Yes*. Or you can sit in Mr. Christianson's office. Because in here we don't talk like that."

Angrily, Billy got up and stomped over to the quiet chair.

"Teacher, you can see that girl's panties," Shane cried.

I turned from Billy to look at Alice, whom I expected to have her dress up around her neck. Instead, she was deep in conversation with her hand. And sitting perfectly normally in her chair. Zane, on the other hand, was under his table, peering through the chair legs to see up Alice's skirt.

"Zane, get back in your chair."

"Mimi doesn't like that boy," Alice announced. "I don't either. I don't really like any of these boys."

"Could you keep your legs together when you're sitting, please?" I replied.

It didn't improve. Alice had one of her funny turns after morning recess. "One, two, three, four. Wrap in a package. Take it to the store," she said in response to my asking her to do a math paper.

Across the room, Jesse had lifted up our huge box of Legos. It was the size of an apple carton and full of zillions of little Legos, and he tipped it. Accidentally. I don't know if he twitched or if he simply misgauged the weight of it or what, but over it went and Legos spilled everywhere.

"Get a broom to clear it up. That'll work faster," I said.

"You're gonna throw it *away*?" Billy cried.

"No. He can sweep it up faster with a broom and pan.

But he's just going to put it back in the box that way. We're not throwing it away."

"Where's the broom?" Jesse asked.

"Who had it last?" I responded.

"Not me."

"Not me."

"Not me."

"Not me."

These responses came so fast, they were almost a chorus. This left only Alice. She went wide-eyed. "Well, not *me*," she said.

We couldn't find the broom, so Jesse was reduced to picking it all up by hand. Billy was desperate to help.

"No, stay in your seat."

Alice said, "I take red. The game is on."

"What game?" Billy asked, perplexed.

"God is good. He takes us to his bosom. He takes us to himself," she replied.

Billy's eyes went wide. "Man, you are *weird*." He shook his head. "I thought Psycho was weird, but, boy oh boy, you are really weird. You know that?"

"Billy." I fixed my eye on him. "Please stop calling Venus 'Psycho.' We've talked about that before. And please get back to work."

"Uh-oh, Teacher! Zane's got a nosebleed!"

I turned. That was an understatement. Blood gushed from Zane's nose and down his shirt. It was on his hands, on the table, on his pants.

"Here, come here, Zane," I said and went across the room to him. "Let's get you over the sink." I grabbed the tissue box.

"Eeuwwww!" Alice cried. "Blood! I'm gonna be sick. I'm gonna be sick."

"No, Alice, you're not going to be sick. Jesse? Could you leave the Legos a minute and come here to help Zane?"

"I *am* going to be sick," she said and started to gag. "Blood always makes me sick."

Abandoning Zane midbleed, I dashed for the trash can by the desk and shoved it at Alice. She promptly vomited into it.

"Eeuwwww!" Billy shrieked.

The only thing I could think to do was sing. The only song that came to mind wasn't too appropriate. "If you're happy and you know it, clap your hands!" I started. "If you're happy and you know it, clap your hands!" Which, of course, I couldn't do because I was holding a garbage can full of vomit. But the boys, bless them, quickly joined in. Even still-bleeding Zane.

Alice looked at us like *we* were nuts.

The afternoon saw another new arrival. Rosa Gutierrez. Middle-aged, definitely on the plump side, and with dark, curly hair pushed up onto the back of her head in a straggly bun held with a brightly colored scarf, Rosa entered the room like she'd always been there. She greeted me in a hearty manner and clapped Billy on the back when she saw him.

"Hey, you are a fine boy! How old are you?" she asked.

"Nine," he replied, a little taken aback. Which impressed me. Anybody who could leave Billy a little taken aback instantly had my respect.

"I'm new," Alice said. "I just came today."

"And she's already barfed," Billy added.

"Well, sweetie, I am new today too."

"Where's Julie?" Shane asked.

"Remember?" I said. "We talked about this the other day. Julie's going to be working at a different school. And Rosa is going to be in our classroom from now on."

Shane wrinkled his forehead. Obviously he didn't remember.

"How come?" Zane asked.

"Because that's what Mr. Christianson decided," I replied. "Now, let's make Rosa feel welcome. Because she's going to be with us every afternoon."

"Okay," Billy said and turned to her. "So, do you sing?"

Rosa proved to be just what we needed. She had been working in the school district for years, mainly with developmentally delayed classrooms, so she was experienced and comfortable with the children. She had a lively, no-nonsense personality and spoke her mind very easily but in a cheerful, good-humored way. And she did sing. A bit off-key and definitely too loudly, but that made her more part of the group than less.

"Lord, I've never seen a room like this, bursting into song

like you do," she said when we started up a rousing round of "High Hopes" while waiting for everyone to get ready to go out for afternoon recess.

"Do you like it?" Jesse asked.

"I think it's screwball," Alice said.

"God has little angels to sing for him in heaven," Rosa replied. "I feel like I have little angels to sing here on earth. That must be a good thing, no?"

"I think it's nuts," Alice said.

"Why's that?" Rosa asked.

"I don't know the words."

"I don't know the words either," Rosa said. "So I just sing la-la-la instead. That's okay, no? La-la-la will do."

"That's right," I said.

"I still think it's nuts," Alice said. "I think this room is just plain weird."

"Well," said Billy in a philosophical tone, "*you've* found the right place to be then."

The day that had started so challengingly ended on a pleasant note. While I took the children down to their rides, Rosa went down to the teachers' lounge and brought a can of soda pop back to the room for each of us. We sat at the table chatting. I found out she was forty-eight and originally from a small village in the state of Chihuahua in Mexico. She'd come to the United States when she was ten as a migrant worker. She'd married Joe, a garage mechanic, in her teens and had six children in quick succession, which included two sets of twins. She'd started working as an aide for the school district when her youngest started kindergarten because the hours coincided with the children's hours. The children were all grown now, all with families of their own, except for her youngest daughter, who was getting married in the fall. "She's a schoolteacher," Rosa said proudly. "Three of mine are schoolteachers. We got education in our blood."

I found out more in that half hour about Rosa than I'd known about Julie in the entire time she'd been with me. We were still chatting when Bob appeared in the doorway.

"Tor?"

I looked up.

"We've got a meeting." He held up his watch and tapped it. "Five o'clock with Social Services. Down in the county offices."

I lifted my eyebrows in question, as I was unaware of a meeting.

"Venus," he said. "They wanted to talk to us before they talked to the press."

Bob and I were ushered into a spacious conference room. It was a bright, airy room, decorated in pale beige tones. A huge oval table took up most of the space. I recognized several of the people there: the director of Social Services, two of the social workers I knew to be involved. Both Officer Millwall and Sam Patterson were there. But there were many more people, including uniformed police. Fifteen people seated themselves around the table. More joined us after the doors were closed and stood against the walls.

"I wanted to have an official briefing on the Venus Fox case," the director said. "I appreciate everyone's involvement in this case and I want to thank all of those who have given their time."

And then came the full story.

Venus had been brought to the hospital unconscious the morning after the second big snowstorm. She was suffering from hypothermia and frostbite. Her mother had told the doctors at the hospital that Venus had wandered out into the night during the storm, which was how this had happened. When undressing Venus to treat her, the hospital staff noticed she was undernourished and had various bruises and abrasions consistent with child abuse. She was x-rayed and discovered to have five broken bones in various states of healing, indicating they had been done over a period of time. There was evidence of twenty-two old breaks, all of which had healed.

The director spoke slowly and calmly as he explained all this, all the hideous little details of what had been broken, whether it was healed or not, where the little abrasions were that indicated she had had her hands tied, how her hair was lightening, indicating the start of malnutrition.

I sat there as cold and unable to move as granite.

"How did hypothermia come into this?" someone asked. I didn't know who he was.

"I'm getting there," the director replied in the patient voice of a teacher with slow students.

That's when I discovered "bad" could always get worse.

The reason Venus had hypothermia was because she was being made to sleep naked in an unheated bathroom. The suspect in all of this was Danny, Teri's live-in boyfriend, and his defense had been that she wet the bed and this was the only place suitable for her. The director said that evidence given during the police investigation indicated that Venus may have been sleeping in the bathroom for several weeks and that apparently she was locked in there most of the time she was at home. She was apparently being fed only when Wanda remembered to give her something. Indeed, Wanda appeared almost solely in charge of her care. Danny forbade the other children from interacting with her.

I lost what he said after that. I'd heard too much. My brain went into overload. I sat, staring at the table. The grain of the wood of that table was all that entered my mind. I would never again hear the word *abuse* and not get a mental picture of the grained white pine beneath the glossy polyurethane of that table.

How had we missed the indicators of this catalog of horrific abuse? That was the only question, and it flooded my mind. I suspect it was the only question in all of our minds. There Venus had been among us – battered, tortured, starved – we had seen her almost every day, yet we had not known. She had been locked in a *bathroom*? Sleeping *naked*? Fed on scraps? For weeks? *Months*?

How had it happened? How had we gone from thinking "something isn't right with this girl" to this? How could we be around her and not know the extent of it?

In the aftermath of that meeting, I felt bereft. I felt it very powerfully as a great hollow maw, as if the marrow had been sucked right out of me. This surprised me. I would have imagined myself to feel horror. Or revulsion – the kind that made people throw up when they encountered something so shocking. But while horror had clouted me during the meeting, afterward I felt only loss.

Loss of what? I wasn't sure. Of my own innocence, I suspect. Of the belief that when I was at the helm, things like this would never happen. Of the confidence that I was somehow better than those people you read about in newspaper articles who never managed to notice the horror going on around them. I had just assumed this wouldn't happen to me. And now it had. I had been in the classroom, in all those private moments reading and watching videos with Venus, and it had *still* happened. Of everybody there at that meeting, it was I who had spent the most time with Venus. Of everyone, I'd had the best chance to identify this. Of everyone, I was the most guilty for not having done so.

Chapter Thirty

Bob and I went out to dinner afterward. His wife, Susan, joined us when she got off work. We picked a small Italian place that looked like some bad 1970s movie set – cheesy mandolin music played rather too loudly, drip candles in Chianti bottles on red-checkered tablecloths – but the food was good and the wine was cheap and plentiful.

We spoke briefly of the case to fill in Susan, but we were both overwhelmed by then to where our conversation seemed stuck in a rut, and we kept returning again and again to the same points. Mainly "How?" and "Why?" Or maybe that was because without answering these two questions, there was nothing much more we could say. And we couldn't answer them.

So we meandered off onto other topics. None of them were very cheerful. Susan had a friend with brain cancer and it looked to be terminal. We discussed that. The food reminded me of Rome and I asked Bob and Susan if they'd ever been there. They said no. Finances just never worked out. Bob talked about how, during his childhood, his father had gone bankrupt and it had left him with a pathological fear of not having enough money. So we didn't get far with a vacation conversation. Finally, we ended up talking about the past, about that first year Bob and I had worked together. Inevitably, it worked its way around to how idealistic we both had been, although we'd been loathe to acknowledge this at the time, thinking we were such "realists." We talked about all the little things along the way that had taught us what true realism was. This conversation served to cloak the fact that I, at least, was still mastering this concept, having that afternoon sustained a body blow to whatever little bit of idealism I had left.

The lawyers involved in the abuse case discouraged me from going up to the hospital to see Venus. It was felt that this, somehow, might be prejudicial to the case, that she might say something or I might encourage a point of view that would harm things.

Everything was in a state of confusion. There were so many parties involved now that it was hard to keep information straight, to find out what was happening, to clarify what I *could* do. Venus's brothers and sisters had all been taken into care immediately, of course, but this meant dispersing them all over town because there were so many of them. All of them were gone from our school within days. Wanda disappeared. I heard that she had been placed in a group home for younger children. But then again I'd heard she had been sent to a supervised adult group home in a neighboring town. Danny was being charged with the crime, but Teri was being charged as an accessory, so they were both detained in jail.

In the end, the best I could do to keep contact with Venus was send things to her at the hospital. So we made up a little booklet. I had each child draw a self-portrait, tell a little bit about what they were doing in school, and say something nice about Venus, if they could manage that. Then we bound it all together with a ribbon, so that extra pages could be added. My plan was to send at least one page each day thereafter, telling her what was happening in class.

Rosa helped Shane do his, while I helped Zane. They just drew pictures and wrote "Get well. Come back soon."

"I'm sorry you're in the hospitale," Billy wrote. "I used to call you 'Siko' and I'm sorry. I never ment to hurt your feelings. I hope you'll come back someday. We are making Play-Doh with salt and oil for our cooking. If you are lucky, I will send you some. I am still going to my AP class. I learned about ants there. If you are lucky, I will send you a picture of them. We have them in a farm. Only it isn't a real farm. It's an ant farm. You wouldn't want to tip it over. Love, Billy."

Jesse wrote, "Dear Venus, Come back. We miss you. I thot you were nice becose you didn't make lots of nosie. We got a new gurl. Her name is Aliss. I was in the hospital ones and got my toncil out. It hurt a lot and gave me a bad sore throte but I got to eat a lot of ice cream. Any time I want. Maybe you can have ice cream. We are not doing anything interesting in class. You are not missing anything here."

And, of course, then there was Alice's contribution. "You don't know me. I am 8. I like rabbits, chipmonks, horses and about every other animel. I don't like boys or scramble eggs. I have small feet for my age. I just came in this class. I don't know why I have to do this becus you don't know me and I don't know you and it seems nuts to do this. I am a girl so we will have two girls in this class whenever you finaly come back. Come back! There are too many boys!!!!! I hope you get well soon. Come back soon. Your frende, Alice."

We had almost two weeks of confused waiting with little news and even less accurate information, because everything was now in the hands of the police and the courts. I heard that Venus had been released from the hospital and was now in foster care, but I was not told where.

On two occasions, Sam Patterson visited my classroom after school and talked to me about my experiences with Venus. She looked at the meager number of things I had that recorded Venus's existence in our class. She had been so reticent to work that there were none of her papers displayed around the room, as there were for the boys. There was little more to show than Venus's place at the table and the She-Ra sword.

On another occasion Bob and I met with the attorney prosecuting the case. He looked over my anecdotal records, which clearly mentioned Venus's numerous absences and my exasperation with them. He talked about my experiences with her. He commented on how frustrating this case was to him because Venus still did not speak to anyone. I asked if he knew what had become of Wanda. He didn't. Bob asked if he happened to know if Wanda was really Venus's biological mother, the way Bob had heard. The lawyer gave a short nod.

"Not a very promising family, is it?" the lawyer finally muttered in a world-weary sort of way.

Bob nodded in agreement.

I was thinking how easy it was to write people off in a few sentences. And how brutally hard it was to accomplish anything, if you tried to do the opposite.

Then, on a Friday morning about ten days later, there was a hump-bump sound up the stairwell outside my classroom. I was standing on a chair and putting up a new May bulletin board when I heard the noise. I paused and turned, trying to discern what it was. It was only 8:20, still fifteen minutes before the bell rang for the children to come in.

Through the window in the door, I saw Bob's head appear. He was carrying something. Rumble-bump against my door and it pushed open. A wheelchair came through with Bob behind it. In his arms was Venus.

"I've got someone for you," he said in a cheerful sort of way.

"Hello!" I said and came down off the chair.

Bob set her in the wheelchair.

She was a changed child in many respects. The long, tangled hair was gone. It had been cut boyishly short. All the crusty dirt was scrubbed away. The scabs and impetigo were gone. She had on a pretty little outfit consisting of a green gingham top and green pants with matching trim. Over bandaged feet, she wore dog-shaped slippers.

Because of the frostbite, she had lost toes on both her feet. She should have been up and walking with the help of crutches, but so far she hadn't tried. I could imagine that. As unresponsive as she had been before, I could guess at the challenge involved in trying to do physical therapy with Venus. As a consequence, she was wheelchair-bound for the time being.

When Bob had left, I knelt beside the chair. "I'm glad you're back," I said.

A moment's hesitation. What to say to her? I wanted to apologize. Desperately. I wanted her to know that I hadn't meant to be so blind, that I most certainly hadn't meant to be an inadvertent party to her suffering. But this was *my* guilt talking. So there was a moment's awkward silence between us.

"I'm sorry you had so many bad things happen," I said softly. "I hope from now on, it'll be better."

She stared at me without responding.

"Do your feet still hurt?" I asked.

For a very brief moment she glanced to her slippers, then back to me. She didn't answer.

"Perhaps soon they will be better. But for now I'll take you over to your table. I'll show you what we're doing now."

The children were delighted.

"Hey, you're back," Billy cried. "Cool! A wheelchair! Can I ride in it?"

"What you got a wheelchair for?" Jesse asked. He walked around Venus's table, leaned down, peered under. "What's wrong with your feet?"

Shane and Zane whizzed by. "I got a present for you!" Shane called. He ran to his basket. "Look. I made this for you." He took out a crumpled piece of tissue paper. The week before we had made tissue paper tulips for art, so this was obviously where he got his idea, but this was just a piece of pink tissue paper. He thrust it under Venus's nose. "It's a paper flower. I made it for you." He set it on her table.

Zane, a little overexcited, pounded on Venus's table and then jumped up on his own. I lifted him down again.

Alice strolled over nonchalantly. "Memories of days gone are a means to resurrect the past," she said.

"Alice, why don't you try introducing yourself?" I suggested.

"The pain and terror of being so incomplete will never go away."

"Okay, well, maybe later," I said. I still hadn't figured out

Alice's weird phrases, but she seemed inclined to say them when feeling threatened, so I left it at that.

The morning went normally. I needed to come down quite hard with the traffic light system to get everyone settled, because there was a party atmosphere in the room. It was less Venus causing such excitement, I suspect, than Venus's wheelchair, which everyone wanted to try themselves or push. Plus, it was our first really sunny, warm spring day, and everyone sensed summer. So there had to be a lot of "mean teacher" behavior to get us back on track.

In the back of my mind, I think I'd expected Venus to be different. I'd expected some cataclysmic change to have taken place in her over the last few weeks because of the way she had evoked it in me. But not so. She was her normal silent, unresponsive self. If anything, she was more silent and unresponsive than before, because she let the boys bounce around her wheelchair in a way that would have provoked a furious explosion in days gone by. As it was, she just sat, immobile, her face a mask.

The difference now was forced intimacy. I had to carry her up and down the stairs on those occasions we did not want to bother with the small, creaking elevator on the far side of the building. I had to take her to the toilet. This involved presuming to know when she needed to go, because, of course, she didn't say. So, at each of the breaks I carried her into the rest room, helped her with her clothes, and lifted her on and off the toilet. It felt strange, this presumptuousness about such private acts, and I felt like I was being forced to cross boundaries I shouldn't, but there was no choice. Instead I focused my attention on trying to convey gentleness, on giving her by osmosis a sense that someone *did* care about her body, that it mattered to me that she not be jostled or have her clothing removed roughly or suffer overlong the discomfort of a full bladder. It became important to me that she know the world was full of people like myself and not just the people she had known.

Wanting to resume some form of normalcy as quickly as possible, I went down to find Venus at lunchtime as soon as I had eaten. She had been wheeled out onto the playground, and one of the playground aides was standing beside her.

"Do you want to come up?" I asked.

Venus lifted her eyes to meet mine. They were enigmatic. Her expression was completely unreadable.

I waited for some response.

Nothing.

"Do you want to come up and watch a video?" I asked.

No response.

"Well, why don't we try?" I said and took the handles of the wheelchair to push her inside.

We went to the elevator and waited for it to arrive. It was a very lethargic thing. I could have walked the stairs two or three times while waiting for it. "It'll be good when you can walk again, won't it?" I said as I set her in the wheelchair outside our room and dug in my pocket for the key. "That elevator is a pain."

I unlocked the door and wheeled Venus in.

"Shall we watch a video? I have a new one. A friend gave it to me."

No response.

I took the tape out of my desk drawer and held it out.

No response. Venus did not move her hand to accept it.

"It's hard getting started again, isn't it?" I asked.

No response.

I laid the video in her lap.

"I'm sorry," I said.

She didn't move.

I knelt down beside the wheelchair and put my hand on her face to make her look at me. "I'm sorry I didn't know what was happening to you, Venus. I'm sorry I didn't do more to help."

She raised her eyes then and met mine.

She looked at me. A long, searching gaze, locking my eyes with hers.

"I didn't know. I really didn't. I didn't know you were in trouble," I said. "If I'd realized, I would have tried to help. I'm really, really sorry I didn't."

Silence then.

She regarded me a moment longer and then dropped her eyes. She looked at her hands in her lap. They'd been folded. Now she twisted them.

Silence.

I didn't know what to say from there. I didn't know quite what to do next.

She looked up. "Do you still got my sword?" she asked in a hoarse half-whisper.

"Yes. Do you want me to get it for you?"

She nodded.

I crossed the room. I'd placed the sword on top of the art cabinet because I was afraid the boys might get a hold of it and inadvertently damage it. Pulling a chair over, I got on it and lifted the sword down. It was a bit dusty.

"Just a minute. Let me wipe it off first." I went over and got a cloth out from under the sink. I rubbed it over the plastic chips to make them shiny. "Here." I held it out to her.

Venus took it in both her hands. It was a slow action. She took it, brought it in close to her, and held it up, all very slowly, as if in a stop-frame film. Taking it by the hilt, she ran her other hand lightly over the design on the blade. Her expression was unreadable.

Extending her arm in a broader movement than I'd seen her make since she'd returned, Venus held it out. It was done very slowly, although not languorously so. It was a thinking kind of slow. Contemplatively slow. As if she were seeing it for the first time and trying to take its measure.

"For the Power of Grayskull," I said quietly and smiled.

She looked at me then. The sword was still extended out in front of her, but she paused and raised her eyes to me.

I smiled.

She didn't. She just stared at me a moment, then dropped her eyes and slowly lowered the sword back into her lap. She placed her other hand over it, pulling it up against her, almost as if to cuddle it to her body.

"It doesn't work," she said softly.

I looked at her.

"It doesn't really work."

Chapter Thirty-one

Rosa was delighted to see Venus. "Look at you! Aren't you pretty? Aren't you just the prettiest little thing, sitting there in that lovely green outfit? You look like a little flower fairy!"

Venus stared at her.

"This is Rosa," I said. "She's our helper in the afternoons now. Remember Julie? Julie works at a different school now. So Rosa comes every day."

No response. Venus didn't even blink.

"And I'm going to help *you* too, little blossom," Rosa said warmly. "We're going to maybe do some math today, no? A nice math sheet? Because I see that's what's in your folder."

Nothing. No response whatsoever.

Alice was just as confident of being part of Venus's life.

"Me and her are going to be best friends," Alice said as she came into the classroom from lunch. "Can we sit together at the same table?"

"So far, it's worked out better when everyone's had a table of his or her own," I said.

"Why? Why is that?" Alice asked. "I noticed that first thing when I came in here. Five kids and five tables. Now six kids and six tables. Why not us guys all sit together and then when those kids who come in from other classes are here, they can have the other tables. Then me and her can sit together, because we're best friends. Huh? What's your name again? You there?"

Venus didn't even turn her head.

"You know what I want to know about this class?" Billy said. "Whatever happened to us being Chipmunks?"

"Chipmunks?" Alice said in surprise.

"Yeah. Way long time back, us guys were all Chipmunks. It was a special club we had, and just us got to be in it and not the kids who came from the other classes. What happened to that? Why did we stop doing it?"

Now that Billy had brought it up, I realized that we had, indeed, forgotten about being Chipmunks. It had happened about the time the traffic light system was introduced. That was about the same time as we started singing too, and it was the singing that had brought us together in a way that being Chipmunks had never really managed to do.

The children started to chatter.

"Hey, not now, gang. Time to do some work," I said.

"But can't we do Chipmunks again?" Billy asked.

"We'll discuss it later. At going-home time, when we have discussion. Now, open your folders, please."

"But what about me sitting at that table with that girl?" Alice asked. She was up out of her seat. "Can't we do that?"

"Yeah, can't we do that?" Billy asked. "Can't we rearrange stuff in here? We've been like this *forever.*" Emphasis went on that last word to make it sound as if I'd subjected him to genuine torture by not changing the seating on a frequent basis."

Even though I'd meant to start work, I got drawn into the conversation. "The last time we tried more than one person at a table, we had lots of fights."

"Yeah. And the last time we tried more than one person at a table was about a million years ago," Billy said. "It was, like, *ages* ago. In my AP class, we get to sit wherever we want. Every day. So I can sit with different kids any time I feel like it."

"In your AP class, folks aren't trying to kill each other," I replied.

"Well, they aren't in here either, are they?" Alice remarked.

And that's when it dawned on me that she was right. We weren't the same group we were when I'd first assigned everyone to their own tables.

"Yeah, so let us. Please?" Billy asked.

"Yes, I wanna too," Jesse chimed in.

"Yeah, me and Jesse. Her and her. And the twins together. That'd work," Billy said. "Pul-leeeeease?"

I grinned. "Okay. We'll try it. Everyone find the place they want."

This was somewhat lost on the twins, who had been fiddling around during this discussion. Their heads turned back and forth in surprise as everyone got up.

"Hey, you guys, you want to sit together? Want to sit there, Shane?" Billy asked.

"How come?"

"He doesn't have to, Billy. Shane, everyone is choosing a new place to sit. If you want to sit somewhere different, you may."

"I want to sit with Billy!" Shane cried.

"Yeah, me too!" Zane echoed. And suddenly, there they were, four at the same table.

"Hey now, I don't think *this* is going to work," I said, coming over.

"Why not?" Jesse asked.

"You're going to get into mischief, if all of you sit together, that's why," I said.

"How do you know?" Billy replied. "You never give us a chance. You never even try to find out if we can be good. You just always think we're going to be bad. *Assume*. That's what you do."

"Yes, well, I know you pretty well," I said. "So it's a safe assumption."

Billy leaned way over across the table toward the

twins. "Okay, now listen up, you two. You can be little buggers, if you want to, and it gets on the lady's nerves. So can you sit still and behave yourselves, if you get to stay here?"

Both boys' eyes went wide.

"Well, can you?"

"Yeah," Shane said.

"Promise?"

Shane and Zane nodded solemnly.

"So, let 'em stay," Billy said to me.

Jesse was sniggering. "Or Billy'll pound 'em," he said in a stage whisper.

"I'll pound *you*, buddy," Billy said and gave Jesse a playful cuff on the shoulder.

Meanwhile, Alice was settling into her place at Venus's table. She chose the chair right next to Venus in her wheelchair.

"I'm eight," she said. "My birthday is January twenty-eighth. How old are you?"

Venus sat with her head down. She didn't even look in Alice's direction.

"I got shiny pencils," Alice said. She reached into her pencil case and took two out. "You can use one, if you want." She lay it over on the table in front of Venus. "Here. That's for you."

No response.

"You can have it, if you want. I'll give it to you."

No response.

"There's a goddess who's got the same name as you. In mythology. Did you know that?"

No response.

"The goddess of beauty. So, you got a famous name. I never heard of anybody else with that name, except you and her."

No response.

"I think you're lucky. Luckier than me. Everybody thinks of *Alice in Wonderland* when I say my name. They always say, 'Seen the White Rabbit lately?' and I *hate* that. I get so sick of people saying that."

Venus had no reaction whatsoever. She just continued staring into her lap.

Alice leaned way over toward her. "How come you never talk?"

"Alice," I said, noticing her, "Venus doesn't like it very much when people come really close."

"Yeah, she might pop you one!" Billy exclaimed and hit his fist into the palm of his other hand with a loud smack. "Done that to me, haven't you, Venus. When she first came, she used to go off like an atom bomb. BOOM!!!!" he shouted *very* loudly.

"Billy, that's enough," I said and gestured for him to sit down again.

The twins couldn't resist this. "BOOM!" shouted Zane and exploded up out of his seat.

"BOOM!" echoed Shane.

"BOOM!" went Billy one last time for good measure.

He gave me a sheepish look and then ducked his head, feigning fascination with the contents of his folder.

Alice heaved a big sigh. "A world of graves and cemeteries," she murmured. "A world of tears and fears."

Jesse smiled blissfully at me. "You know what? I just love it in this class."

There was no need now to stay in with Venus at recess. Indeed, the aides who had been specially hired to police her at lunchtime had also been released from duty. Wheelchair-bound, Venus was not much of a threat to anyone. I decided, however, I wanted to continue that special time alone with her. So when the others went thundering down the stairs for recess, I had Rosa take them out and I remained behind.

"Do you want to go to the toilet?" I asked, because I thought I'd better get that chore out of the way, if it was necessary.

Venus regarded me.

It occurred to me that somewhere along the line I, like so many others around her, had come to the point where I usually did not expect her to respond. Despite my many years of experience working with children who were electively mute – a psychological disturbance where the child who can speak refuses to do so – which should have given me a better understanding of speech refusal, I'd grown accustomed to her silence. Yet she could speak. She'd proven that. So, I thought, here was the right time to start afresh with her. After this break, after the trauma, we'd come to a good place to establish a new relationship. Thus, when she didn't answer me this time, I didn't let her off the hook. Instead, I waited, keeping her locked in my gaze.

She looked down.

"Venus, do you want to go to the toilet now?"

Silence.

"You know, it is going to be much more helpful if you talk. I know you are not used to talking. I am sure it is a little scary getting started. But it will be much better to talk. So, do you want to go to the toilet now?"

No answer.

I waited.

Silence.

I waited.

Silence is a funny thing. Most of us cannot tolerate much of it. Ninety seconds is about the maximum for most of us before discomfort sets in. One of the tricks for dealing with speech refusal, I've found, was learning to be comfortable with much longer silences. To keep everyone's mind focused on the "conversation," as it were, by reasking the question if it appears attention is wandering, but not to rush in unnecessarily and fill the silence. So I continued to wait.

Finally, she gave a faint nod.

If I was going to start over afresh with Venus, I had to go the full nine yards. No good settling for "halfway there." It was tempting, of course, to do that. Poor child, just back at school from traumatic abuse, still suffering from her injuries. It was very, very tempting to be sympathetic, to reinforce the smallest gestures and rejoice in those. Certainly, a large part of me wanted to do that. But the greater part said, "Now or never." For her own benefit, as well as mine, Venus needed to start responding reliably, preferably verbally, and as I knew she was capable of speaking, I did not think I was demanding too much. So, I said, "I'm sorry, what?"

No response.

"Do you want to go to the toilet now, Venus?"

She nodded more straightforwardly.

"Pardon?"

No response.

"I'm sorry, I didn't hear you."

She nodded very plainly.

"Pardon?"

She looked up at me, her eyes clouded with puzzlement. Clearly she couldn't figure out why I didn't understand.

I cupped my hand behind one ear and tipped it toward her. "Pardon? I didn't hear you."

She gave an obvious nod, her eyes fixed on mine.

"I didn't hear you."

A pause. She looked away, looked back at me, looked down in her lap. Then, "Yes." Very quietly.

"I'm sorry. A little louder," I said.

"Yes." It wasn't quite a full voice but it was close enough.

I smiled. "You want to go to the bathroom?"

"Yes."

"Okay. I'll take you."

In my experience with children who refused speech I had found that once a child began to speak, it was important to keep demanding it at regular intervals until it became established. So, once we were in the rest room, I put the brakes on the wheelchair and said, "Do you think you can stand long enough on your feet so that we can get your pants down?" because the previous visits to the toilet had been marred by the difficulty of lifting a child of her size up while at the same time removing clothing.

No response.

"Pardon?"

No response.

I sat back on my heels.

Venus looked at me.

"Do your feet hurt a lot?"

No response.

I waited.

Nothing.

I waited longer.

Slowly she nodded.

"Pardon?"

No response.

"Pardon?"

"Yes," she said at last, her voice soft.

And so it went. Sentence by sentence. Question by question. "Are you done?" "Do you want help wiping?" "Can you pull your pants up, if I help steady you?" "Can you reach the water?" "Do you want me to give you a paper towel?" She answered all of them. Eventually. It took us more than the twenty minutes of recess. The children had been back in the room ten minutes by the time Venus and I returned, and Rosa had already started them on their art project.

"Look what I'm doing!" Alice said and pointed to the clay she was modeling.

I wheeled Venus over to her place at the table. "Shall I get you some clay?" I asked.

No response.

"Pardon."

"Yes," she said.

So I did.

Chapter Thirty-two

Because of her extensive problems, both physical and emotional, Venus had been placed on her own in a foster home, in which the parents were specially trained to deal with the seriousness of her problems. Her other siblings had been scattered among different foster homes around the town. Wanda was placed in a neighboring community where she now lived in a supervised adult group home and took part in a special sheltered workshop.

I was very impressed with Venus's foster mother, Mrs. Kivie, who came in to see me toward the end of Venus's first week back. She and her husband had had considerable experience fostering children who had suffered abuse, and while she had not dealt with a child who had Venus's emotional problems, she felt confident of coping. More importantly, she showed genuine warmth toward Venus when talking to her and helping her, using the kind of empathic gestures that aren't put on just to make a good show in front of the teacher. Her smiles, her words, her touches were there for Venus.

In this newfound warmth, I think we all expected Venus to blossom quickly. Cared for, supported, and encouraged for the first time in her life, she was now in a position to make the progress that circumstances had previously denied her. However, as the early weeks of May passed, this didn't happen.

Venus did now talk, but there was not an overnight change in her speech. Every single utterance was hard-won. She never responded directly to anything without long gaps, whether it was in class or in private with me. And there was virtually no spontaneous speech. She responded when spoken to and seldom said more than one word.

That was the only obvious progress we made. Nothing else happened. Venus remained closed, quiet, and if I had to put a word on it, depressed.

Depressed? Once I thought that, I realized, yes. Depression was what it appeared to be. This caught me by surprise, not only because it seemed so out of context – why would she be depressed now when everything was at last going right? – but also because her behavior had always been so "closed down" that one could have easily mistaken it for depression. However, previously I had never had the sense that it was. Despite her often catatonic behavior in class, there was an inherent liveliness to her, whether it was in her explosive reaction to the boys or when we shared time playing She-Ra together. Now, nothing.

Venus didn't want to go back to our She-Ra cartoons. She didn't react in the playful way she had before to our She-Ra games. She was easier and more compliant in the classroom, doing more of what was set before her, and giving little indication of her previous "dangerous" status, where she attacked without provocation. I'd wanted improvement, but not at this cost.

The day that occurred to me, I stopped by the office after school and phoned Ben Avery, the school psychologist. In the way of most school psychologists, he was far too busy to be able to come over and see Venus immediately. His caseload now extended to almost two thousand students, and he was responsible for overseeing the districtwide assessment testing that always took place in May, so it wasn't a matter of dropping what he was doing to deal with a child who needed a psychological evaluation. He promised, however, to come over and observe her at the first opportunity. In the meantime, we chatted. He said that depression might be expected in light of all the disruption in her life. I said it seemed strange that going from appalling conditions to a warm, loving family would make someone depressed. Ben replied something about the human mind being even stranger.

I mentioned it later to Bob. I knew Venus was having some kind of psychological help. I didn't know the details beyond that because, from my rather lowly status as her teacher, I wasn't in the position to have such information shared with me, but I thought he could pass it on.

The final person I phoned was Mrs. Kivie. I said I was concerned about Venus's unusually subdued behavior and wondered if it was depression. She said yes, she'd thought Venus was very quiet but that this wasn't unusual in her experience with abused children. It took some adjusting to all this change. She told me that Venus was under the care of a psychiatrist from the hospital and he was aware of the problem and that was about all we could do.

And "all we can do" seemed to *be* about all we could do. No one had any particular advice for helping Venus over this new hump in the road. In the end, I could figure out nothing beyond being supportive and patient and continuing to nudge her forward, even when she was unmotivated to try.

Unexpectedly, my best ally proved to be Alice. Alice was not put off by Venus's remote behavior. Indeed, I suppose if you were used to talking to your hand, talking to a person, even one inclined to totally ignore you, was still an improvement. Thus Alice happily chatted to Venus and interacted with her, as if Venus were participating in everything.

Alice was particularly good about schoolwork. She would whiz through her own, have a little chat with Mimi, and then launch into getting Venus to do her folder.

"Hey, you wanna do this?" she'd ask. "I'll help you." She would open Venus's folder and take out whatever was on top. "Look, a math paper. Adding. You want me to help you?" Alice would then pull her chair right over next to Venus's and lay Mimi out on the table, palm upward. "Two plus three," Alice would say. "Here's how you do it. Mimi, show us three. There. There's three fingers. Now, you just count two more. Five. See that? See how it's done?"

Venus often didn't say a thing. Indeed, Alice not only did all the talking, but she usually did every single one of the math problems herself as well, but she achieved a better feat. She managed to get Venus to write them down. "You write it," Alice would say. Venus would just sit. "No, you write it. Mimi's busy, 'cause she's doing the counting. *You* write it." And eventually Venus would pick up the pencil and write the number.

I left them to it. On the surface, it appeared neither girl was doing what she was supposed to. Alice was spending much more time on Venus's work than on her own, and Venus was actually never doing much of the work in her folder herself, but there *was* something going on between these two. While Venus often appeared to be totally ignoring Alice, I could tell this wasn't so. She *did* write down things Alice told her to. She didn't pull away from Alice the way she did when one of the boys came around her wheelchair. And during those occasions when Alice was busy with her own activities at the table, particularly when she was engaged in one of her long conversations with

Mimi, I'd often see Venus watching her. It was a furtive sort of watching. Venus watched only with her eyes and almost never turned her head even a little, but she was watching.

At the beginning of the year because the boys had been so aggressive and unable to control themselves, we'd never developed the habit of having a morning discussion, as I'd always had with my other classes. At that point, they simply could not sit still long enough without trying to kill one another, so we whipped through the necessary role-taking and lunch money collection and got on with activities that allowed me always to keep them at least ten feet apart.

I'd missed this discussion period very much. It was a good transition period between home and school, giving children an opportunity to talk about things that had happened at home or caused problems or upset. It was a good opportunity for communicating among ourselves so that we could deal with any difficulties in the class that arose. And it gave a more democratic feel to what was actually a benign autocracy. But the boys just couldn't cope.

As the year wore on and the children became more settled, we did eventually develop an equivalent of morning discussion. This sprang up at the end of the day instead. About the time the traffic light system starting taking effect and the boys had begun to work a little better, there was a tendency for everyone to finish up their work a little sooner than I'd anticipated, giving us ten or fifteen minutes left over. To keep the peace, I'd started asking them each to tell me one good thing that had happened during the day and one bad thing. They all enjoyed this. Billy, of course, was the one who kept asking if we could do it again the next day, and soon we had instituted a regular period at the end of the day to "de-brief," as it came to be known.

"De-briefing" began to fill out. We still did the best thing/worst thing, but we also talked about other things. I used it to introduce necessary discussions about such matters as caring for others' property, putting oneself in others' shoes, and the ethical problems with popular playground codes such as "finders/keepers, losers/weepers." We settled disputes about whose reading book was whose even when they were *exactly* alike, where you could put your running shoes without making the room smelly, and this didn't mean out the window, and what precisely constituted "looking at me funny." We planned parties, acknowledged successes and other special events, and discussed changing certain class rules. And sometimes, if I came across a good activity in a book or teaching magazine that would provide a "thinking experience," we did that.

One such "thinking experience" posed this possibility: if you could ask anybody in the whole world one question and get it answered, what would it be? I thought it might be the jumping-off place for a good conversation.

Billy leaped in enthusiastically, waving his hand. "Pick me! Pick me! Pick me!" he squealed.

"Okay," I said.

"Welllll ... ," he replied in a dramatic tone, "I'd ask to God. And I'd ask 'What really happens to you when you die?'"

"That's a good question," I said.

"I'd ask God what's in the future," Jesse said. "That's what I want to know."

"Yeah, like when you're going to die," Billy chimed in cheerfully. "'Cause that'd be interesting to know. Did you ever stop to think that, like, one particular day on the calendar is going to be the day you died on? Like, for instance, February first. Say, you're going to die on February first. But every year you go by February first, not knowing. Not knowing that's going to be the second most important day in your whole life, except for your birthday. And, like, maybe it's on a Thursday. So every week you go by a Thursday and *that's* the day you're going to die on."

"Thank you for that cheerful thought," Jesse said.

"But isn't that *interesting*? Did you ever think of that before?"

"Yes, very interesting," I said. "And no, I admit, I hadn't thought of that."

"But you're going to *die* on that day. And it just seems ordinary. We don't know. It seems like an ordinary day, but it's going to be *so* important to us someday."

I smiled at him. "It *is* very interesting. I'll agree with you. Shall we give others a chance to pose their questions too? Alice?"

"I'm asking Mimi," she said, holding her hand out in front of her.

"I'd ask Mickey Mouse," Shane said. "I'd ask him if he liked living at Disneyland."

"I'd ask my grandma what I'm going to get for my birthday," Jesse said, "because my birthday's in June and I don't want to wait!"

"Hey, no fair!" Billy cried. "Jesse already had a turn. If he gets another turn, I get another turn."

"Billy, settle down, please. We can have more turns, but let's let everyone have their first turn. Alice, have you thought of anything?"

"The stars shine all over the sky. The wind is gone, like sorrow."

I raised an eyebrow. The psychologist consulting on Alice's case said stress caused her sudden weird utterances. I wasn't sure what she would find stressful about this sort of discussion, but then I still had no real idea why Alice could be perfectly appropriate one moment and off in outer space the next. It was so abrupt on some occasions as to seem almost medical. As if she was having an odd kind of seizure. But no one I mentioned this to had ever heard of seizures like this.

"Alice, that's not actually a question. Can you give more?"

She blinked, as if coming out of a sleep.

Zane raised his hand, a behavior he was learning to imitate from Billy, who had learned it in his AP class. "I'd like to ask Goofy if he liked living at Disneyland."

"You and Shane will know lots about Disneyland, won't you?" I replied and smiled. Zane wiggled with pleasure and nodded.

I turned yet again to Alice. "What about you?"

She was consulting Mimi again.

Next to her was Venus. Venus had her head turned and she was looking right at Alice, watching her talk to Mimi. I ordinarily would not have even thought of including Venus in this discussion, but my sense at that moment was that she was very present in the conversation.

"Venus?"

Billy, detecting this irregularity, jerked forward in his seat, no doubt ready to query me on why I was asking Venus something when it wasn't what we usually did. I put out a hand toward him to silence him, and he fell back in his seat.

Venus looked over at me.

"If you could ask anyone in the whole world a question, who would you ask?"

There was a long pause. I saw Venus draw in a deep breath. Her eyes flitted from me to the others in the room to Alice. Then there was a moment of staring into space and I thought I'd lost her. I didn't reask the question. I wasn't too sure how long to wait. I hesitated.

Then Venus looked back to me. "Alice," she said softly.

"You'd ask Alice?"

She nodded faintly. "I want to know, why does she talk to her hand so much?"

Chapter Thirty-three

Venus's depression remained. It clung to her like a cobweb. She sat hunched over in her wheelchair day after day, as if she were stuck to it. She always seemed tired to me, her movements slow and sluggish, as if everything were too much of an effort.

In spite of this, she was making progress. She was interacting more. She did talk, after a fashion, with Alice. She did answer yes or no, if one waited long enough. And as with the discussion during de-briefing, she did very, very occasionally begin to participate in class. It was still not what I'd term spontaneous, but it was inching closer.

The one thing, however, we could not do was get her to try standing on her feet or walking. She remained steadfastly in the wheelchair, and no matter how much physiotherapy she was given, how much encouragement, how much reassurance from the doctors, her foster parents, me, or anyone else about how she *could* now try regaining normal movement and no longer needed the wheelchair, Venus refused to try. She was an absolute deadweight on those occasions when I lifted her to her feet. Except for when I took her to the toilet and needed her up enough for me to adjust her clothing, she would not even attempt standing, much less taking steps.

The third week of May there was a big conference over Venus, and everyone met in an effort to coordinate her extended care. It was the first time all the people now involved with her were together in one place, and it included social workers, her foster mother, the child psychiatrist who'd been appointed by the hospital, Sam Patterson, who was still processing the abuse case for the police, two physiotherapists, and, of course, Bob, Rosa, and me. Everyone talked about what kind of progress Venus was making and where we needed to go. I told them about how depressed she seemed, and the psychiatrist said that, yes, this was normal in such a case. It happened quite often. I asked why. He said something rather fuzzy about mourning all that she had lost. At which point somebody else said, "Like what? Sleeping naked in the bathroom? Being beaten until her bones were broken? Not much to mourn in losing that."

The psychiatrist gave a faint shrug in understanding and then a quick gesture of helplessness with his hand. "I guess it's all she had."

The physiotherapists discussed how important it was to

get her walking again because her muscles were deteriorating from lack of use. Her feet were going to cause her problems if she did not start bearing weight on them, because the areas where the toes had been amputated were healing without the feet being allowed to create a new weight-bearing configuration. A long discussion ensued about the psychological ramifications of recovery from amputation.

In the end, I think we all got a bit waylaid by the idea that Venus was missing these amputated toes. Someone suggested this was behind her depression, and several others nodded sagely. She was mourning her loss of wholeness. That made sense.

Not to me. Undoubtedly this loss was distressing to her, but I couldn't imagine it was all that was behind such an all-encompassing depression or her refusal to stand or walk. Indeed, we got waylaid generally while discussing depression and the physical importance of getting her back on her feet until we finally lost the plot. People started into long discourses on theories of depression, and the conversation locked into party lines, the psychiatric people supporting psychological reasons, the physiotherapists supporting physical reasons, the social workers going off on some completely different tangent involving care in the community. Despite the skills of all these high-powered professionals – the kind of people I'd so wanted involved with Venus from the beginning, indeed, the kind of professional expertise I would have wished for all my children – we found it hard to identify the source of real problems, much less come up with any real solutions. I was glad to attend the meeting and glad to see so many people from different disciplines involved, but I came away frustrated.

Life in class went on. Four of us – Jesse, the twins, and I – had birthdays in late May or early June, so we decided to have a group celebration. We made plans for a big party of the kind we hadn't even dared contemplate at Halloween or Christmas. I promised to bake a special cake. Rosa was going to bring ice cream. As Shane and Zane were birthday boys, their mother volunteered to bring cookies, and we were going to stir up our very own fruit punch as part of cooking in the early afternoon.

Because we hadn't managed any really serious parties earlier in the year, I wanted to go all-out and give the children a day to remember. So on the afternoon before, I allowed the last thirty minutes before going-home time to be spent "decorating," which was a bit of a recipe for disaster, as it involved a lot of leaping around from table to table to hang streamers, which resulted in some wild behavior from the twins, who needed no encouragement to jump and climb on furniture, and a lot of bossing from Jesse, who, since Billy was away at his AP class, claimed this chance to run the show. But we managed it, and the bell rang before anyone killed anyone else. Or themselves.

The day of the party, the twins showed up in ties and

little suits. I hadn't meant it to be *that* kind of party and was worried that they might spoil their clothes if things got rowdy, which I feared inevitably would happen, but they were both anxious to show off their "dress-up" clothes.

"This is my wedding suit," Shane said proudly.

"What? You got married?" Billy asked and laughed. "Who'd you marry? Alice?"

Shane made a fist and shook it fiercely.

I pointed to the traffic lights up on the chalkboard. Less and less often I was actually carrying the disks. The boys were more able to control themselves now without my having always to reward or punish with the disks, so I wanted to ease us away from such a highly structured approach. Nonetheless, the threat of the traffic lights still worked well. All I had to do was point and the more controlled children, like Billy, would get the message.

"Take it back!" Shane shouted.

"I was just joking," Billy said and looked over at me with an expression of disdain. "Nobody here can take a joke. You guys would never last a minute in my AP class. *There*, everybody jokes."

"Take it back!" Shane shouted again.

"I wouldn't want to marry pukey old you anyway," Alice responded from her seat.

"Billy," I said menacingly.

"It was *just* a joke."

"Jokes only work if everyone finds them funny," I said.

"Okay, sorry, Shane. I didn't mean it," Billy muttered.

"Guess what," Zane said. "At the wedding, Shane peed in his pants. Right in the church and it went on the floor."

"Take it back!" Shane shrieked in horror.

And so the rest of the morning went.

Venus too had arrived at school dressed for a party. She was wearing a lovely little frilly pink top and matching pants and she did look really pretty. Alice commented on it when she first saw Venus arrive in the morning, but it was Rosa who made the big fuss when she came in the afternoon.

"Look at you, little blossom! Aren't you just the beautifulest thing?" She swooped down and kissed Venus on the cheek. I would have expected Venus to pull away in surprise, but she didn't. Indeed, I think there might have been a smile touching Venus's lips then, just slightly.

We tried to carry on a normal day for as much of it as possible. We intended to have the party in the forty-five minutes between afternoon recess and going-home time, so it wasn't until recess itself that Shane and Zane's mother arrived with the cookies and I laid out the cake I'd brought. It was chocolate and made in the shape of a little train. To avoid too much squabbling, I'd made an individual freight car on the train for each child, putting his or her name on the side of it and decorating each car with *exactly* the same number, color, and kinds of candy and frosting. I put my name on the engine and Rosa's on the caboose.

In order to keep the party from caving in entirely, I kept things fairly structured. We'd play games for the first fifteen minutes, then we were going to listen to some relaxing music while making a party hat to wear, then eat our cake, cookies, and ice cream the last fifteen minutes. If there was any time left over, I had gotten permission from Bob to let everyone go outside on the playground early, as I reckoned that was just about all the excitement any of the children could cope with indoors without going homicidal.

For the game Billy wanted to play Twister, which he had brought from home. This consternated me a little, as I suspected it was just an elaborate means for looking up Alice's skirt, but I promised one game. Surprisingly, this came off quite well. Alice was relatively modest in her moves, and the boys seemed preoccupied with twisting themselves up in as many crazy positions as possible. Indeed, everyone was laughing so much that I agreed to a second game.

Venus, of course, did not join in. I encouraged her to call out the colors, but she wouldn't do it. She did spin the spinner for me a couple of times, but beyond that, she just watched.

Rosa, not wanting to see her sidelined, came over while we were getting ready to play the second game of Twister. "You can come help me make the things ready for our hats, no?"

Venus looked at her.

"We will make beautiful hats, no? You can make a pretty pink one to go with your lovely pink clothes. Doesn't she look beautiful today, Torey? That pink makes you so pretty. Come on, you come help me, beautiful child." She took hold of the handles and wheeled Venus's chair over to the table where the art materials were being laid out.

I started up the new game of Twister. The boys and Alice played enthusiastically and, indeed, very happily. There was a bit of pushing and shoving, but it was all taken in the spirit of the game.

We were just about to the end when Rosa came over to me. She leaned close to my ear and said, "There's something wrong with little Venus."

I looked over. I couldn't see because the back of the wheelchair was toward me.

"She's crying," Rosa said. "She started to cry when I took her over. I said, 'What's the matter?' but she will not say. I thought maybe she did not want to leave the game. I said, 'You want to go back? I don't mind,' but she will not say. She just cries. So, I think perhaps it is best to get you."

I nodded. "Can you finish this off?" I gave her the spinner for the game, rose, and went over to where Venus was sitting.

She was indeed crying, her mouth pulled down in a grimace of tears, her cheeks awash, but she made almost no noise.

I knelt down beside the wheelchair. "What's the matter, sweetheart?"

She just cried.

Rising, I lifted the box of tissues from the shelf and pulled one out. Kneeling back down, I reached over and wiped the tears from her cheeks. If anything, this made her cry harder.

I caressed her head. "What's wrong, Venus?"

It was unusual for her to cry. The last time had been in those weeks just before the abuse was discovered and I still smarted with the thought that I had not been sufficiently sensitive to her distress, that if I'd taken a little more time with her then, the horrible episode that had landed her in the hospital might have been prevented.

Nonetheless, the same pressures that had been on me then were on me now. Venus refused to talk. And then the game was over and the other children came bounding over, clamoring for attention.

I rose up on my feet. "Could you oversee this?" I asked, feeling horrible as I did so because it was a lot to ask of Rosa, but I wanted just a little time alone with Venus.

"Sure, muffin," she said and patted my shoulder in a rather motherly way. "You get on with God's work."

I wheeled Venus and the box of tissues out into the hallway. There wasn't much of any place else to go, what with her wheelchair and the layout of the building.

I knelt down beside the wheelchair again and touched her face. She still cried, softly and inconsolably.

Several minutes passed with me crouched on the floor beside her. It was an uncomfortable position. I was either going to have to sit all the way down on the floor, which put me in a rather awkward position to comfort her, or else I was going to have to stand. Neither worked well.

Finally I rose. "Here, here's what we're going to do," I said to her and put the brakes on the wheelchair. Then I reached down and lifted her up into my arms. Sitting down in the wheelchair myself, I set her on my lap. Wrapping my arms close around her, I held her.

She pressed her face into my shirt and cried.

Beyond the door behind us I could hear the other children. Voices went up and down. Excitement made them loud, but I didn't hear anything that sounded too dangerously near fighting. I murmured thanks to whatever power might be listening for having sent me Rosa.

I looked down at Venus. She was all snot and tears. Taking one of the tissues, I wiped her face.

"Can you tell me what's wrong?" I asked.

She shook her head.

"You just need to cry?"

She nodded.

"That's all right. You cry. Sometimes we feel that way."

She nodded and took the tissue from my hand. She pressed it against her nose.

"Sometimes that's all there is to do about life," I said.

She nodded.

Minutes passed. I could tell by the shrieks of glee beyond the door that Rosa had brought out the cake.

I ran my hand across Venus's forehead, the kind of caress used to push back hair, except that hers was too short.

"You know what?" I said. "I think you are a *very* special little girl. I mean that. I don't think I've said that to you.

I meant to, but sometimes we forget to say things to people. Especially good things. But I think you are so special. I always have. Right from the first day of school. Do you remember that? I do. You were up on your wall. I thought you looked beautiful."

Rather than reassure her, this seemed to upset her more. Venus broke into renewed tears.

"I'm glad you're in my class. I'm glad I got to be your teacher."

She wept.

I pulled out a clean tissue. Gently, I dabbed her cheeks. "What's wrong, lovey?"

"I wanna go home," she cried.

"You want to go home?" I asked.

She nodded.

"What's the matter? Aren't you feeling well?"

"I want to go *home*."

"Shall we call your foster mother?"

"No," she said and sat upright on my lap. She looked at me full in the face. "No. I want to go home to *my* home." And with that she really started to cry. She fell forward against me and sobbed.

"Ah," I said and finally understood.

She cried. Cried and cried and cried. Wrapping my arms tight around her, holding her there in the wheelchair in the hallway, I kept her as close as I could.

Reduced at last to snuffles and heavy hiccups, Venus continued to lie against my breast. Damp and rather sticky, I mopped the tears as best I could until we had a small soggy mountain of tissues with us there in the wheelchair.

"I want to go home," Venus murmured tearfully yet again.

"Yes, of course, sweetheart."

"I want Wanda."

"Yes."

"She calls me 'beautiful child.'"

"Yes. And is that what happened? Rosa called you 'beautiful child' and it made you think of Wanda?"

Venus nodded. "I want her to be here."

"Yes, I can understand that. It's very hard for you, isn't it?"

Venus nodded.

"You must feel very frightened by everything that's happened. It must be very scary being by yourself in a new home with a new family."

"I didn't want this," she said in a very tiny voice. "I just wanted it to stop, that's all. I didn't know they were going to take me away."

And the enormity of what had happened to Venus suddenly became real to me too. Up until that moment I had seen it all only from my own perspective. It hadn't even occurred to me that there was another. Here was a child living in the most appalling conditions. Even without the hideous abuse, her home situation had been awful with its poverty, motley assortment of half-siblings and "mother's boyfriends," poor supervision, and lack of care. The only solution to us on the outside – we, in the educated middle class – had been to "rescue" this girl. "Save" her from her environment by taking her out, giving her a new home, new parents, new clothes, and in the process, a new identity. This not only seemed right, it seemed desirable. Of course, she would want it. Of course, she would grow and develop normally and everything would turn out fine.

Now, for the first time, I realized that in the process of rescuing Venus, we had also destroyed everything she loved.

"I'm really sorry, Venus," I said softly. "I really, really am. You must miss your mom and your brothers and sisters very much."

She nodded.

"Do you ever get a chance to see them?"

She shook her head.

There was a small pause.

"Well, maybe that can change," I said.

Again the pause while I considered what could be done.

"I can't say for sure. I don't know what rules the police and the social workers have about visiting, so I'll have to check. But shall I do that? Shall I see if you can visit with your brothers and sisters?"

"Wanda?" she asked and looked up at me.

"Yes, Wanda too. Shall I look into that for you?"

She nodded.

A moment or two passed quietly. Venus lay against my breasts. She wasn't crying any longer.

"I wish I could make magic with my She-Ra sword and

magic everything back again, before everything happened," she said softly. "I wish that could be real."

"Yes, I can understand."

"I wish everything was back like it was before and I could go home," she said. "And my mom would be there and Wanda and everyone and it would be just like it was."

"Yes. Sadly, what was happening, what Danny was doing to you was wrong. It's against the law. And when parents or other adults show that they can't take care of children, then other people have to come to take over that job."

"I'd take my She-Ra sword and magic him to death."

"Yes, I can understand your feelings."

"I'd magic my mom back. My mom never done nothing. I'd magic my mom back and Wanda and my brothers and magic it the way it was before Danny came. I'd magic a special spell so no bad men could come hurt my mom again. Or Wanda. Or me. Or beat up on my brothers. Or my sister Kali. 'Cept I wouldn't magic her back 'cause she was always nasty to me. I'd magic all that stuff with my She-Ra sword."

"That'd be good, wouldn't it?"

Venus nodded.

There was a long moment's silence.

She sighed heavily.

"I think they're just about done in the classroom," I said, listening to the noise beyond the door. "Shall we go back in?"

Venus didn't respond.

"You could have your piece of cake. Did you see it? I made it in the shape of a train and there's one whole car just for you. It has your name on it."

"No. I don't wanna."

"Why not?"

"I don't like chocolate," she said.

"You *don't*?"

"No."

"You never said. Never in all this time!" I laughed. "Remember clear back in the beginning? Clear back in those first weeks and I was trying to get you to eat M&Ms?" I asked. "No wonder you wouldn't eat them. And there was me, sticking them in your mouth!"

Venus giggled. It was an unexpected sound, small and tinkly.

"You think that's funny?"

"Yeah," she said. "I thought they tasted like throw-up."

I laughed too.

"Well, shall we go in and have some punch then?" I finally said. "And some cookies? They're sugar cookies with pink icing. You *do* like sugar, I hope."

Another giggle. "Yeah."

I rose and set her back down in the wheelchair. "Okay, then. Let's go have goodies."

Chapter Thirty-four

Since Venus had returned, I'd endeavored to continue the special time we'd spent together during afternoon recess, even though she no longer required this kind of supervision to keep her out of trouble. I did it in part because I felt Venus needed this continued one-to-one, which she just could not receive in the hurly-burly of the classroom, but I did it also because I enjoyed it myself. My favorite part of teaching was this intricate process of connecting with a child, of looking for, finding, and bringing the phoenix from the ashes.

We never really went back to the She-Ra cartoons or the comics. No doubt this was partially due to her confinement in the wheelchair. Soon after her return to class, I realized how physical our interactions in regards to She-Ra had been. It had not simply been a matter of reading the comics or watching the videos. Much of our relating had revolved around the games of chase with the sword or Venus's twirling change into She-Ra. There was no way to duplicate this without watering it down in a way that did nothing but emphasize her current disability. Above and beyond this, I remained sensitive to the issues Julie had brought up about the quality and racial suitability of She-Ra. I had to admit, she wasn't the best heroine I could find, and this rather ruined her for me.

As a consequence, what we usually ended up doing during that twenty minutes each afternoon was reading. I lifted Venus down onto the floor in front of the bookshelf and she went through the assortment of storybooks there to choose one. Then we cuddled up on the pillows and read. She liked this. And I think she liked the freedom and comfort of being out of the wheelchair for a while too. She wouldn't crawl in front of the other children, but she did quite happily there alone with me. She also snuggled up with me on the pillows in a way she'd never done in earlier times.

We read quite widely from among the books – Greek myths, picture books, and the whole of A. A. Milne's *Winnie-the-Pooh* – but Venus's favorite was a thin book of verse called *Father Fox's Pennyrhymes*. It was liberally illustrated with humorous little pen-and-ink drawings of foxes dressed in old-fashioned country clothes and getting up to some very silly antics. Venus loved to pore over the drawings, which were very detailed.

It was during these times that Venus began to speak with genuine spontaneity. "Look at the little bugs there," she'd say and run her fingers over four teeny little bugs standing on a tree branch. "And lookit, there's some more there. And there's some worms."

"How many bugs?" I asked.

"One, two, three, four," she replied, counting them very precisely with her fingertip. "And then there's one, two, three, four here."

"How many all together?"

"One, two, three, four," she said, counting over. A pause while she located the others. "Five, six, seven, eight. Eight."

"How many worms?"

"Two." She ran her finger along the picture. "There's a lot of things on that branch. Those bugs. I think they're ants. And then there's a ladybug. And mouses. And worms. And birds. And the foxes. And ..." She leaned closer to the page. "I don't know what those are. What are those?"

"Squirrels, maybe?" I suggested.

Venus nodded. "Squirrels. And then more mouses. And birds. And bugs."

"Can you count them all?"

"One, two," and she kept counting right up to the correct number of twenty-four. And thus it was with *Father Fox's Pennyrhymes* that I discovered Venus really did know her numbers and, indeed, could manage simple adding and subtraction.

The verses themselves had the strong rhythm of nursery

rhymes. *Mister Lister sassed his sister. Married his wife because he couldn't resist her.* Venus quickly learned them and enjoyed saying them in a lilting singsong.

Her favorite of all the rhymes was one called "Dilly Dilly."

Dilly, Dilly, Piccalilli. Tell me something very silly. Well, there was a chap, his name was Bert. He ate the buttons off his shirt.

Every time we came to that, Venus laughed. Every time she said it, she laughed. No matter how gloomy the day had been, no matter how sad she had seemed in class, "Dilly, Dilly" always cheered her up.

So, *Father Fox's Pennyrhymes* was the book Venus pulled out most often.

Then, on the Monday following our birthday party, Venus was going through the books on the shelf when she came across a paperback. It was a follow-up to *Father Fox's Pennyrhymes* called *Father Fox's Feast of Songs*. It was a thin little paperback songbook. Several of the popular rhymes from the first book had been set to music, plus a few new songs. This book had never proved very popular with the children for the understandable reason that most of the pages were musical score, and in my classrooms I'd almost never had any instruments other than a tinny xylophone that could play that kind of music and even fewer students who knew how. I'd let it stay in the bookshelf because it contained more of the same marvelous pen-and-ink illustrations and kids always enjoyed those, but for the most part, this was a book that ended up shunted to the bottom of the pile or the back of the shelf.

"I didn't know you had this," Venus said as she opened it. "What's this?"

"Musical notation. That's a songbook. They've written music to go along with some of the rhymes from the other books. That's how you write music down."

Venus crawled over to me with the book and sat down. "Sing the songs," she said.

"I can't."

She looked up at me.

"I can't read music," I said.

Her brow furrowed. "You sing other songs."

I nodded. "But that's because I already know the tune. See, these notes, they tell me what the tune of the song is. But I don't know this song, so I'd have to read these notes to find out."

"So, sing it."

"Except I can't read them."

Again she looked up. Again her brow furrowed.

"I don't know how to read them," I said. "I know what the names of the notes are. And I know what these lines are called. But I don't know how to put it all together to make the song. It's like reading words. Sometimes you will know what the letters are and you can see how they go together, but you still don't know what the word is that they make because you can't read it."

"And you can't read this?" she asked.

I shook my head. "Nope."

"Why not?"

"Because I haven't learned how."

There was a pause. She was scrutinizing my face very carefully.

"Are you stupid?" she asked at last. It wasn't sarcastic. The way she asked it, clearly it was a genuine question.

"On this, I suppose, yes, I am a bit. Because I was taught how when I was little, but I never understood it well enough to learn it."

Venus looked back down at the book. A pause in the conversation lengthened into a thinking silence. She touched the page with one finger, tracing over a quarter note.

"I'm stupid too," she said quietly.

"Everybody's stupid about some things. Everybody has things they can't do. There's nobody in the whole world who can do everything," I said.

"I thought you could," she said softly, still not looking up.

"I *wish* I could," I replied. "But I can't. Even teachers don't know everything."

A pause.

"That's all right," she said, her voice still soft. "I like you anyway."

"Yes, I like you too. A lot."

She smiled up at me. "Yes. I know."

Life seeped slowly back into Venus after her big cry at the birthday party. It wasn't a dramatic change but more of a shading, the way night fades into day. In class she became more responsive, especially to Alice.

Alice was a right little character, who was forever thinking up odd tricks. One of her favorites was to write Venus's name on her papers and then make this out to be a big joke when they came back in Venus's folder instead of hers. It struck me more as silly than funny, but Alice thought it was hilarious. And then Venus caught the joke.

"Look," she said one afternoon. "I'm Alice." She'd written Alice's name on the top of a page in her own folder.

"Oh, I have two Alices today," I cried in mock surprise.

"Call me Alice," Venus said and smiled.

"Call *me* Alice," said Alice. The two of them seemed to find this really funny. They both laughed uproariously. This, in turn, made Rosa and me laugh.

"You guys are nuts," Billy said.

"No, we're Alice!" Alice cried, and again, she and Venus fell about laughing.

"You ought to tell them off," Billy muttered to me. "You'd tell *me* off for laughing like that. You don't treat boys the same as you treat girls in this class."

"I don't pay any attention to whether you are a girl or a boy, Billy. When I treat people differently, it's because they have different needs," I said.

"So they need to laugh?"

"They're not hurting anything by laughing."

"Humph," he muttered. "I liked them better when they were quiet all the time."

Then we were into the last week of school. I was trying to clear things up in the classroom as we went along, so that on the last day I did not have to stay too late closing the room down. I was going to be in the same room the following year and, indeed, Venus, Alice, and the twins were all due to come back. Nonetheless, because of school policy, everything had to be cleared from the rooms except school property, and those things would need to be stored in drawers and cupboards that were taped shut on the last day. Consequently, whenever there were a few spare minutes during that last week, I encouraged the children to help me sort things out and prepare them to be put away for the summer.

Jesse, in particular, enjoyed this activity. He had a real tidy streak in him and always found organizing and cleaning things an enjoyable pastime. Tuesday of that week dawned overcast and very wet, so the children stayed in for morning recess. When this normally happened, the recess aides organized indoor games in the classrooms with the children. On this morning, Jesse, who had been straightening out the bookshelf, asked if he could be excused from the games and keep working. This seemed reasonable to me, so I said he could and then went on down to the teachers' lounge for my break.

About five minutes into my break, there was a loud knock on the door. It was one of the boys from the third-grade class next door to mine. "Miss Hayden, you got to come quick. That one boy of yours is in a fight with the girl in the wheelchair."

I shot out of the teachers' lounge. The third-grader ran with me.

"I would've got the aide but I couldn't find her," he said, "and I was scared he was gonna hurt that girl."

"That's all right. I'm glad you came."

"She sounded like he was killing her."

Cursing the silly idea that two aides could supervise eight classrooms of children, I sprinted up the stairs two at a time. I had been able to hear the yelling from the bottom of the stairwell.

By the time I got into the classroom, both of the aides were there too. Venus was out of her wheelchair and on the floor. Billy was crying. Jesse had a bloody nose. Alice was huddled over in the corner, being comforted by Mimi, who stroked her lovingly on the cheek. The twins were all but bouncing off the walls.

"What is going on?" I demanded.

"She went psycho!" Billy howled and pointed at Venus. "She tried to kill Jesse! I was just trying to settle her down!"

Whatever the third-grader had thought, Venus seemed to have come off the better in this, as she was clearly unhurt. Sitting on the floor, she gave Jesse and Billy a very evil glare.

"She *did* try to kill me," Jesse said. "She got out of her chair and I didn't even know she could stand up and she was gonna grab me." He had his hand cupped over his nose. Blood dripped through his fingers.

"Come here. Get over the sink, Jesse." Putting a hand

on Jesse's shoulder, I encouraged him in the right direction.

Billy, weeping more with outrage than anything else, trailed after us. "And I wasn't doing *anything*. She hit me and I wasn't doing anything, 'cept trying to be a good Samaritan and help poor Jesse before he got his lights knocked out."

"There's times to be a good Samaritan and times when it's not such a good idea," I said.

"I wasn't doing *anything*! That girl just went psycho. Again!"

"How did you get a nosebleed?" I asked Jesse. "Did Venus hit you?"

"No, I bumped it on Billy's head when he jerked back. He was trying to keep her from hitting me and he hit me instead."

"But not on purpose! I don't deserve to get in trouble. I was just minding my own business," Billy howled.

"Yes, okay. Let's get things settled down first and then I'll hear all sides of it. Can you help Jesse here? Can you stay with him while I sort the twins out?"

Snorting up his tears dramatically, Billy nodded.

I turned. And that's when I saw her. Beside the bookcase, Venus had pulled herself up on her feet. She reached over and grabbed her She-Ra sword, which lay on the back of the bookcase. Pulling it against her, she cradled it a moment and then looked back at the wheelchair. Tentatively, she turned, still clutching the cardboard sword.

I watched without speaking, without moving.

There was maybe seven or eight feet between where Venus stood and where her wheelchair was. I could tell by her expression that she was trying to gauge if she could make it. Putting a hand out to steady herself on the bookshelf, she took a faltering step. She stopped, teetered briefly but remained upright. She then looked around and saw me watching her.

"Do you want help?" I asked.

She didn't answer immediately. For a moment it was the old, closed, unresponsive Venus looking at me. Then she nodded faintly.

I crossed the room to her and put one hand under her elbow, the other on her shoulder to steady her.

She didn't move and I could sense she'd expected me to pick her up and put her back in the wheelchair.

"Just go slowly. I'll keep hold of you. You won't fall."

"You ought to send her to Mr. Christianson's," Billy shouted from across the room. "You ought to punish her! She tried to kill me and Jesse. Just like in the old days."

I looked at him. The temptation was to tell him to shut up, already. Blather, blather, blather. That was our Billy.

Instead, I started to sing. "High hopes, I've got high hopes. I've got high, apple pie in the sky hopes. All problems are just a toy balloon. They'll be bursted soon. They're just bound to go pop! Oops there goes another problem kerplop!"

It was ludicrous. One of those absolutely, dazzlingly

absurd moments, standing there, balancing Venus and singing "High Hopes" to Billy while Jesse bled, the twins ran maniacally around, and Alice talked to her hand. But it worked. Venus managed to hobble slowly back to her wheelchair. Jesse, a huge wad of tissue held to his nose, joined the singing because he loved the kerplop part of this song. So did Billy. He made a loud, juicy sound by rubbing his hand, wrist, and arm practically up to his elbow under his nose. Then he begrudgingly started to sing. We started the song over at the beginning and did actions for the ant and the ram in the song, and this caught Shane and Zane, who wanted to be ants and rams too. Only Alice was left. I approached her and encouraged her to wave her arms in conducting motions. She looked imploringly at Mimi and Mimi must have said yes. Alice joined in too.

It took us two full rounds of "High Hopes," plus half a dozen choruses before everyone looked in a halfway reasonable mood. I stopped the song. "Okay. Recess is well and truly over, because look at the clock. It's ten to. Places, please."

"Aren't you even going to send her to the quiet chair?" Billy muttered.

"*You* get to work. If you're the innocent party here, I don't need to talk to you, do I? So you show me I have no reason to think you are a troublemaker."

Billy made a face and took his seat.

When the boys had their work out, I went over to Venus at her table and pulled out a chair.

"I can't allow people to hurt one another in here," I said quietly. "That's a class rule."

Venus stared at me.

"Can you explain why you got so upset?"

"He tooked my She-Ra sword," she murmured. She still had the cardboard sword clutched in her lap.

"I didn't either!" Jesse shouted from his table. "I didn't take her stupid sword. I was just straightening up. I just was moving it to put stuff away."

"Thanks, Jesse, but I'll take care of it. You take care of your work."

When I looked back at Venus, she was tearful.

"Your She-Ra sword is very important, isn't it?"

She nodded.

"Jesse wasn't going to hurt it. He was just cleaning, just helping me get ready for the end of the year."

"He said 'I'm going to throw it away,'" she murmured.

I smiled at her and reached over to touch her cheek. "No, he wouldn't throw it away. I wouldn't let him. He was just talking. Your sword's safe."

A pause.

"And you know what?" I said.

"What?" she asked.

"I saw your sword doing magic."

Venus looked up at me.

"It made you walk." I smiled. "I saw that. Your magic sword made you able to walk."

Chapter Thirty-five

And then it was the last day.

On this occasion the last day wasn't even a whole day. It was just a half day. In years gone by I'd planned a picnic or other outing for the last day, but with so little time, this wasn't possible. Nonetheless, I wanted some last way to celebrate our year together, so I suggested to the children's families that instead of picking them up at lunchtime, that they come into the school and join us for a pizza party. This idea was met with general enthusiasm. The twins' mother and Billy's and Alice's mothers were coming, as was Jesse's grandmother. Venus's foster mother was coming too.

After Venus's and my discussion on the day of the birthday party, I had alerted Social Services and her foster parents to how much Venus missed her brothers and sisters.

Efforts had been made to let her see her brothers, who did not live too far away, but she had yet to see Wanda again, largely because Wanda was now living in a sheltered group home about thirty miles away.

I felt strongly about bringing Wanda and Venus together again. If Wanda was Venus's biological mother, Venus knew nothing about it, as she always referred to Wanda as her sister. However, there was no denying there was a special bond between the two of them. Regardless of their blood relationship, my suspicion was that it had been Wanda, inept as she might have seemed to others, who had managed to keep Venus alive during the horrific period of abuse. It seemed grossly unfair now to keep the two apart. As a consequence, I suggested that it would be very nice if Wanda could also join us for the pizza party at lunchtime.

Arranging this proved to be a logistical nightmare. I must have made at least ten calls to Social Services to clear everything and then another half dozen to the staff of the group home and to Venus's foster family to organize picking up Wanda and getting her to the school on time. Venus's foster mother agreed to drive Wanda back to her group home in the afternoon. Indeed, Mrs. Kivie said she had to stop out at the mall after lunch and if Wanda wanted, she could come shopping with them first. But we couldn't get anyone to bring Wanda. Absolutely no one at the group home or from Social Services was willing to travel the sixty-mile round-trip to pick Wanda up and bring her to us. In the end, Rosa volunteered to do it.

The children and I spent the morning finishing up all the last-minute details. There were things to pass out, bits of bureaucracy to be completed, the finally taking down, handing out, and putting together. Everyone had brought big paper grocery bags to put their things in.

When all was completed, I took out their work folders.

"Oh, no!" Billy cried. "Work? You're gonna make us work on the last day of school?"

"Oh no! Oh no!" echoed the twins and then Jesse and finally Alice. Even Venus groaned.

"No, this is going to be different. Do these look different to you?" I said, holding up the folders.

"*No*," Billy retorted.

"Look closely. What's different?"

All the children craned to study the folder I was holding in my hand.

"Nothing," Billy said. "It's our work folders. That one's Shane's."

"Anybody else?" I asked.

"I don't see nothing," Zane said.

"It's thick," said Shane.

"That's right. See all the papers in the folders? You know why? Because these are *all* the papers you did. All year long."

"Wow," Jesse said. "All of 'em?"

"Yep. And I'm going to hand them out to you. You can take them home now. They're for you to keep. But before you stick them in your bags, let's look through them. Let's see how far everybody has come since last September."

The children accepted their folders as I gave them out. Only Alice's and Venus's were thin, Alice's because she'd only arrived at the beginning of May, and Venus's because she hadn't started doing any real paperwork until about the same time.

"Wow, look at this," Jesse said. "I was doing single-digit adding when I first came. I can do multiplication now."

"Well, I wasn't reading. Look at this. It's first-grade stuff, practically," Billy said.

"I was *coloring*!" Shane said.

"Who'd think I'd go to AP class," Billy said as he thumbed through his papers.

"I remember this. Remember this, guys?" Zane said, holding up a Halloween poem.

The boys were well occupied, paging through their folders, so I went over to Alice and Venus's table. I hunkered down beside Venus's wheelchair.

"You know what I was thinking?" I said. "Wanda is coming at lunchtime and I was thinking maybe you would like to give her a surprise."

Venus looked at me expectantly but didn't speak.

"I don't think Wanda knows you are in the wheelchair and I'm thinking that this might frighten Wanda a little."

Venus's eyes narrowed as she listened to me.

"So, while the boys and I are going through their folders, I was thinking maybe you would like to practice standing. Like you did the other day when you got your She-Ra sword. Maybe you could practice taking a few steps. Then, when Wanda comes, you could show her how well you are doing. Then she wouldn't be frightened by the wheelchair because she'd know you were getting better."

Venus didn't speak.

"What do you think?"

Pulling her lower lip in under her teeth, Venus just regarded me.

"I could help," Alice volunteered. "I could hold your hand so you didn't fall."

"That sounds like a good idea," I said. "What do you think? Do you want to try?"

There was a long moment's hesitation. Venus studied my face, dropped her eyes, then glanced briefly at Alice. Finally she nodded. "I'll try."

And she did. I stayed a few moments, helping her stand in front of the wheelchair, steadying her while she took a few faltering steps. Then Alice took over. Holding onto Venus's hands, she carefully guided Venus's steps. Venus didn't last long on her feet. Less than ten minutes of trying and she was too tired to try any longer, but she had managed it. She had gotten to her feet and walked with Alice's help. More importantly, she had wanted to.

And then the last fifteen minutes. Everything was taken down, sealed up, put away. The children sat at bare tables in a bare classroom.

I passed out lined school paper. "Okay, here's what we're going to do in the time left. Everybody got a pencil? Okay.

Now, I want you to think back over the whole school year, over everything we did, over all the things that happened, and I want you to write down what you liked best. You tell me what your favorite thing this year was. If you need help spelling, just ask and I'll write the word on the board. But you write down your favorite part of the whole school year. And when you're done, fold it up and put it in this box up here. I'm going to save these until I get home and then I'm going to read them and I'll be able to remember all the fun things we did together."

All six children bent studiously over their papers and wrote. Billy was first done. He folded his paper and put it in the box.

"If you want to go down to the front door, you can watch for parents coming and tell them how to get up here," I said.

Then Jesse and Alice finished.

"If you want to go down to the cafeteria, you'll find the paper plates and things we'll need for our party. You can lay them out on the tables. There's going to be fifteen people. You can set fifteen places."

Zane and Shane and Venus completed their papers. Zane took Venus's too and put them all in the box.

"Zane and Shane, you want to go down and help Billy meet people and show them into the cafeteria? Venus, you come with me. We'll go phone to make sure the pizza man is coming with our delivery."

We were in the main office when I saw Rosa coming up the school drive with Wanda. Wanda hadn't changed a bit. She looked a little cleaner perhaps, but not a bit tidier. And she hadn't lost any weight. She waddled along behind Rosa.

"Look," I said to Venus. "Look who's coming."

We were behind the big counter in the office and Venus couldn't see over it. I leaned down to pick her up so that she could see, but she stood up from the wheelchair before I could get there. Hanging on to the counter, she pulled herself up to see Wanda coming into the office.

"Beautiful child!" Wanda shrieked when she saw her. "Beautiful child!"

Clinging to the counter, Venus pulled herself around it and fell into Wanda's voluptuous hug.

"Beautiful child," Wanda said again and held her tight.

Eyes closed, head back, Venus smiled broadly, happily, uninhibitedly.

And then it was the end. The pizza was eaten. Everyone was chatting excitedly about their summer plans. Zane and Shane were getting impatient to get theirs started. They raced around the cafeteria, empty except for us, until their mother decided it was time to take them home. This brought our lunch party to a close.

I hugged them, one by one.

Billy started to cry. "I'm not coming back. I miss you already. I don't want to go. This was the best class in the whole world and I'm not coming back. They are. All those guys are, but I'm not!" he wailed. "It's not fair!"

"I'll miss you too. But we'll see each other next year."

"And me too!" Jesse said. "I'll be gone, but not gone. You'll see me too."

"Bye. Bye."

"Bye."

And they left, one by one.

"And I'll see you," I said to Venus. I leaned over her wheelchair and kissed her forehead. "Have a good summer."

"Bye," she said.

"Bye-bye. And good-bye to you, Wanda. I'll see you too next year, I'm sure."

And they were all gone.

I was left with Rosa in the emptiness of the cafeteria. We cleared up the mess of pizza boxes and paper plates, cups, and napkins. Then I wished Rosa a good summer and climbed the stairs up to the room to get the last things and lock the door.

Picking up the box where the children had put their papers, I unfolded them one by one.

Shane's said: *I like them trips to afika*, meaning, I assumed, the many imaginary journeys we had taken, like our first one into the woods.

Jesse's was next. He wrote: *I liked the party. The party was at 2:40 and we had choclit cake like a train and Kool-Aid and pretzels and cake and ice ceram and the ice ceram was Butter Brikle and a hole bunch of candy on the cake. I love you. XOXOXOXOXOXOX.*

I picked up Billy's. *I like the way you always laughe with us, Miss Hayden. You like us. You make us smile. You sing with us. I wish you would all ways be my taecher forever. I love you vary much. I hope you have a nice summer. I will miss you. Love, Guillermo Manuel Gomez Jr. (Billy).*

Zane's said: *I like you when you help us.*

Alice wrote: *You'ev helped us when we've had, a very bad problme. And you made us lauph a long time, well, that's all I have to say now good-by thank you for the ordeal.* I laughed when I read that. "Thank you for the ordeal" summed up the year quite well.

And last of all I took out Venus's and unfolded it, laying it flat on the table. It said: *I am happy.*

Epilogue

Billy, after leaving our class, continued to go from strength to strength. Diagnosed officially as dyslexic the following year, he continued to struggle with reading but caught up sufficiently with his other work to be considered for full-time placement in the AP class in sixth grade. He has continued on successfully through school and has entered university.

Jesse went on to fourth grade in our school with resource help and adapted successfully to regular education. He graduated from high school and is studying for a business degree.

Shane, Zane, Alice, and Venus all stayed with me the following year. Shane and Zane continued to have serious problems with academic achievement, and they both remained in full-time special education throughout their school career. They are now both in sheltered programs.

Alice was mainstreamed in the middle of the second year in our class, joining a regular fourth grade in our building. She adapted well, although she returned regularly to see her friends in our class. In fifth grade, her family moved and I have since lost track of her.

Venus also was mainstreamed in the middle of her second year in our class. A year younger than Alice, she went into third grade and continued to have learning support two hours a day to help her with her lagging academic skills. She continued with this arrangement through middle school and then went on to high school as a full-time regular student. She is now employed in the office of a construction company.

Venus remained in the same foster home throughout her childhood and adolescence and was never reunited with her siblings, although she continued to see several of them on a regular basis. Danny was convicted of child abuse and sentenced to fifteen years in prison. Teri was convicted as an accessory and sentenced to four years. Wanda continued to live in sheltered group living. She died at age thirty of a respiratory ailment.

Also by **Torey Hayden** and available from **HarperElement**

One Child

She was a wild, violent six-year-old, lost in a world of anger and torment – until a brilliant young teacher reached out

Six-year-old Sheila was abandoned by her mother on a highway when she was four. A survivor of horrific abuse, she never spoke and never cried. She was placed in a class for severely retarded children after committing an atrocious act of violence against another child.

Everyone thought Sheila was beyond salvation – except her teacher, Torey Hayden. With patience, skill and abiding love, she fought long and hard to release a haunted little girl from her secret nightmare, and nurture the spark of genius she recognized trapped within Sheila's silence. This is the remarkable story of their journey together – an odyssey of hope, courage and inspiring devotion that opened the heart and mind of one lost child to a new world of discovery and joy.

'Page after page proves again the power of love and the resiliency of life.'

Los Angeles Times

The Tiger's Child

The story of a gifted, troubled child
and the teacher who refused to give up on her

Sheila was a deeply disturbed six-year-old when she came into Torey Hayden's life – a story poignantly chronicled in *One Child.* Over the course of five remarkable months, this dedicated special-education teacher profoundly touched the life of this abandoned, abused little girl. Then Torey lost touch with the child she had helped to free from a hellish inner prison of rage and silence. But seven years later, Sheila was back, now a gangly teenager with bright orange hair – no longer broken and lost, but still troubled and searching for answers.

This marked a new and extraordinary chapter in a story of dedication and caring – one that would test the strength and heart of both Sheila and her one-time teacher. Torey would once again answer the call to help Sheila, this time guiding her through a difficult yet glorious transition into young womanhood.

'Torey Hayden deserves the kind of respect I can't give many people. She isn't just valuable, she's incredible. The world needs more like Torey Hayden.'

Boston Globe

Ghost Girl

The true story of a child in desperate peril – and a teacher who saved her

Jadie never spoke, never laughed and never cried. She spent every waking hour locked in her own private world of shadows. But nothing in Torey Hayden's experience had prepared her for the nightmare Jadie revealed to her when she finally persuaded her to break her self-imposed silence. It was a story too painful, too horrific for Hayden's professional colleagues to acknowledge.

But Torey Hayden could not close her ears … or her heart. A little girl was trapped in a hell of unspeakable memories. And it would take every ounce of courage, compassion and love that one remarkable teacher possessed to rid the 'Ghost Girl' of the malevolent spirits that haunted her.

'A testament to the powers of caring and commitment.'

Publishers Weekly

'An amazing story.'

Washington Post

Just Another Kid

Each was a child no one could reach,
until one amazing teacher embraced them all

'*Just Another Kid* is not just another book. This remarkable teacher's memoir reminds us that love takes many forms.'

New York Times

No other teacher had been able to handle these six emotionally damaged children. Three were recent arrivals from conflict-ridden Ireland, horribly traumatized by the nightmare of war. Then there was an eleven-year-old boy who had never known life outside an institution; eight-year-old Mariana, who was dangerously excitable and sexually precocious; and Leslie, seven years old, yet completely unresponsive and unable to speak.

These were the children entrusted to Torey Hayden, the extraordinary special-needs teacher who refused to give up on them. Torey was determined that every child should experience joy, hope and a future free of fear. With compassion, patience, and most of all love, she knew that miracles could happen.

Twilight Children

Three Voices No One Heard – Until Someone Listened

'Hayden's books are unapologetic tear-jerkers.'

The Times T2

Two children trapped in a prison of silence and a woman suffering in the twilight of her years – these are the cases that would test the extraordinary courage, compassion and skill of Torey Hayden and ultimately reaffirm her faith in the indomitable strength of the human spirit.

While working in the children's psychiatric ward of a hospital, Torey was introduced to seven-year-old Cassandra, a child who had been kidnapped by her father and was found dirty, starving and picking though rubbish bins to survive. She refused to speak, so Torey could only imagine what she'd been through. Drake, by contrast, was a charismatic four-year-old who managed to participate fully in his pre-school class without uttering a single word. Then, there was Gerda, eighty-two, who had suffered a massive stroke and was unwilling to engage in conversation with anyone. Although Torey had never worked with adults, she agreed to help when all other efforts had failed.